Easy and Exciting Way to Work with Avocado!

A Comprehensive Collection of Avocado Recipes

The Ultimate Avocado Cookbook

BY: Alicia T. White

License Note!

I know you've read this and seen this in many other books and movies. Still, there's a reason why authors and filmmakers are so adamant about protecting their copyrights despite it being so annoying for you to see yet again… The thing is, lots of people infringe on copyrights, and this greatly affects our work negatively.

Thus, here we go again just so things are clear:

Do not make any print or electronic reproductions, sell, re-publish, or distribute this book in parts or as a whole unless you have express written consent from me or my team.

I spent over 4 months working on this cookbook, so I protect it like it's my baby! I know you can understand the value of working hard on something and wanting to protect your end product, so please help me by not infringing on the copyright or letting others do so.

Thanks!

Table of Contents

Introduction

The majority of people have only developed the habit of eating avocados raw.

If this is your story, you've been eating avocados incorrectly!

This statement is not to say that eating avocados raw is a sin or wrong, but that you have not been eating avocados to their full potential and are about to begin a new journey with this book!

So, I welcome you to this cookbook, where you will learn how to cook with avocado in various ways.

This recipe book will discover more reasons to keep avocados on your grocery list every weekend!

If you don't think you've eaten as many avocados as you should, this recipe book will prove you wrong!

All you have to do to be proven wrong is turn the page!!!

OOOOOOOOOOOOOOOOOOOOOOOOOOOOOOOOOOOOOOO

Avocado Salads

OOOOOOOOOOOOOOOOOOOOOOOOOOOOOOOOOOOOOOOO

1. Chicken Caprese Avocado Salad

Prep Time: 5 minutes

Total Prep Time: 10 minutes

Serving Size: 2 servings

List of Ingredients:

- 1 skinless, boneless chicken breast
- Salt and pepper
- ½ a cup of fresh mozzarella balls cut in half
- 1 ripe avocado, peeled, pitted, and cut into cubes
- 6 ounces of mixed fresh salad
- ½ a cup of cherry tomatoes cut in half
- ¼ cup of fresh basil, chopped

List of Ingredients for The Balsamic Vinaigrette

- 1 clove of minced garlic
- 1 tsp. of dry basil
- 1 tbsp. of Dijon mustard
- 1 tbsp. of lemon juice
- ¼ cup of balsamic vinegar
- 1/3 cup of olive oil
- Salt and pepper

OOOOOOOOOOOOOOOOOOOOOOOOOOOOOOOOOOOOOOOOO

Methods:

i. Preheat the grill to 200 degrees C.

ii. In a medium-sized bowl, combine the balsamic vinegar, lemon juice, Dijon mustard, basil, garlic, and salt and pepper. Whisk together thoroughly until the oil and the vinegar are combined.

iii. Season the chicken breast with salt and pepper and cook it on the grill for 5 minutes on each side. Once cooked, remove from the grill and slice into cubes.

iv. Divide the salad into three small bowls and top with the grilled chicken, mozzarella balls, basil, cherry tomatoes, avocado, and spring mix.

v. Drizzle the balsamic vinegar over the top and serve.

2. Grilled Chicken and Avocado Salad

Prep Time: 10 minutes

Total Prep Time: 15 minutes

Serving Size: 4 servings

List of Ingredients:

- 2 skinless, boneless chicken breasts
- 3 tbsp. of extra virgin olive oil
- Kosher salt
- Ground black pepper
- ½ a cup of mayonnaise
- 2 cloves of grated garlic
- ¼ cup of diced red onion
- 3 tbsp. of minced chives
- 1 large iceberg lettuce head sliced into 4 chunks
- 2 avocados, peeled and pitted

OOOOOOOOOOOOOOOOOOOOOOOOOOOOOOOOOOOOOOO

Methods:

i. Preheat the grill to 200 degrees C.

ii. Drizzle 1 tbsp. of olive oil over the chicken and season with salt and pepper.

iii. Cook the chicken for 5 minutes on each side.

iv. Once the chicken is cooked, please remove it from the grill and shred it with a fork.

v. Add the chives, red onion, garlic, red wine vinegar, remaining olive oil, mayonnaise, salt, and pepper to a medium jar. Put the lid on the jar and shake well.

vi. Serve the iceberg wedges with half an avocado, shredded chicken on top, salad dressing, garnish with chives and serve.

3. Lemony Crab Salad and Avocado

Prep Time: 10 minutes

Serving Size: 4 servings

List of Ingredients:

- 5 ripe but firm avocados
- 1 tbsp. of grated lemon zest
- 5 tbsp. of fresh lemon juice
- 1 pound of crab meat
- ½ a cup of diced radish
- ¼ cup of light mayonnaise
- ½ a cup of fresh chopped basil

OOOOOOOOOOOOOOOOOOOOOOOOOOOOOOOOOOOOOOOO

Methods:

i. Slice 4 of the avocados in half. Chop one avocado into cubed pieces.

ii. Drizzle the lemon juice over the avocados.

iii. In a large bowl, combine the lemon zest, diced avocado, basil, mayonnaise, radishes, crab meat, and the remaining lemon juice.

iv. Stuff the salad mixture into the avocado halves and serve.

4. Avocado Salad in a Jar

Prep Time: 20 minutes

Total Prep Time: 10 minutes

Serving Size: 4 servings

List of Ingredients:

- 2 tbsp. of red wine vinegar
- 1 tbsp. of Dijon mustard
- 1 clove of minced garlic
- 1 tsp. of Worcestershire sauce
- 1 tbsp. and 1/3 cup of olive oil
- Kosher salt
- Ground black pepper
- 1 cherry tomato, halved
- ½ a pound of skinless, boneless chicken breast
- ½ a tsp. of garlic powder
- ½ a tsp. of lemon pepper
- 4 hard-boiled eggs cut into quarters
- 4 slices of bacon, cooked and crumbled
- 1 avocado, peeled, pitted, and chopped
- 1 tbsp. of lemon juice
- ½ a cup of blue cheese, crumbled
- 2 large romaine lettuce heads, chopped
- 2 tbsp. of chopped chives
- 4 Mason jars

OOOOOOOOOOOOOOOOOOOOOOOOOOOOOOOOOOOOOOO

Methods:

i. Make the vinaigrette in a medium-sized bowl by whisking together the Worcestershire sauce, garlic, Dijon mustard, and red wine vinegar. Slowly add the olive oil, whisking as you pour, and season with salt and pepper.

ii. In a large frying pan, heat the remaining olive oil.

iii. Season the chicken with salt, pepper, and garlic powder.

iv. Cook the chicken for 4 minutes on each side.

v. Once cooked, transfer the chicken onto a chopping board and slice it into small chunks.

vi. Put the avocado into a small bowl and add the lemon juice. Toss to coat.

vii. Pour 2 tbsp. of the dressing into each Mason jar.

viii. Layer the jar with the salad ingredients.

ix. The salad can be refrigerated for up to 4 days if tightly sealed.

x. Before serving, shake the jar thoroughly to coat the salad in the dressing.

5. Avocado Salad with Cumin and Lime Vinaigrette

This creamy, excellent, spicy avocado salad is a healthy and creative addition for lunch or dinner.

Prep Time: 25 minutes

Serving Size: 8 servings

List of Ingredients:

- 1 tbsp. of cumin seeds
- ¼ cup of lime juice
- ¼ cup of fresh cilantro leaves, chopped
- ½ a cup of whole cilantro leaves
- 2 tbsp. of rice vinegar
- 1 tbsp. of honey
- Kosher salt
- Ground black pepper
- ¼ cup of olive oil
- ¼ cup of vegetable oil
- 4 cups of arugula leaves
- 2 pounds of ripe tomatoes
- 4 large ripe avocados
- 1 large red onion
- 1 tsp. Of ground cumin

OOOOOOOOOOOOOOOOOOOOOOOOOOOOOOOOOOOOOOOOO

Methods:

i. In a frying pan at medium-high heat, toast the cumin seeds for about 5 minutes or until aromatic.

ii. Release the frying pan from the heat and set aside to cool the cumin seeds.

iii. Whisk together the toasted cumin seeds, honey, vinegar, chopped cilantro leaves, ¼ tsp. of black pepper, and 1 tsp. of salt in a medium-sized bowl.

iv. Top the arugula with the red onions, avocados, and tomatoes on a serving plate.

v. Drizzle half of the vinaigrette over the top, followed by the cilantro leaves, and serve with the remaining vinaigrette on the side.

6. Raspberry, Avocado and Chicken Salad

Prep Time: 10 minutes

Total Prep Time: 25 minutes

Serving Size: 4 servings

List of Ingredients:

- 2 tbsp. of fresh lemon juice
- 2 tbsp. of low-fat sour cream
- 1 tbsp. of pure honey
- 1 tsp. of Dijon mustard
- Salt and pepper
- 1 tsp. of poppy seeds
- 1 pound of boneless, skinless chicken breast in halves
- ½ tsp. of olive oil
- 1 avocado
- 1 pound of raspberries
- 6 ounces of mixed greens
- ¼ cup of sliced toasted almonds

ooooooooooooooooooooooooooooooooooooooo

Methods:

i.   Preheat the grill to 200 degrees C.

ii.   Combine the mustard, honey, sour cream, lemon juice, 1/8 tsp. of salt, 1/8 tsp. of pepper, and the poppy seeds. Stir to combine.

iii.   Season the chicken with salt and pepper.

iv.   Cut the avocado in half, remove the seed and rub oil into the cut side.

v.   Grill the chicken for 10 minutes and the avocado for 5 minutes.

vi.   In a large bowl, combine the greens, raspberries, and 1 tbsp. of dressing. Toss to combine.

vii.   Serve the salad on plates, topped with avocado, chicken, raspberries, and almonds.

7. Guacamole Salad

Prep Time: 10 minutes

Serving Size: 5 servings

List of Ingredients:

- ¼ cup of extra virgin olive oil
- The juice of 1 lime
- ¼ tsp. of cumin
- Kosher salt
- Ground black pepper
- 1 pint of cherry tomatoes sliced in half
- ½ a cup of corn
- ½ a finely chopped medium red onion
- 1 minced jalapeño
- 2 ripe avocados, peeled, pitted, and cut into chunks
- 2 tbsp. of chopped cilantro

ooooooooooooooooooooooooooooooooooooooo

Methods:

i. Whisk together the cumin, lime juice, and olive oil in a small bowl, and season with pepper and salt to make the dressing.

ii. Mix the salad ingredients in a large bowl with the dressing and serve.

8. Shrimp Stuffed Avocado Salad

Prep Time: 5 minutes

Total Prep Time: 7 minutes

Serving Size: 4 servings

List of Ingredients:

- 2 pitted avocados
- 2 tbsp. of extra virgin olive oil
- ½ a pound of raw deveined shrimp
- 1 cup of cherry tomatoes sliced in half
- ½ a cup of corn
- ¼ cup of Greek yogurt
- The juice of 1 lemon
- Kosher salt
- Ground black pepper
- Basil

OOOOOOOOOOOOOOOOOOOOOOOOOOOOOOOOOOOOOOO

Methods:

i. Scoop out the flesh of the avocado but leave some around the edges. Chop the avocado into cubes and set it to one side.

ii. Heat the olive oil in a frying pan over medium heat.

iii. Cook the shrimp for 7 minutes, then allow them to cool before chopping them into small pieces.

iv. Combine the corn, tomatoes, shrimp, avocado, Greek yogurt, lemon juice, salt, and pepper in a large mixing bowl.

v. To mix, toss everything together.

vi. Divide the salad into 4 avocado halves and sprinkle with basil.

9. Breaded Chicken Cobb Salad

Prep Time: 15 minutes

Total Prep Time: 20 minutes

Serving Size: 4 servings

List of Ingredients:

- 1 pound of skinless, boneless chicken breasts
- 1 cup of bread crumbs
- 2 lightly beaten eggs
- 2 tbsp. of extra virgin olive oil
- 1 large head of Romaine lettuce
- 2 cups of cherry tomatoes cut in half
- 1 cup of corn
- ½ a cup of crumbled blue cheese
- 1 avocado, peeled, pitted, and diced
- ½ a pound of bacon, cooked and sliced into pieces
- Kosher salt
- Ground black pepper
- Ranch dressing

OOOOOOOOOOOOOOOOOOOOOOOOOOOOOOOOOOOOOOOO

Methods:

i. Preheat the oven to 200 degrees C.

ii. Line a baking tray with parchment paper.

iii. Place the chicken in a shallow bowl and season it with salt and pepper.

iv. Whisk the eggs in a separate shallow bowl and put the bread crumbs into another shallow bowl.

v. Dip the chicken into the eggs and then into the breadcrumbs.

vi. Arrange the breaded chicken onto the baking tray.

vii. In a large frying pan, heat the olive oil over medium-high heat.

viii. Cook the chicken for 4 minutes on both sides.

ix. Place the chicken back onto the baking tray and bake for 10 minutes.

x. When the chicken is cooked, remove the tray from the oven and allow it to cool down.

xi. Transfer the chicken onto a plate and cut it into chunks.

xii. Arrange the lettuce onto serving plates, and top with the chicken, bacon, avocados, blue cheese, corn, and tomatoes.

xiii. Season with salt and pepper, drizzle the ranch over the top, and serve.

10. Avocado and Shrimp Salad

Prep Time: 4 minutes

Total Prep Time: 6 minutes

Serving Size: 4 servings

List of Ingredients:

- 1 pound of medium shrimp, deveined and peeled
- 1 tbsp. of vegetable oil
- 5 cups of arugula
- 1 sliced avocado
- 1 diced mango
- ½ a medium red onion
- ¼ cup of extra virgin olive oil
- The juice of 2 limes
- A pinch of sugar
- A pinch of cumin

OOOOOOOOOOOOOOOOOOOOOOOOOOOOOOOOOOOOOOO

Methods:

i.   In a large frying pan, heat the oil over medium heat.

ii. Cook the shrimp until they become opaque. This process should take approximately 4 to 6 minutes.

iii. Combine the onion, mango, avocado, shrimp, and arugula in a large salad bowl.

iv. Mix the cumin, sugar, lime juice, and olive oil in a small jar. Tightly screw a lid on the jar and shake thoroughly.

v.   Arrange the salad onto plates, drizzle the dressing over the top, and toss to combine.

Avocado Sandwiches

OOOOOOOOOOOOOOOOOOOOOOOOOOOOOOOOOOOOOOOOO

11. Avocado and Turkey Sandwich

Prep Time: 10 minutes

Serving Size: 8 servings

List of Ingredients:

- 3 loaves of sour bread dough
- 2 ripe avocados, peeled, pitted, and sliced
- 3 tbsp. of salsa
- 3 strips of roasted red pepper
- 1 pound of thinly sliced smoked turkey
- 3 slices of red onion rings
- 1 ounce of sliced pepper jack cheese
- 2 Romaine lettuce leaves

oooooooooooooooooooooooooooooooooooooo

Methods:

i. Make a shell out of the bottom part of the bread by tearing out the inside.

ii. Mix the salsa and avocado, and mash thoroughly in a small bowl.

iii. Spread the avocado mix onto the shelled-out bread.

iv. Layer with cheese, turkey, onions, slices of avocado, lettuce, and turkey.

v. Top with the rest of the bread. Cut into triangles and serve.

12. Turkey Bacon and Avocado Hummus Sandwich

Prep Time: 10 minutes

Serving Size: 4 servings

List of Ingredients:

- 1 ripe avocado, peeled, pitted, and cut into slices
- 8 slices of whole grain bread
- ½ a cup of hummus
- 8 strips of cooked turkey bacon
- 1 tomato cut into slices

OOOOOOOOOOOOOOOOOOOOOOOOOOOOOOOOOOOOOOO

Methods:

Spread the hummus onto all slices of bread.

Layer 4 slices of bread with 2 slices of avocado, 2 strips of bacon, and 2 slices of tomato.

Top with the remaining slices of bread.

13. Grilled Chicken and Avocado Sandwich

Prep Time: 20 minutes

Serving Size: 8 servings

List of Ingredients:

- 4 boneless chicken breasts
- 12 ounces of Italian dressing
- 3 tbsp. of fresh rosemary
- 1 loaf of ciabatta bread
- Olive oil
- 2 ripe avocados, peeled, pitted, and sliced
- 2 medium-sized ripe tomatoes, sliced
- Fresh ground pepper

OOOOOOOOOOOOOOOOOOOOOOOOOOOOOOOOOOOOOOO

Methods:

i. Preheat the grill to 200 degrees C.

ii. Combine the rosemary and dressing in a small bowl and whisk together thoroughly.

iii. Marinate the chicken for 15 minutes.

iv. Grill, the chicken for approximately 5 minutes on both sides.

v. Slice the bread into 8 pieces.

vi. Brush the bread with olive oil and arrange them on the grill.

vii. Top the bread with the chicken and remaining sandwich filling and serve.

14. Apple, Feta and Avocado Sandwich

Prep Time: 10 minutes

Serving Size: 4 servings

List of Ingredients:

- 1 ripe avocado, peeled, pitted, and cut into slices
- 2 tbsp. of lime juice
- 2 tbsp. of olive oil
- 1 tbsp. of fresh mint, chopped
- 1 ½ cups of baby arugula
- 1 apple, sliced and cored
- ¼ English cucumber sliced and peeled
- 6 slices of feta cheese
- 8 slices of whole wheat bread

OOOOOOOOOOOOOOOOOOOOOOOOOOOOOOOOOOOOOOOO

Methods:

i. Combine the arugula, salt, mint, oil, and lime juice in a medium bowl.

ii. Arrange the avocado on 4 slices of bread.

iii. Top with feta cheese, cucumber, and apple.

iv. Top with the rest of the bread.

v. Slice into triangles and serve.

15. Turkey, Brie and Avocado Panini

Prep Time: 15 minutes

Serving Size: 4 servings

List of Ingredients:

- ½ a cup of olive oil
- 3 tbsp. of balsamic vinegar
- 1 large clove of garlic, minced
- Salt and pepper
- 8 ounces of thinly sliced turkey
- 10 ounces of brie, sliced
- 2 ripe avocados, peeled, pitted, and cut into 12 slices
- 1 16-ounce ciabatta bread

ooooooooooooooooooooooooooooooooooooo

Methods:

i. Preheat the grill to 200 degrees
ii. In a small bowl, combine the garlic, vinegar, olive oil, salt, and pepper. Whisk together thoroughly.
iii. Layer the bread with avocado, cheese, and turkey, and drizzle the dressing over the top.
iv. Top with the remaining bread and cut into triangles.
v. Grill for 3 minutes and serve.

16. Chickpea and Avocado Sandwich

Prep Time: 10 minutes

Serving Size: 4 servings

List of Ingredients:

- 1 can of chickpeas rinsed and drained
- 1/3 cup of diced celery
- 1/3 cup of medium onions, diced
- ½ a ripe avocado, peeled, pitted, and sliced
- The juice of ½ a lime
- 1 tsp. of Kosher salt
- Black pepper
- 1 sliced tomato
- 8 slices of whole grain bread

OOOOOOOOOOOOOOOOOOOOOOOOOOOOOOOOOOOOOOO

Methods:

i.   In a small bowl, combine the onion, celery, and chickpeas, and mash with a potato masher.

ii. Add the lime juice and avocado, season with salt, pepper, and cumin, and continue to mash.

iii. Spread the mixture onto 4 slices of bread.

iv. Top with the tomatoes.

v.   Serve with the remaining bread, and cut into triangles.

17. Veggie and Avocado Sandwich

Prep Time: 5 minutes

Serving Size: 1 serving

List of Ingredients:

- 1 whole wheat pitta round
- 1 ripe avocado, peeled, pitted, and mashed
- 2 tbsp. of sliced baby mushrooms
- 2 tbsp. of grilled artichoke hearts
- 1 red bell pepper, diced
- ½ a cup of sundried tomatoes
- 1 tsp. of dried rosemary
- ½ a tsp. of olive oil

OOOOOOOOOOOOOOOOOOOOOOOOOOOOOOOOOOOOOOOOO

Methods:

i.   Slice the pitta bread open down the middle.

ii. Spread the avocado inside the bread.

iii. Layer with the remaining ingredients and serve.

18. Egg Salad with Avocado Sandwich

Prep Time: 10 minutes

Serving Size: 4 servings

List of Ingredients:

- 1 avocado, peeled, pitted, and sliced
- 6 hard-boiled eggs
- 1 tbsp. of white wine vinegar
- 1 tsp. of Dijon mustard
- ½ a tsp. of salt
- ½ a cup of minced onion
- 2 tbsp. of chopped chives

ooooooooooooooooooooooooooooooooooooooo

Methods:

i. Peel the eggs, and take the yoke out of two of them.
ii. Chop up the rest of the eggs.
iii. In a small bowl, combine the eggs, avocado, onion, mustard, vinegar, and salt. Mash the ingredients together.
iv. Spread the mixture over 4 slices of bread.
v. Top with the rest of the bread, cut into triangles and serve.

19. Hass Avocado Halftime Sandwich

Prep Time: 10 minutes

Serving Size: 4 servings

List of Ingredients:

- 1 tbsp. of olive oil
- ¾ tbsp. of lemon juice
- ½ tbsp. of chopped dill
- Salt and black pepper
- 1 skinless, boneless, grilled chicken breast
- ¼ cup of diced cucumber
- 1/8 cup of red onion finely chopped
- ¼ cup of diced tomato
- ¼ cup of diced red pepper
- 1 ripe avocado, peeled, pitted, and diced
- 1/8 cup of low-fat feta cheese, crumbled
- 1 cup of baby spinach
- 2 slices of whole wheat pitas, cut into two

ooooooooooooooooooooooooooooooooooooooo

Methods:

i. Place all the ingredients into a medium-sized bowl and stir to combine.

ii. Stuff the mixture into the pitta halves and serve.

20. Ploughman Avocado Sandwich

Prep Time: 15 minutes

Serving Size: 1 serving

List of Ingredients:

- 3 slices of thick rustic bread
- 2 ounces of honey mustard
- 1 ounce of finely chopped chives
- 5 ounces of sliced corned beef
- 1 ripe avocado, peeled, pitted, and sliced
- 4 slices of Irish cheddar cheese
- 1 large Portobello mushroom, sliced and roasted
- 1 sliced medium tomato

ooooooooooooooooooooooooooooooooooooo

Methods:

i. Preheat the oven to 200 degrees C.
ii. Spread the honey mustard over three slices of bread and sprinkle with chives.
iii. Layer with cheese, corned beef, and avocado.
iv. On the other slice of bread, layer with mushrooms, tomato, and cheese.
v. Bake both parts of the sandwich in the oven for 2 minutes.
vi. Remove the sandwich from the oven and top with the third slice of bread.
vii. Slice into triangles and serve.

Avocado Smoothies

OOOOOOOOOOOOOOOOOOOOOOOOOOOOOOOOOOOOOOOO

21. Avocado Combo Smoothie

Prep Time: 5 minutes

Serving Size: 2 servings

List of Ingredients:

- ½ cup of coconut milk
- 1 avocado, pitted, peeled, and sliced
- 1 banana, pitted, peeled, and sliced
- 1 medium apple, sliced into chunks
- 1 stalk of celery, sliced into chunks
- 1 1-inch piece of ginger, peeled and sliced
- 1 cup of ice

OOOOOOOOOOOOOOOOOOOOOOOOOOOOOOOOOOOOOOOO

Methods:

i. Place all the ingredients into a food processor and blend until smooth.

ii. Pour into glasses and serve.

22. Strawberry and Avocado Smoothie

Prep Time: 5 minutes

Serving Size: 2 servings

List of Ingredients:

- ½ an avocado, pitted, peeled, and sliced
- 2/3 cup of strawberries cut into halves
- 4 tbsp. of natural low-fat yogurt
- 6 ounces of semi-skimmed milk
- 1 ½ cups of ice
- Lemon juice
- Honey

OOOOOOOOOOOOOOOOOOOOOOOOOOOOOOOOOOOOOOOO

Methods:

- Blend all of the ingredients in a food processor until smooth.
- Pour into glasses and serve.

23. Avocado Acai Smoothie

Prep Time: 5 minutes

Serving Size: 2 servings

List of Ingredients:

- 1 ½ cup of soy vanilla milk
- 1 ½ banana, peeled and chopped
- 1 cup of frozen or fresh blueberries
- 1 cup of frozen or fresh strawberries
- 1 cup of acai juice
- 1 cup of ice

OOOOOOOOOOOOOOOOOOOOOOOOOOOOOOOOOOOOOOO

Methods:

i.   In a food processor, combine all ingredients and blend until smooth.
ii. Pour into glasses and serve.

24. Tropical Peach and Avocado Smoothie

Prep Time: 5 minutes

Serving Size: 2 servings

List of Ingredients:

- 2 cups of peaches, sliced
- 1 banana
- ½ an avocado
- 1 cup of ice
- 1 ½ cups of orange juice

OOOOOOOOOOOOOOOOOOOOOOOOOOOOOOOOOOOOOOOOOOO

Methods:

i.   Blend all of the ingredients in a food processor until smooth.
ii. Pour into serving glasses and serve.

25. Green Goblin Halloween Treat

Prep Time: 5 minutes

Serving Size: 2 servings

List of Ingredients:

- 1 ½ banana, peeled and sliced
- ½ a cup of vanilla or soy milk
- ½ a cup of non-dairy milk, vanilla flavor
- 1 tsp. of matcha green tea powder
- ¾ cup of peaches or watermelon
- ¼ avocado, peeled, pitted, and cut into chunks
- A handful of fresh spinach
- 1 cup of ice

OOOOOOOOOOOOOOOOOOOOOOOOOOOOOOOOOOOOOOOOO

Methods:

i.   Place all the ingredients into a food processor and blend until smooth.

ii.   Pour into serving glasses and serve.

26. Spinach, Blueberry and Avocado Smoothie

Prep Time: 5 minutes

Serving Size: 2 servings

List of Ingredients:

- 2 cups of orange juice
- 2 cups of spinach
- 1 cup of frozen or fresh blueberries
- 1 banana
- 1 cup of ice
- ½ an avocado

OOOOOOOOOOOOOOOOOOOOOOOOOOOOOOOOOOOOOOOO

Methods:

i. Blend all of the ingredients in a food processor until smooth.

ii. Pour into serving glasses and serve.

27. Avocado and Cucumber Smoothie

Prep Time: 5 minutes

Serving Size: 2 servings

List of Ingredients:

- ½ a long cucumber, cut into cubes
- ½ a large avocado, peeled, pitted, and cut into chunks
- ½ a cup of whole-milk yogurt
- 1 tbsp. of chia seeds
- 1 tbsp. of honey
- 1 cup of ice

OOOOOOOOOOOOOOOOOOOOOOOOOOOOOOOOOOOOOOOO

Methods:

i. Blend all of the ingredients in a food processor until smooth.
ii. Pour into 2 serving glasses and serve.

28. Avocado Chocolate Smoothie

Prep Time: 5 minutes

Serving Size: 2 servings

List of Ingredients:

- 1 ½ banana
- ½ a large avocado, pitted, peeled, and chopped
- 2 tsp. of raw cacao powder
- ¾ cups of soy or vanilla milk
- 1 cup of ice
- A pinch of salt

OOOOOOOOOOOOOOOOOOOOOOOOOOOOOOOOOOOOOOO

Methods:

i.   In a food blender, combine all the mixtures and process until smooth.

ii.   Pour into glasses and serve.

29. Berry-Cado Smoothie

Prep Time: 5 minutes

Serving Size: 2 servings

List of Ingredients:

- 1 ¼ cup of orange juice
- ½ an avocado, pitted, peeled, and chopped
- ¾ cup of the fresh or frozen berries
- ½ a cup of the fresh or frozen strawberries
- 1 peeled kiwi
- ½ a cup of ice
- ½ a banana, peeled and slices

OOOOOOOOOOOOOOOOOOOOOOOOOOOOOOOOOOOOOOOOO

Methods:

i. Combine all of the ingredients in a food processor until fluffy.
ii. Pour into serving glasses and enjoy.

30. Avocado and Blueberry Smoothie

Prep Time: 5 minutes

Serving Size: 2 servings

List of Ingredients:

- 1 cup of ice
- 1 cup of orange juice
- 1 cup of Greek yogurt, non-fat
- ¾ cup of fresh or frozen blueberries
- ½ a banana, sliced and peeled
- 1 avocado, pitted, peeled, and chopped

OOOOOOOOOOOOOOOOOOOOOOOOOOOOOOOOOOOOOOOOO

Methods:

i. Place all the ingredients into a food processor and blend until smooth.

ii. Pour into glasses and serve.

Author's Note

Not many people do this, but I grew up under difficult circumstances where nothing was handed to me, and the only way forward was with your best effort. At some point, people started recognizing me for my talent in the kitchen despite my young age, and I've only worked harder from there!

Because I am constantly trying to improve my work, I would really appreciate your help. Sure, I always ask my friends and family for their feedback on my newest projects but, whether they want to accept it or not, there's always some sort of bias because they don't want to hurt my feelings by criticizing my work. Thus, I need a neutral pair of eyes — that's where you come in!

If you're up for it, I would appreciate you telling me what you think of my cookbooks. Are the recipes easy to follow? Did you get stuck somewhere? Are the measurements laid out? Any suggestions you may have are welcome. After all, cookbooks are only helpful when you actually understand them! Incorporating your ideas and suggestions into my new projects will be my show of eternal gratitude because you can only be the best at something by constantly improving and being open to change.

Thanks!

Alicia T. White

About the Author

Alicia had a tough childhood and had to take care of her siblings early. Although they often helped her with making the beds and washing, Alicia was responsible for cooking since she was the oldest of six. Being in the kitchen was still very difficult at her age, but she learned her way around the stove and oven throughout the years.

Whereas her first dishes were practically inedible, burnt rice and mushy pasta… Eventually, she turned to the oven for help as many of the dishes she wanted to make were too complicated. Nonetheless, her baked casseroles were amazing! Most importantly, they were simple and required way less clean-up.

At first, they were simple pasta bakes, but once Alicia got the hang of things, she was baking all sorts of meals. When it came to spreading the word of her delicious cooking, having 5 siblings was extremely advantageous. Soon, neighbors were placing orders for some of her casseroles! Eventually, Alicia was doing so well with the business that she hired extra help. Now it's one of the most affordable yet popular weeknight casserole services in the mid-West!

Today, she still lives with her siblings and is working hard to teach them about the family business that led them out of poverty. She likes to publish cookbooks on casseroles and one-pot meals in her free time— basically anything quick and easy. Her motto is, "If a seven-year-old can't make it, it isn't simple enough!"

Contents

Bentley Hunaudieres, a prototype not confirmed for production. Picture courtesy of Auto Express.

Motoring Pioneers

1895 – 1905

There were other internal combustion engined vehicles before it - notably the pioneering Daimler, Benz, Panhard and de Dion-Bouton - but the Lanchester first made in Birmingham in 1895 was revolutionary. Whereas the others consisted of engines installed in derivatives of carts, carriages and tricycles, the first Lanchester of 1895 was a homogenous motorcar. Frederick Lanchester's subsequent designs incorporated perfectly balanced engines (the Lanchester harmonic balancer is still used by dozens of motor companies). From soon after 1900 Lanchester also employed the first disc brakes and utilised an epicyclic semi-automatic gearbox. There was full pressure lubrication, shaft drive and a full-width body when everyone else used running boards. After making thousands of cars without compromise Lanchester joined Daimler of Coventry in 1931.

1905 – 1915

Gottlieb Daimler's successful prototype of 1895/6, along with the contemporary experiments of Carl Benz, started the motor industry. In addition to Germany, Daimler licensed production in Paris to Panhard et Levassor and also to Coventry Daimler (a firm nowadays owned via Jaguar by Ford). The Panhard system of front engine, rear wheel drive (by chains) and steering wheel was widely copied. Many customers were introduced to Daimlers in France by the Austrian Consul-General at Nice. Seeing the lower-built and more sporting Panhards he asked Daimler to come up with something similar. Panhard owned Daimler's French rights so a new name was needed and the Consul's daughter's name of Mercedes was chosen. By 1902 most of the latest German Daimlers with mechanically operated valves, pressed steel frames and gate-change gearboxes were called Mercedes. Following the first 6 litre 35 horsepower type a whole range of smooth, sleek and powerful models evolved. In the mid-1920s Daimler merged with its old rival Benz to create the new marque of Mercedes-Benz.

1915 – 1925

The Cadillac Motor Car Co. was named after the founder of 18th century Detroit. It made single cylinder cars from 1903 and within three years had the world's largest motor factory. In 1909 it became the jewel in its crown of the infant General Motors Corporation. All the latest luxury features were incorporated into the increasingly complex Cadillacs. Late in 1911 the Delco electric starter became a major innovation and within two years there was electric lighting and coil ignition too, which won for Cadillac the RAC's coveted Dewar Trophy. In 1914 came Cadillac's real tour de force, the world's first mass produced V8 engine which provided smooth and seamless power for thousands of wartime staff cars and then powered some of the top luxury cars of the 1920s and beyond.

1925 – 35

Henry Ford had worked for the company that became Cadillac before setting out on his own. The Ford Motor Co. outsold all its rivals by 1906 and in the following year introduced its immortal Model T. This became the sole Ford car available until 1928. It featured one of the world's first monobloc four cylinder engines with detachable cylinder head. It's epicyclic easy-change transmission was worked by pedals and, with constantly lower pricing, motoring became accessible to the masses. A peak 1,817,891 were built in America in 1923 (they were also made in England from 1911) and by the end a staggering fifteen million had been turned out of Detroit.

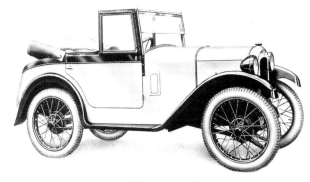

1935 – 45

Herbert Austin and William Morris did more than anyone to copy Ford's mass production ideas in Britain. Austin tried a similar 20-horsepower, one-model policy after the First World War but horsepower tax made smaller engines essential. He made a successful 12 and then sketched his immortal 7hp car on the proverbial cigarette packet. Launched in 1922 it was like a big four cylinder car in miniature rather than a skimpy cyclecar exemplified by the Morgan three wheeler. The 100,000th was sold in 1929, and the British total eventually reached 300,000. It became so popular in Japan that Datsun came up with a near replica. It was also adopted in Germany by none other than BMW and was also made in France and in America, where it indirectly led to the creation of the Jeep.

The First Millennium

1945 – 55

This was the era of the peoples' cars like the Renault 750, Citroen 2CV, Morris Minor and Austin A30 but, most famous of all after an inauspicious start, became the Volkswagen. Conceived in the 1930s as Hitler's peoples' car, 335,000 Germans placed orders but only 210 of the air-cooled, horizontally opposed four cylinder cars had been built when war intervened. Some military derivatives followed and the factory was destroyed by the Allies. To help put Germany back on its feet British soldiers re-commissioned the factory to build Beetles and Major Ivan Hirst ran the operation until handing it back to German control in 1948. The first sales to America, where it became Number One Import, took place in 1949 and in 1972 the Beetle finally overtook the Ford Model T's sales record. Well over twenty million were ultimately built, from 1979 mostly in South America.

1955 – 65.

Andre Citroen brought American-style mass production to France in 1919. He died of cancer in 1935 soon after one of the great landmark cars of the era, familiarly known as the 'traction avant' had been launched. Its monocoque construction, independent suspension and front wheel drive showed the shape of things to come but frightened off many buyers. The ultimate expression of Citroen's vision came with the streamlined DS of the mid 1950s. This had self-levelling hydro-pneumatic suspension, front wheel drive, and power assistance to its steering, gearchange and, for the first time on a family car, front disc brakes. Some, including a less complex ID version, were built at Slough in Britain. Roadholding, and particularly ride, far surpassed that of any rival for at least the next ten years.

1965 – 75.

The Mini burst on a startled world in 1959. Its designer Alec Issigonis had already brought us the popular post-war Minor but most preconceived ideas were abandoned for the Austin Seven and Morris Mini-Minor, as the Minis were originally known. A fraction over ten feet long (305 cms to be precise) it had all-round independent suspension and seated four in comfort with lots of cleverly thought out storage space around them. The 848cc four cylinder engine was placed transversely under the diminutive bonnet with gearbox and drive to the front wheels below. Roadholding with a wheel at each corner was a revelation and, when higher performance Cooper versions arrived in the 1960s, BMC basked in the glory of one of the greatest rally cars, at any rate until the arrival of the Audi Quattro in the 1970s.

1975 – 85

Volkswagen made many attempts to break the Beetle mould but all met with commercial failure until 1974. Then the Golf arrived as the complete antithesis to the Beetle, for it featured not a rear mounted air-cooled engine but a front mounted water-cooled unit.

The many fans of the Beetle were horrified, but at last VW had a modern winner and after years of loss making and being beaten into Germany's second spot by Opel, it returned to the top in 1976 (thanks also to the new Passat and the acquisition of Audi). Whilst the Golf followed a concept pioneered by others it soon earned an enviable reputation for strength and build-quality. The GTi high performance version opened up a whole new and trendy market place whilst at the same time the diesel model became one of the most trusted workhorses of the fuel conscious 1980s.

1985 – 2005

MPVs are now an established part of the motoring scene, enjoyed by families who started by liking the idea of a big 4x4 but did not need the off-road capabilities. However in 1984, when the Espace with its boxy shape and extra row of seats arrived, there was nothing quite like it. Sales were initially disappointing but as rival designs arrived, and massive resources were spent on promotion the whole idea began to attract droves of admirers. The Espace was underpinned by the front-wheel driven Trafic van and was actually created not by Renault, but by its associates at aeronautical engineers and sports-racing car manufacturer, MATRA (Mecanique Avion Traction). The Espace has been continually refined and improved over the years and continues to be the yardstick by which the other MPVs are measured. Without the benefit of hindsight it is difficult to say which will have been the landmark car as we enter the new Millennium. However a major pointer to the future has to be the introduction of a highly sophisticated compact car from one of the best known exponents of luxury cars in the world: the Mercedes A-Class.

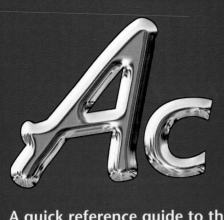

A quick reference guide to the 333 cars within this guide

Make	Model	Page		Make	Model	Page		Make	Model	Page
Hyundai	Atoz	59		Mitsubishi	Colt	85		San	Storm	133
	Accent	59			Carisma	84			Streak	133
	Lantra	59			Galant	85		Saturn	EV1	107
	Sonata	58			Magna	85			LS	107
	XG	58			Eclipse	86			SL	107
	Coupe	59			FTO	86		Seat	Arosa	109
Isuzu	Trooper	57			3000GT	86			Ibiza	108
	VehiCross	57			Space Star	85			Cordoba	108
Jaguar	S-Type	60			Space Wagon	86			Toledo	109
	XJ8	61			Space Runner	86			Alhambra	109
	XK8	61			Space Gear	87		Skoda	Felicia	110
Kia	Pride	63			Pajero Pinin	87			Octavia	110
	Mentor II	62			Shogun	87		Shelby	Series 1	111
	Shuma	62			Challenger	87		Spectre	R45	111
	Clarus	63		Mitsuoka	Galue	133		Subaru	Justy	113
	Carnival	63			Type F	133			Vivio	113
	Sportage	63		Morgan	Plus 4	88			Impreza	113
Lada	Samara	64			Plus 8	88			Legacy	112
	110	64		Nissan	Micra	90			Forester	113
	Niva	64			Almera	90		Suzuki	Alto	115
Lamborghini	Diablo	65			Primera	89			Swift	115
Lancia	Ypsilon	67			QX	90			Baleno	115
	Delta	67			200SX	91			Wagon R	115
	Lybra	66			Skyline	91			Jimny	114
	Kappa	67			Serena	90			Grand Vitara	114
	Z	67			Terrano II	91		Tata	Indica	133
Land Rover	Defender	69			Patrol	91			Safari	133
	Freelander	68		Oldsmobile	Alero	93		Toyota	Yaris	116
	Discovery	69			Intrigue	92			Corolla	117
	Range Rover	69			Aurora	93			Prius	117
Lexus	IS200	70			Bravada	93			Avensis	117
	GS300	71		Opel	Corsa	123			Camry	118
	LS400	71			Astra	123			MR2	118
	SC300	71			Vectra	123			Celica	119
	RX300	71			Omega	124			Picnic	118
Ligier	Ambra	132			Tigra	124			Previa	118
Lincoln	LS	72			Zafira	122			RAV4	119
	Continental	73			Frontera	124			Colorado	119
	Town Car	73		Perodua	Nippa	100			Amazon	119
	Navigator	73		Peugeot	106	95		TVR	Chimaera	121
Lotus	Elise	74			206	94			Griffith	121
	Esprit	74			306	95			Tuscan Speed Six	120
Mahindra	CJ	132			406	95			Cerbera	121
Marcos	LM	75			806	95		Vauxhall	Corsa	123
	MantaRay	75		Plymouth	Prowler	100			Astra	123
	Mantis	75		Pontiac	Grand Am	97			Vectra	123
Maserati	Quattroporte	79			Firebird	97			Omega	124
	3200 GT	79			Grand Prix	97			Tigra	124
Mazda	121	77			Bonneville	96			Zafira	122
	323	77			Montana	97			Frontera	124
	626	77		Porsche	911	98		Venturi	Atlantique	125
	Xedos 6	78			Boxster	98		VW	Lupo	126
	Xedos 9	78		Proton	Compact	99			Polo	127
	MX-5	78			Persona	99			Mk1 Golf	129
	RX-7	78			Perdana	99			Gol	128
	Demio	77		Reliant	Robin	132			Golf	127
	Premacy	75		Renault	Twingo	102			Beetle	127
MCC	Smart	80			Clio	101			old Beetle	129
Mercedes	A-Class	80			Megane	102			Bora	128
	C-Class	81			Laguna	103			Passat	128
	E-Class	81			Safrane	103			Sharan	128
	S-Class	81			Kangoo	102			Microbus	129
	SLK	82			Scenic	102		Volga	3111	133
	CLK	82			Espace	103		Volvo	S40/V40	131
	SL	82		Rolls-Royce	Silver Seraph	21			S70/V70	131
	V-Class	81		Rover	Mini	105			S80	130
	M-Class	82			200	105			C70	131
Mercury	Sable	83			400	105		Westfield	SEi	125
	Grand Marquis	83			75	104			FW400	125
	Villager	83		Saab	9-3	106		Zil	4104	133
	Mountaineer	83			9-5	106				
MG	MGF	105								

NEW FOR 2000

September is a vital time in the world motor industry calendar. Each year a major motor show alternates between Paris and Frankfurt, and in 1999 it was the turn of the German city to host the event where a massive number of new models were unveiled to the public. Here we bring you the most tantalising cars that will hit the streets over the next 12 months. It looks like being a bumper year.

Audi A2

A direct competitor for the Mercedes A-Class, the A2 is just as technically advanced, with an aluminium body and space-frame chassis keeping weight down, economy high. It is unlikely to reach the UK before 2001.

Audi TT Roadster

The massive success of the TT coupe delayed the launch of the roadster, but this enticing prospect goes on sale soon. The rigid body ensures the handling is as sharp as the coupe.

Audi RS4

Subtlety goes out of the window with the RS4. Based on the A4 Avant, it gains massive wheel arches, quattro four-wheel-drive and, best of all, a 2.7-litre twin-turbo V6 producing 380bhp!

BMW X5

BMW may own the Range Rover brand but that has not stopped it producing its own luxury 4x4. BMW says that the X5 is aimed at fast road use rather than providing the all-round ability of the British car.

BMW Z8

Bond's new car is an altogether more effective weapon than the Z3, even though it still relies on retro design ideas. This time, however, BMW M5 V8 power ensures that performance matches the promise.

Cadillac DeVille

A new platform, fresh bodywork and an arsenal of high-tech gizmos worthy of a Star Wars spaceship. The new DeVille even gets Night Vision to help you see in the dark!

Citroen Picasso

Citroen's answer to the Renault Megane Scenic, with a return of the design flair we used to take for granted from the French manufacturer. The Xsara provides the mechanical specification beneath the stylish body.

Chrysler Neon

The car with the bug-eyed headlights and cute smile grows-up for 2000. Longer, wider and more spacious than before, with improved comfort but the same vocal 2.0-litre engine.

Daewoo Tacuma

Daewoo's mini people carrier offers both sporty and executive styles plus an abundance of space on its Nubira-derived chassis. 1.8, 2.0 and a new turbo diesel will be on offer. UK sales start in late 2000.

Ford Fiesta

A fresh corporate nose, a new 1.6 and the option of automatic transmission are the key points of this facelifted Fiesta, but the all-new model is still a few years away.

Ford Excursion

The Excursion has the dubious honour of being the world's biggest and heaviest sport-utility vehicle. It has engines to match, rising up to a 7.3-litre V8 turbo-diesel, and can carry nine people. Size matters.

Fiat Punto

Fiat replaces the Punto with this all-new model even though the original still held up well. Improvements in refinement and quality are the main aims, but the two body styles add extra interest.

Hyundai Santa Fe

Hyundai expands its range with its first ever sport utility vehicle. Style is high on the agenda, but the 3.0-litre V6 should ensure strong performance too.

NEW FOR 2000

Lotus 340R

Take the Lotus Elise, arguably the finest sports car of its generation, and make it lighter, more powerful and better handling. The 340R is aimed as much at the race track as the road, but guarantees thrills wherever it goes.

Mercedes-Benz CL Coupe

Last year Mercedes-Benz launched the outstanding S-Class saloon. Now it is the turn of the coupe derivative, without doubt the best-looking that Mercedes has offered. The prices are equally impressively high.

Morgan 4/4

Morgan reintroduces the four-seater with more space and improved safety features. A four seater sports car is an incongruous idea, but Morgan sells a couple a week, from its overall weekly production of eleven cars.

Mercedes-Benz SLR

What started out as a styling exercise is now promised for production, albeit in very limited numbers. McLaren, Mercedes' partner in Grand Prix racing, will build the SLR in England.

Mitsubishi Pinin

Having dominated many markets for years with its full-sized Shogun/Pajero, Mitsubishi launches a smaller version, the Pinin, to compete in the "lifestyle" arena. This one is built in Italy.

Mitsubishi Eclipse

The latest version of the Eclipse was designed in the States for US buyers. It looks good and is bags of fun to drive too. A soft top version follows soon.

Nissan Almera

The 2000 Almera, to be built in the UK, features less adventurous styling than the old model, probably a good thing. 1.5 and 1.8-litre petrol engines, plus a new 2.2 direct inject turbo-diesel, provide the power.

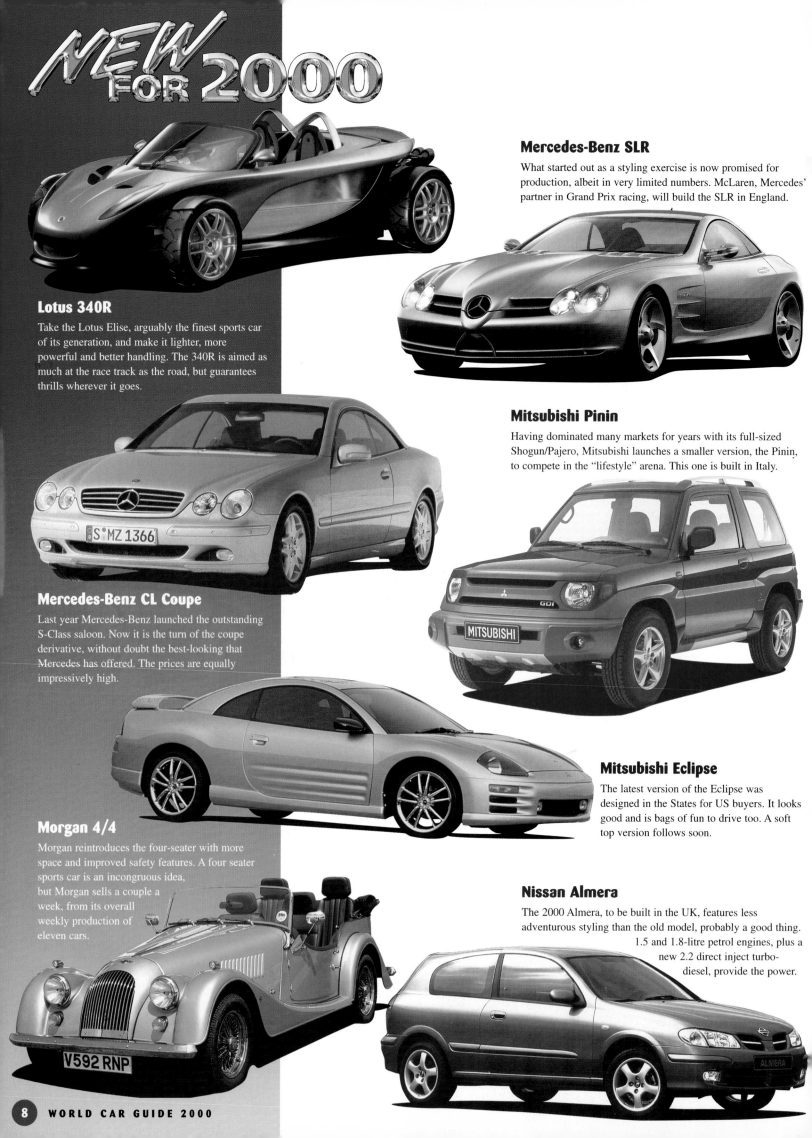

Nissan Almera Tino

Derived from the new Almera hatchback, the Tino follows the latest vogue by offering lots of space and great versatility within a compact package. The Japanese version has been re-engineered for Europe and will be built in Spain.

Oldsmobile Aurora

Gone is the visual impact of the old car, but this new Aurora has plenty to offer luxury car buyers, not least a 4.0-litre V8 and leather lined comfort for five.

Peugeot 206 Convertible

Peugeot could steal the show for affordable convertibles with the forthcoming 206. With a steel roof like the Mercedes SLK, it offers the comfort and security of a coupe in winter.

Peugeot 607

It has been a long time since Peugeot produced an executive model that had much appeal to buyers outside France. The new 607 certainly seems to have the style to succeed, but has it the charisma?

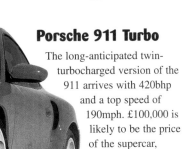

Porsche 911 Turbo

The long-anticipated twin-turbocharged version of the 911 arrives with 420bhp and a top speed of 190mph. £100,000 is likely to be the price of the supercar, which arrives in Summer 2000.

Renault Avantime

Few believed that Renault would have the gall to turn this show car into a production reality, but it is happening. Based upon the V6 Espace chassis, the Avantime is being sold as luxurious coupe.

Renault Clio Sport V6

It may look like a beefed up Clio but, oh yes, it's far more than that. It has room only for two for a start, and the 3.0-litre engine sits behind the front seats and pushes out 250bhp. Just like a Boxster S in fact.

NEW FOR 2000

Rover 25

Re-launched as the "premium" competitor for the Fiesta, Peugeot 206 and Polo, this facelifted version of the 200 gets a restyle like the 75, new seats and uprated suspension for sportier handling.

Renault Scenic RX4

Add four-wheel-drive, raised suspension and a heap of body armour to a Scenic and you get the new RX4. With the Scenic's legendary space and versatility, it should compare well with the lifestyle off-roaders.

Seat León

The great looking new Toledo is transformed into an even sexier hatchback, the León. Seat has tried to combine coupe looks with family practicality, so there is a wide range of engines to suit every need.

Skoda Fabia

Skoda's all new supermini is positioned between the Felicia and Octavia and is the first on VW's new small car chassis. Sales start in Europe at the end of 1999, in the UK in 2000.

Saturn L Series

Saturn moves into bigger cars with saloon and estate based loosely on the Opel/Vauxhall Vectra. Ding-resistant plastic body panels, in Saturn tradition, feature as do 2.2 and 3.0V6 power units.

Strathcarron

This exciting new British sports car project comprises a light composite-chassised roadster powered by a Triumph motorcycle engine. Its 600kg weight should ensure strong performance, the sub-£20,000 price should ensure strong sales.

Toyota Yaris Verso

Toyota takes its acclaimed Yaris supermini and pumps it up to make a baby MPV. The extra height and length improves space for people and passengers; power comes from a new 1.3-litre engine.

Toyota Celica

A dramatic redesign for Toyota's Celica, now smaller and sportier than the coupes of the past. Both versions get a 1.8-litre engine, the 140bhp model appears late in 1999, the more powerful 180bhp Celica in 2000.

Vauxhall/Opel Astra Coupe

Spiritual replacement for the Calibra, the Astra Coupe arrives in the summer with a choice of three two-litre engines of up to 188bhp. It will be built by Bertone, the Italian coach builder and designer.

Vauxhall Speedster

Lotus will build this dynamic new sports car that will go head-to-head with the new Toyota MR2. Based upon the chassis of the Lotus Elise, but with a 2.2-litre engine and more comfort, the omens are good.

Volkswagen Concept D

Concept D is the prototype for a new luxury car from Volkswagen, with the style of a coupe but four-door practicality. Technically highly advanced, the range of V10 and W12 engines puts it in a class of its own.

Toyota MR2 Roadster

The styling may not be to everyone's taste, but the third generation MR2 is a true sports car again. A mid-engined convertible, the 140bhp 1.8 VVT-i engine pitches it straight against the MGF and Mazda MX5.

Vauxhall/Opel Agila

Lacking a contender in the increasingly popular town car category, General Motors has teamed up with Suzuki to take the next generation Wagon R and transform it into the Agila with European engines.

Volkswagen Polo

The Polo gets a new look for the Millennium, with bigger headlights, stylised dashboard and a galvanised body with a 12-year corrosion warranty. Twin airbags, ABS brakes and a new 125bhp GTi model add further appeal.

UK BEST SELLERS

Ford Fiesta

100

There are over 250 models of car on sale in the UK, but if you listen to the manufacturers, who would like you to think that a 2.0 LX is a completely different car to the 2.0 GLX, the number rises to over a couple of thousand. So making a sensible decision about which to choose is never going to be easy. One thing is certain, however. If you pick the easy route and buy the class best seller, you are likely to miss out on some wonderful alternatives. Here we run through the choices, the graphs showing how well each car sells compared with the most popular in its class.

2 Ford Focus

99

3 Vauxhall Astra

92

4 Vauxhall Corsa

84

5 Vauxhall Vectra

81

6 Ford Mondeo

78

7 VW Golf

70

8 Renault Clio

68

9 Renault Megane

66

10 Peugeot 206

53

THE TOP TEN

Budget Buys

That the Ford Ka outsells its nearest rival here more than twice is proof enough of the blue oval's draw. Not that the Ka is without merit; its Fiesta base provides a good drive, while cheeky style compensates somewhat for the grand price and compact accommodation. The Skoda Felicia is due for replacement soon but, deservedly, keeps picking up awards anyway thanks to its talents. Just a few years ago, buying a budget car would have meant picking up a cheaply made also-ran - like the Suzuki Swift - but newer models like the Daewoo Matiz and Fiat Seicento go to show how far the market has come recently.

Pick of the bunch: Skoda Felicia

1. Ford Ka 100
2. Skoda Felicia 48
3. Fiat Seicento 31
4. Daewoo Matiz 25
5. Suzuki Swift 16

Superminis

In a tight market segment with small profit margins and extremely competitive pricing, the top spot is vied for by The Big Two - Ford and Vauxhall. The Fiesta, due for substantial alteration in 2000, is a considerably better car than the dated Corsa, and the Vauxhall's other major competitors are newer too. The Clio, new in 1998, is a reasonable bet, whilst the all new 206 and the VW Polo both prove competitive. Missing out on top five spots are the old Fiat Punto - the new version debuts late in '99 - and Toyota's excellent new Yaris.

Pick of the bunch: Toyota Yaris

1. Ford Fiesta 100
2. Vauxhall Corsa 84
3. Renault Clio 68
4. Peugeot 206 54
5. VW Polo 46

Small Family Cars

No surprises at the top - Ford's Focus narrowly leads the Vauxhall Astra and Volkswagen Golf. All are fine cars with different and appealing virtues, whilst Renault's Megane shows a strong fourth place thanks in part to class leading safety features and attractive pricing. The partly-replaced Escort is still finding some favour outside the top-five, as is Rover's 200. The all-conquering Focus is perhaps the best all-rounder, but the Astra scores highly in terms of driver appeal and practicality, without the controversial looks. The Golf's interior quality feels better than both, whilst the ageing 306 is still an enjoyable, stylish drive.

Pick of the bunch: Volkswagen Golf

1. Ford Focus 100
2. Vauxhall Astra 93
3. VW Golf 71
4. Renault Megane 67
5. Peugeot 306 53

Medium Family Cars

In the big fleet market sector, selling cars means offering comfy cruising, high equipment levels, competitive pricing and heavy discounting. Ford and Vauxhall rule, with their constantly upgraded ranges. The Mondeo has the edge over the Vectra in terms of driver appeal, but the Peugeot 406 betters both and a mid-1999 facelift with a superb diesel keeps it on the pace. The Rover 400 is fighting a class above its weight, whilst the Renault Laguna scores mostly on pricing, equipment and style. Just outside the top five sits the VW Passat, with an interior that feels a class apart from all its rivals, while the driving experience is fine and the diesel is great.

Pick of the bunch: Volkswagen Passat

1. Vauxhall Vectra 100
2. Ford Mondeo 98
3. Peugeot 406 48
4. Rover 400 41
5. Renault Laguna 39

Compact Executive Cars

There is no doubt who rules this class: the excellent new BMW 3 Series behaves like a baby 5 in terms of quality, style and refinement. It's not cheap though, especially when compared to the Lexus IS200 newcomer. The IS200 misses out in this top five but the driving experience, price, equipment levels and looks make it a sure-fire winner. The Audi A4 was revised early in 1999 to keep it competitive, whilst Rover's new 75 should sell well - its interior is superb. Mercedes' C-class looks a bit dated and expensive in this company now. Alfa's 156 still fails to make it anywhere near the top five, but is undoubtedly a fine machine.

Pick of the bunch: Lexus IS200

1. BMW 3 Series — 100
2. Audi A4 — 40
3. Mercedes C-Class — 40
4. Saab 9-3 — 24
5. Volvo S/V70 — 20

Executive Cars

Competitive pricing and 'Buy British' fleets keep the Vauxhall Omega in the top spot here, despite it needing a facelift - due late in 1999. Otherwise, the still brilliant BMW 5 Series leads the way in both sales and driver appeal. Mercedes' E-class is a quality but pricey item. The Audi A6 has Teutonic appeal whilst the Saab 9-5 attracts in a more relaxed manner. Jaguar's new entry into this market, the S-Type, wins plaudits for its refinement. A further batch of fine cars sell in fewer numbers: the Alfa Romeo 166, Volvo S80 and Lexus GS300 all put up a good case for themselves.

Pick of the bunch: BMW 5 Series

1. Vauxhall Omega — 100
2. BMW 5 Series — 98
3. Mercedes E-Class — 81
4. Audi A6 — 47
5. Saab 9-5 — 43

Sports Cars

The MX-5 continues to dominate UK sports car sales thanks to its cute looks, cast-iron reliability, residual values and, of course, the fact that it is simply superb to drive. Cast-iron reliability is a phrase less-associated with the MGF, but that doesn't stop owners loving the way they look and the way they go. Buyers of BMW's 1999 revised Z3 can expect great build too and, though expensive, residual values and kudos are surpassed only by far more pricey models like the Mercedes-Benz SLK, let down only by its coarse engine. Porsche's incredibly successful Boxster is easily worthy of its top-five spot.

Pick of the bunch: Porsche Boxster

1. Mazda MX-5 — 100
2. MGF — 82
3. BMW Z3 — 76
4. Mercedes SLK — 47
5. Porsche Boxster — 34

Coupes

Ford's Fiesta-based wonder, the Puma, continues to pull in the young and young-at-heart, with styling that still turns heads and a chassis that still turns corners like little else at the price. Its larger Cougar stablemate also offers the looks, but is a bit short on ability. BMW still shifts large quantities of its impressive 3 Series, updated in June 1999 with the new version. The C-class based Mercedes CLK is gaining in popularity as a swift executive express too now that supply is up. Vauxhall's cute Tigra still appeals on a style level too, even though it has been around for a few years.

Pick of the bunch: Ford Puma

1. Ford Puma — 100
2. Ford Cougar — 68
3. Mercedes CLK — 63
4. BMW 3 Series — 56
5. Vauxhall Tigra — 51

Luxury Cars

That the Jaguar XJ8 range starts at 'just' £35,000 is not the only reason it tops the UK luxury sales charts. Its fine looks, sumptuous gentlemen's club-like interior and wondrous refinement also assure the top spot. A bit less English Heritage feel is given by its German counterparts. The solid-look-and-feel BMW 7 Series and Audi A8 are both 1999 revised models which provide rewarding driving experiences, superb refinement and great build quality. Meanwhile, the all-new, all-conquering Mercedes-Benz S-class is the reason for the other Germans' revamps: it resets class standards. Lexus' LS400 is a fine car too, but lacks the ambience of its rivals here.

Pick of the bunch: Mercedes-Benz S-class

1. Jaguar XJ8
100
2. BMW 7 Series
67
3. Mercedes S-Class
50
4. Audi A8
21
5. Lexus LS400
8

Off-Roaders

Despite reliability scare stories the trendy new Freelander eclipses all-comers here. Its blend of road-going qualities and fashionable good looks maintain the appeal enough to make it outsell its nearest rival, the 1999 revised and much improved Discovery, by nearly two-to-one. For those who choose roads more often than fields, Honda's CR-V is an excellent, car-like choice, as is the Toyota RAV4. Another recently revamped car, the Vauxhall Frontera, still appeals on its rugged looks and image but in truth, it lags behind most competitors. The wide and diverse range of choice in this sector means that there's something for everyone, even if it doesn't make the top sellers listing.

Pick of the bunch: Land Rover Freelander

1. Land Rover Freelander
100
2. Land Rover Discovery
62
3. Honda CR—V
41
4. Vauxhall Frontera
39
5. Toyota RAV4
30

MPV's

Despite the fact that they're based on the same car, Ford's Galaxy outsells its Volkswagen Sharan sibling by three-to-one and the Seat Alhambra by five-to-one. None is a poor choice, handling reasonably well and accommodating large families comfortably. The same can be said of the popular Chrysler Voyager, especially convenient despite the bad press surrounding its safety. Renault's evergreen Espace is also offered in Grand form, which makes it a useful, if expensive, travelling tool. Although a late-comer to the party, the seven-seat Vauxhall Zafira features highly and betters the Megane Scenic – not included here because it only has seating for five.

Pick of the bunch: Vauxhall Zafira

1. Ford Galaxy
100
2. Chrysler Voyager
42
3. Renault Espace
35
4. VW Sharan
33
5. Vauxhall Zafira
23

Exotics

Includes a mixed-bunch of supercars and long-legged GTs, with the latter dominating sales. Porsche's new 911 continues recent Porsche themes – a bit more pace, a bit more subtlety, a bit more refinement, a bit more like Jaguar's sublime XK8. The Coventry cat is a real competitor to the new 911, quite unlike Ferrari's F355, replaced in 1999 by the 360 Modena. The Ferrari is the definitive sports car in this section and narrowly misses a top-five sales spot. Mercedes-Benz's SL and BMW 8 Series are still impressive, but Aston's DB7 shows both how to go Grand Touring, with the Vantage version boosting it right up the desirability index.

Pick of the bunch: Porsche 911

1. Porsche 911
100
2. Jaguar XK8
92
3. MercedesSL
38
4. BMW 8 Series
14
5. Aston Martin DB7
12

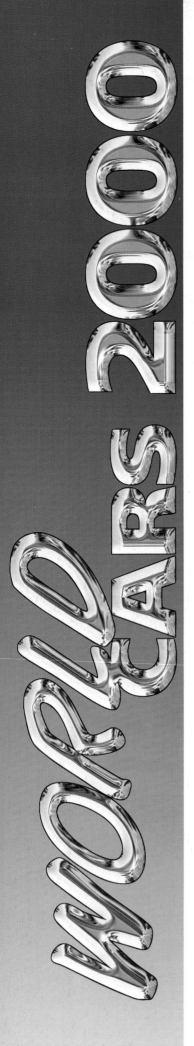

WORLD CARS 2000

The World Car Guide 2000 is the most comprehensive source around for information on the world's automobiles. And, with more than 110 pages dedicated to over 300 models from 60 manufacturers, this year's edition is the biggest and best yet – it's our definitive guide to motoring at the end of the 20th Century.

Since the 1999 edition, we have driven hundreds of new models and interviewed dozens of company directors, designers, and engineers. Add the fact that our vastly experienced team of testers have driven nearly every model in the world, across every continent, and you can see why the insight you get here is one you can trust. As always, each car entry gives you details of the range plus the model which exhibits the best all-round characteristics. While it would have been all too easy to pick the most expensive version of each car, cost has been included in the equation too, so that our Best All-Rounder represents a fine blend between its qualities as a car and its value for money.

Determining the country of manufacturer becomes increasingly confusing. Is a Ford Fiesta a "British" car? It may be but there is a 50:50 chance that it has been built in Spain. How about the BMW Z3 – German? No, it comes from the USA. Toyota Avensis – Japanese? Wrong again, it is built in Britain. But even "built" is confusing, for what the manufacturer usually means that is where the final assembly takes place. The new

Peugeot 206 is built in France and England, but the British models use imported body panels, engines, gearboxes and suspension. Does it all matter? Probably not, because all manufacturers make doubly sure the new factories they build produce cars to the same or even better standards than the original.

Car entries in the catalogue contain a limited amount of technical data, but for a fuller account, a comprehensive database is included after the main catalogue section. It contains information on almost every model listed in the main catalogue section, although occasionally data on the newest cars was not available before we went to press.

Finally, we give you a comprehensive listing of new car prices for the UK market. We wait until the last possible minute before going to press to make sure this is as up-to-date as possible. But, as car prices change on a regular basis, check out the most recent costs in the weekly magazine Auto Express, or visit www.autoexpress.co.uk, and see full specs with option prices, too.

Picking the Right Car

Cars usually fall into a number of convenient categories, an idea usually supported by the industry, although there are those brave enough to develop new concepts, such as Mercedes-Benz with the radical A-Class. But in general new cars follow old trends. So the Ford Focus is much the same size as the Escort, even though, as things always go, it will be a touch longer and roomier, a bit quicker and marginally more economical.

At the other extreme a fascinating blend of mechanical components can be used to produce several cars from the same basic ingredients. The Volkswagen Group is a master of this. Take one floorpan, pick from a selection of engines, transmissions and suspensions, then design a range of distinctive body styles. Volkswagen's result is the Golf, new Beetle, Audi A3, Audi TT, Skoda Octavia, Seat Toledo and Seat Leon. Or simpler still, take the same vehicle and just stick a different badge on it – what you get is the Citroen Synergie, Peugeot 806, Fiat Ulysse and Lancia Z. Economic realities mean that these type of deals can only increase. Below are listed the most significant on the market today.

Small Cars

Ford Fiesta and Mazda 121
Mazda's 121 is identical to the Ford Fiesta, built on the same production line in Dagenham. But despite a far better warranty on the 121, the Fiesta outsells it a hundred times in the UK.

Peugeot 106 and Citroen Saxo
Peugeot facelifted the 106 for 1997 with a new nose, tail and interior. Citroen adopted the car at the same time with only subtle changes to the exterior, plus a different dashboard.

Suzuki Swift and Subaru Justy
In earlier incarnations there was the original Subaru Justy. Now it is merely a four-wheel-drive version of Suzuki's Swift. Both are built in Hungary.

Seat Arosa and Volkswagen Lupo
Volkswagen's just-launched Lupo may look distinctly charming, but it has been around for well over a year wearing the clothes of the Seat Arosa.

VW Polo, Seat Ibiza and Cordoba
VW owns Seat, and all these small cars are similar under the skin. The Polo saloon and Estate use the Cordoba body with very few changes.

Family Cars

Audi A3, Seat Leon, Seat Toledo, Skoda Octavia, Volkswagen Golf, Volkswagen Beetle
This one is cleverer than most, because the Octavia and new Toledo have been made to look like they are a class bigger than the Golf and Audi, while the Beetle is different again. Oh, and the Audi TT coupe is also based on the same chassis.

Rover 400 and Honda Civic
Originally a Honda design, Rover restyled it and inserted its own engines. In 1997 Honda had a make-over on its five-door Civic and in 1999 Rover did the same with the 400/45, so the two cars look increasingly different. Both cars are manufactured in the UK. Confusingly, three-door and saloon Civics are of a different generation.

Volvo V40 and Mitsubishi Carisma
Built in the same factory in Holland, with the same underpinnings, but distinctly different bodies and engines. About as different as you can get with a jointly developed car.

MPVs or People Carriers

Citroen Evasion, Citroen Synergie, Peugeot 806, Fiat Ulysse, Lancia Z
A joint venture between the French PSA company (Citroen and Peugeot) and Italian Fiat (Fiat and Lancia). Same engines in all, differences in trim.

Ford Galaxy, Volkswagen Sharan and Seat Alhambra
Built in a Portuguese factory. Turbo-diesel and V6 engines from VW, but each company uses its own 2.0-litre.

Off-Roaders

Isuzu Trooper and Opel Monterey
Sold for several years in the UK by Isuzu and in Europe by Opel, before Vauxhall muscled in during 1994. Vauxhall sales have been poor, and the Monterey has been dropped in the UK.

Isuzu Rodeo and Vauxhall/Opel Frontera
The Japanese-manufactured Rodeo is little seen in Europe, but it is also built in England and sold as the Frontera throughout the European Community.

AC

The British sports car maker has not had an easy time of it over the years. It has had a number of owners and partners, most of whom have been troubled by the tricky reality that AC have, for far too long, relied on just a single model designed over 40 years ago, to form the core of the business. There is no denying that what we all think of as the Cobra (but can no longer be called that for legal reasons) is a highly charismatic vehicle, but there is a limit to the number of buyers willing to pay £70,000 for such a basic fun machine. For 2000 it has a been joined by the more affordable CRS carbon-fibre-bodied model. Progress is also being made with the Ace and Aceca, luxury convertible and coupe, with bodies built in South Africa and then shipped to the UK for assembly.

Body styles:	Convertible, coupe
Engine capacity:	4.6V8, 5.0V8, 5.0V8 supercharged
Price from:	£70,000
Manufactured in:	England

Ace/Aceca

After years producing its uncompromising roadster, AC needed a more luxurious model to tempt a greater audience. Hence the Ace, a modern rival to the Mercedes-Benz SL and Jaguar XK8 and the newer Aceca, effectively the Ace in coupe form. On paper they seem impressive, with a US-sourced 5.0-litre V8 delivering supercar performance, but AC's limited resources mean the design is too dated and flawed. The interior is beautifully trimmed in traditional wood and leather but mass-produced Ford switchgear spoils the effect somewhat. Under its latest owners the Ace and Aceca have progressed nicely - there is a Lotus twin-turbo V8 on the way - but they remain a brave way to spend upwards of £70,000.

Best All-Rounder: Ace 4.6 V8

Body styles:	Convertible
Engine capacity:	5.0V8 supercharged
Price from:	£40,000
Manufactured in:	England

Superblower

The roads may be awash with look-alike kit-cars, but the Superblower is the only Cobra which can wear the AC badge with pride – and legally. The price has always been the off-putting factor – £70,000 for the aluminium-bodied model – but now AC has bowed to the inevitable by offering a sub-£40,000 carbon fibre alternative. In its hairiest incarnation the Cobra thrills with a huge supercharged V8 engine producing an awesome 355bhp. But at this price almost all competitors will be more comfortable, practical and safer than the AC. Still, the brutish straight-line performance, old-fashioned handling and famous name may be enough to part some enthusiasts from their money.

Best All-Rounder: Cobra 5.0V8

ALFA ROMEO

Flushed with the success of the 156, Alfa Romeo now needs to make sure that the impetus is not lost with the rest of the range. As always the emphasis with Alfas is an enticing sporting nature that no-one – not even BMW – can manage to emulate. The GTV and Spider fulfil that role admirably, the new 166 is also impressive to drive, though its appearance may be too understated for some. Recent developments on the 156, which include the Selespeed transmission with steering wheel gearchange control, keep Alfa at the forefront. All that is needed now are replacements for the rather tired 145 and 146 – due soon.

Body styles:	Hatchback
Engine capacity:	1.4, 1.6, 1.8, 2.0, 1.9TD
Price from:	£14,500
Manufactured in:	Italy

Alfa Romeo 145/146

In the shadow of more hyped and more recent competition, Alfa Romeo's Ford Focus class contenders are often overlooked. Characterful, the 145 'bread van' 3-door hatchback offers a smidgen more sporting pretence than the more mature 146 5-door. Both are sprightly though, with their choice of cracking 1.6, 1.8 and 2.0-litre petrol engines. But time is starting to tell for the 145 and 146; even a recently re-vamped interior and exterior cannot hide some awkward ergonomics. Interior packaging has never been any Alfa's raison d'être; enthusiastic, vocal engines, sharp steering, brow-raising looks and entertaining chassis rightly still find more favour with Alfa devotees.

Best All-Rounder: 146 1.8 Twin Spark

Alfa Romeo 156

Not only did it win European Car of the Year 1997, Alfa Romeo's best ever upper-medium contender is still winning plaudits two years after its launch. The initial range of 1.8, 2.0-litre and 2.5 V6 petrol engines has been boosted with the introduction of a five-cylinder turbo-diesel which really does credit to Alfa Romeo's sporting heritage. An estate looks like making a debut too, whilst the Selespeed clutchless transmission, introduced in spring '99, is a real boon for enthusiastic driving. Of course, it's the looks which seal it for most people, but the way this Alfa satisfies in everyday use makes it a great complete package.

Body styles:
Saloon

Engine capacity:
1.6, 1.8, 2.0, 2.5V6, 1.9TD, 2.4TD

Price from:
£18,000

Manufactured in:
Italy

Best All-Rounder: 156 2.0 Selespeed

Alfa Romeo 166

Gone is the crisp style of the 164, the new 166 offering a blend of curves that is perhaps a bit too subtle. But there can be little argument about the quality of what lays beneath. The chassis is based upon that of the Lancia Kappa, the engines are familiar lusty units that makes even the biggest of Alfas so good to drive: 2.0-litre, a 2.0-litre turbo V6 with 205bhp (mainly for the Italian market), a 190bhp 2.5V6 and 226bhp 3.0V6. There is also a sporty common-rail 2.4-litre, five-cylinder turbo-diesel. Inside there is considerable comfort for four, a great driving position and a quick, precise gearshift. But the 166 is not just for enthusiasts, there is a grace about the car too.

Body styles:
Saloon

Engine capacity:
2.0, 2.0V6, 2.5V6, 3.0V6, 2.4TD

Price from:
£23,400

Manufactured in:
Italy

Best All-Rounder: 166 2.5V6

Alfa Romeo GTV

The GTV is a perfect blend of soft curves and subtle menace. Even four years on from its introduction there is little to touch its style, and it is just as good to drive. Power comes from either a 155bhp 2.0-litre Twin Spark or a 3.0-litre 24-valve V6. Both are lively, extremely eager to rev hard and make the most glorious noise. The V6 is a truly rapid machine, though the front-wheel-drive chassis can be a little twitchy when asked to transmit every last 226 bhp. Inside there is a revised and much improved fascia, though the GTV remains a car for two – the rear seats and boot are so small it's silly.

Body styles:
Coupe

Engine capacity:
1.8, 2.0, 2.0 turbo 3.0V6

Price from:
£22,200

Manufactured in:
Italy

Best All-Rounder: GTV 3.0 V6 24v

Alfa Romeo Spider

The Spider manages to offer even more visual appeal than the GTV on which it is based, and anyone looking for a sports car that stands out alongside a Mazda MX–5 or Honda S2000 needs look no further. Mid-term revisions have improved the interior, added an adjustable steering wheel and enhanced the flexibility of the 2.0-litre engine. But the combination of front-wheel-drive and a considerable amount of weight means that the Alfa Spider struggles hard to compete on the road with much of the competition. A hood that is awkward and the tiny boot don't help the argument either. But as a style statement the Spider remains a winner.

Body styles:
Convertible

Engine capacity:
1.8, 2.0, 2.0 turbo

Price from:
£23,600

Manufactured in:
Italy

Best All-Rounder: Spider 2.0

ASTON MARTIN

With the backing of Ford, Aston Martin has gone from strength to strength. The DB7 is now the best selling Aston Martin of all time and was joined in 1999 by the breathtaking Vantage. £90,000 is a great deal of money in anyone's terms, but the Vantage offers the promise of 420 bhp V12 performance for little more than half the price of the equivalent Ferrari. And who could argue with those looks? The V8 has become a bit of an old stager now, answering a small need from those who find that the DB7 does not offer enough exclusivity, but in reality too elderly to compete on equal terms with the more modern competition.

Aston Martin DB7

The DB7 has been the saviour of Aston Martin, raising its profile by offering a car that, even though it starts at £85,000, has multiplied sales. New for 2000 is the Vantage, powered by a 6-litre, 420bhp V12 developed by owner Ford. Like the "standard" car it uses many Jaguar and Ford components, but the craftsman built wood and leather interior and kudos of the badge make it worth the extra. The coupe DB7 is a grand tourer of the old school, with ultra refinement and mile munching ability, but even the six-cylinder model is capable of surprising supercars with its 165mph performance and supercharger-boosted mid-range punch. The Volante convertible is more of a cruiser, but open-top cars don't come much more desirable.

Best All-Rounder: DB7 Vantage

Body styles:	Coupe, convertible
Engine capacity:	3.2 supercharged, 6.0V12
Price from:	£85,000
Manufactured in:	England

Body styles:	Coupe, convertible
Engine capacity:	5.4V8, 5.4V8 twin-turbo
Price from:	£149,500
Manufactured in:	England

Aston Martin V8/Vantage

The cheapest Coupe may cost more than most people's mortgages, but for die-hard Aston Martin enthusiasts the V8 and Vantage are still the real thing. Hand built by craftsmen using skills almost extinct elsewhere in the industry, cars are made exactly to the customer's specification, down to the colour of the seat piping; it is even possible to specify a shooting brake body. And while this Aston Martin may have the luxury and quality to match – or even better – a Rolls Royce, each is capable of scaring most drivers with its massive V8 engine. For something special, pick the V8 Volante – an open-top gentleman's club on wheels – or the awesome tuned 550bhp Vantage, one of the fastest and most exclusive cars in the world.

Best All-Rounder: Aston Martin V8 Coupe

BENTLEY & ROLLS ROYCE

Now that the dust has settled in the battle for who is going to own the Rolls-Royce Motor Cars, it is helpful to spell out the details. Volkswagen has bought the company, but BMW has bought the Rolls-Royce name. VW owns the factory and will continue building both makes there until the end of 2002. From that point BMW will take on Rolls-Royce and is certain to bring out all-new models, which it will build elsewhere. Volkswagen, of course, are now in the slightly embarrassing situation of building two cars – the Arnage and Silver Seraph – powered by BMW engines. But having brought engine production back to Crewe this year, the Arnage will get the option of the long-running 6.75-litre twin turbo too.

Rolls-Royce Silver Seraph

Body styles:	Saloon
Engine capacity:	5.4V12
Price from:	£155,000
Manufactured in:	England

Bentley Arnage

Body styles:	Saloon
Engine capacity:	4.4V8 twin-turbo
Price from:	£145,000
Manufactured in:	England

Bentley Arnage/Rolls-Royce Silver Seraph

The final new car produced by the "old" company was, as became commonplace, developed in two slightly different directions to become either a Rolls-Royce or a Bentley. Both move the boundaries far from the earlier cars, relying on technical input from BMW including, in the Arnage, a 4.4-litre twin-turbocharged V8, five-speed automatic transmission and computer-controlled suspension, braking and stability control systems. The Silver Seraph gets a BMW-derived V12 engine instead, and suspension tuned more towards comfort than the Bentley's sporting set up. None of this is at the exclusion of sumptuous luxury in either car, of course.

Bentley Azure and Continental

Body styles:	Coupe, convertible
Engine capacity:	6.8V8 twin-turbo
Price from:	£200,000
Manufactured in:	England

Bentley Azure and Continental

For those who disdain the prospect of a BMW-powered Bentley, the Continental coupes or the Azure convertible provide the answer. The Continental R and Azure share the old Turbo R saloon's formidable twin-turbo 385bhp 6.75-litre engine and consequently the decidedly un-regal performance. While there is no way that cars of this size could ever feel truly sporting, agility is not a top priority and there is plenty of sheer grip. Those who crave for yet more performance, together with yet more exclusivity, can take the Continental T. Inside there is a rather tasteless aluminium dashboard, but its 400-plus bhp gives almost Ferrari-like performance.

AUDI

Audi used to be the glamourous end of the Volkswagen Group, but now Lamborghini and Bugatti are also in the fold, that position is less clear cut. No matter, for Audi has its own trump card, the TT, which is drawing customers into the showrooms like never before. This Hungarian-assembled sportster has generated massive waiting lists, but the rest of the Audi range has had to be content with mild revisions to maintain the interest. Over the past year the main thrust has been to introduce ever-faster versions of the four-seaters, although the turbo-diesels continue to get better and better – the latest is a 3.3-litre V8 for the A8.

Body styles:	Coupe, convertible
Engine capacity:	1.8 turbo
Price from:	£26,700
Manufactured in:	Hungary

Audi TT

The TT has to take the prize for the most daring car to be introduced in the last decade. Few motor show concept cars make it to final production, but the TT coupe – and soon the roadster version – look almost identical to the wild show car. The TT gets two engine options, both 1.8-litres and both turbo-charged to produce 180bhp or 225bhp. Quattro four-wheel drive is compulsory on the more powerful model, with front wheel drive an option on the 180. The result is a breathtaking sports car, with dynamic or just plain explosive acceleration, depending upon your choice of engine, and leech-like roadholding. You have to drive around some transmission jerk in the quattro, but otherwise there's little to fault in the TT.

Best All-Rounder: TT 220bhp

Body styles:	Convertible
Engine capacity:	1.8, 2.6V6, 2.8V6, 1.9TDi
Price from:	£22,300
Manufactured in:	Germany

Audi Cabriolet

Audi bases its Cabriolet on a superseded car, in this case the 80 saloon. This may seem a strange thing to do but some judicious development and continuing UK demand have helped keep sales ticking along. The inside is much like the old 80, and like the exterior, it hasn't dated too much. The slab-like dashboard is functional and solid, with a quality feel which puts many new prestige cars to shame. The driving experience is more cruiser than sports car, with steering that lacks enough feel for the enthusiastic driver. But if a head turning, relaxed cruise is your bag, then the Cabriolet still competes.

Best All-Rounder: Cabriolet 2.6

Audi A3

It may be the same underneath as the Volkswagen Golf, but the smallest Audi still exudes the sort of quality and style which lifts it into a higher class. And it needs to, for it's pricey for a hatchback of this size. The range has been expanded recently, with the addition of five-door hatchbacks as well as higher performance versions with four-wheel-drive, including the stunning S3. The range starts with fine 1.6-litre and 1.8-litre petrol engines, but the 110bhp turbo-diesel is a real star, with 45mpg economy and real GTi style performance. Allied to comfort and style, the A3 still offers sufficient cachet to deserve its market niche.

Body styles:
Hatchback

Engine capacity:
1.6, 1.8, 1.8 Turbo, 1.9TDi

Price from:
£15,200

Manufactured in:
Germany

Best All-Rounder: A3 1.9 TDI SE

Audi A4

Despite a mild makeover early in 1999, the Audi A4 is now the oldest car in a tough class that features the BMW 3 Series, Alfa 156 and the new small Lexus. It remains, however, an impressive compact executive saloon with fine handling and refinement blended with top quality, style and comfort. The Avant is more of a lifestyle estate than a load lugger while the four-wheel-drive quattro models offer unrivalled roadholding in this class. The A4 range gets continually stronger with a new more powerful 1.8 Turbo model with 180bhp. But the smooth 2.4-litre V6 petrol and torquey 150bhp V6 diesel are the cream of the crop, with the tempting entry-level 1.6-litre models under-powered.

Body styles:
Saloon, estate

Engine capacity:
1.6, 1.8, 1.8 Turbo, 2.4V6, 2.7V6 Turbo, 2.8V6, 1.9TDi, 2.5TDi

Price from:
£17,500

Manufactured in:
Germany

Best All-Rounder: A4 2.4SE

Audi A6

The A6 is Audi's seriously viable alternative to the BMW 5-Series and, like the BMW, is available in saloon or estate forms. The bold, fashionably-styled body houses a variety of refined engines ranging from a 1.8-litre Turbo through to a 2.8 V6, and includes punchy turbo-diesels. This year also sees the addition of a 4.2 V8 to rival BMW's M5. Inside, the cabin is faultlessly designed and screwed together, the cockpit's ambience clinical but impressive. Accommodation front and rear is excellent too and there's ample luggage space in both body styles. Refinement is good, even though the ride quality can be a little firm, a compromise to ensure taut handling. The A6 is a fine car indeed.

Body styles:
Saloon, estate

Engine capacity:
1.8, 1.8 Turbo, 2.4V6, 2.7V6, 2.8V6, 4.2V8, 1.9TDi, 2.5TDi

Price from:
£23,200

Manufactured in:
Germany

Best All-Rounder: A6 2.5 V6 TDi

Audi A8

Audi's BMW 7-Series rivalling flagship is not just pretty to look at, but is a real technological tour-de-force thanks to its all-aluminium space-frame bodyshell. Keeping the weight down means economy and performance are class-topping, with discreet looks that rival Mercedes and BMW. 1999 saw some improvements, notably more powerful V8 engines; all of which are now coupled to four-wheel-drive. That gives real roadholding advantage, something missing from the comparatively sluggish front-wheel-drive 2.8. For occupants there is space and comfort by the bucket load, so though the A8 may look expensive alongside Jaguar's finest, it is an underrated luxury alternative. Topping out the range is the S8 – a supercar in all but looks.

Body styles:
Saloon

Engine capacity:
2.8V6, 3.7V8, 4.2V8, 2.5TDi

Price from:
£37,600

Manufactured in:
Germany

Best All-Rounder: A8 4.2 quattro

BMW

In its carefully thought-out manner, BMW continues with its mixture of new car launches and upgrades. During 1999 the 3-Series range was extended with the addition of the coupe and touring derivatives, leaving just the Compact and convertible models from the old model range still running. The Z3 received a mild makeover and some new engines at the lower end of the range, and the 5-Series and 7-Series got state-of-the-art turbo-diesels. The big news for 2000 is the four-wheel-drive X5 and the Z8. The first moves into dangerous new territory for a company that has a sporting image others would die for. But the Z8 – Bond's next car - with M5 power, will undoubtedly make up for it.

BMW 3-Series

The definitive small executive car moves up several steps in its latest incarnation – what else would you expect from BMW? While some may mourn the move to more luxury and refinement, BMW knows its market well and there is no doubt that these saloons and coupes are highly impressive driving machines as well as offering sophistication. There's a predictable range of engines, from a 1.9 four-cylinder through to a 2.8-litre six, but there are some new models too, a smooth 1.8 and a powerful 2.0-litre direct-injection turbo-diesel. Space has always been a bugbear, but it keeps getting better, and now there is reasonable room for four adults. Still running in the previous style are the Convertible and Compact; both will be replaced in time.

Best All-Rounder: 323i

Body styles:	Saloon, coupe
Engine capacity:	1.9, 2.0, 2.5, 2.8, 2.0TD
Price from:	£15,000
Manufactured in:	Germany

BMW 5-Series

The handsome looks of the 5-Series are more than skin deep – this remains the pace-setting executive car despite the strength of the competition. Saloon or estate, and from the humble but impeccably refined 2.0 to the stunning new M5, each 5-Series provides a fine balance of refinement with driving pleasure. As well as the character of its engines, the 5-Series excels in its ride and handling. The only thing even approaching a weak point is that there is still not as much rear legroom as in its direct rivals, even though this aspect has been improved over the previous generation model. The Touring offers a uniquely sporting driving experience for a big estate, but less load space than direct rivals.

Best All-Rounder: 528i SE

Body styles:
Saloon, estate

Engine capacity:
2.0, 2.5, 2.8, 3.5V8, 4.4V8, 4.9V8, 2.5TD, 3.0TD

Price from:
£24,600

Manufactured in:
Germany

BMW 7-Series

The 7-Series is long-established as one of the favourite 'director level' cars. Although the entry-level 728i is less than half the price of the top level 750iL, there is very little to visually differentiate one model from another within the 7-Series range, reflecting just how strong the image is. Both the 740i and 750i are available in long wheelbase form for that extra rear legroom. Compared with its direct rivals the Mercedes-Benz S-Class and Audi A8, the 7-Series lies somewhere in between in its driving experience – not as stiffly sprung as the Audi but firmer than the Mercedes. All the engines are superbly refined and responsive, including the highly impressive new V8 turbo-diesel.

Best All-Rounder: 735i

Body styles:
Saloon

Engine capacity:
2.8, 3.5V8, 4.4V8, 5.4V12, 2.5TD, 3.0TD, 4.0TD

Price from:
£37,600

Manufactured in:
Germany

New!

BMW Z3

BMW's Z3 roadster has been a resounding sales success, and now gets a redesign that tidies up the rear end with an aggressive look to match the front. There are new engines too. There's also an outrageous coupe derivative which in the UK is available only in 320bhp 'M' form, but in other countries it can be bought as a 2.8 too. The Z3 scores by offering a level of comfort, class and quality unavailable in an MX-5 or MGF, though either of these are arguably better sports cars. The new 2.0-litre six cylinder Z3 is a good balance of performance and price, and it makes the right noises too, but the new budget 1.9 (called the 1.8) is lifeless. The critics choice is the gutsy 2.8, but that's getting expensive.

Best All-Rounder: Z3 2.0

Body styles:
Convertible

Engine capacity:
1.9, 2.0, 2.5, 2.8, 3.2

Price from:
£20,000

Manufactured in:
United States

BMW X5

It may seem a little odd that BMW - owner of Rover - is launching its own hugely expensive 4x4, but the X5 is a very different beast to the Range Rover. A "Sports Activity Vehicle", the X5 is aimed primarily at fast road use, like all BMWs. First to be launched is the 4.4-litre V8 with close to 300bhp and a price tag around £45,000; after that will come a cheaper six-cylinder petrol and turbo-diesel versions. Built in the US alongside the Z3, the X5 goes in sale in Europe and the States late in 1999, with UK buyers having to wait until autumn 2000.

Best All-Rounder: Too soon to say

Body styles:
Estate

Engine capacity:
2.8, 3.2, 3.5V8, 4.4V8, 2.9TD

Price from:
£32,000 (est)

Manufactured in:
United States

BUICK

Will Buick ever break out of its over-60s, retirement crowd image any time soon? Don't hold your breath. Starved of new models that even hint of youthful style and excitement, GM's once-powerful division continues to appeal to older buyers who want well-built, reliable, dependable, good ol' American-built transportation at a fair price. Even though traditional luxury car buying Americans are going crazy for upscale off-roaders, Buick won't get one until 2002. That said, the latest LeSabre continues to be America's best-selling full-size luxury car, and the flagship Park Avenue is a hot choice for America's country club set.

Body styles:	Saloon
Engine capacity:	3.1V6, 3.8V6, 3.8V6 s'ch'd
Price from:	$18,800
Manufactured in:	United States

Buick Century and Regal

The Century is the first rung on the Buick ladder. It's a clean-cut, rounded, but rather uninspiring-looking family four-door. The standard 3.1-litre V6 gets an extra 15bhp power boost for 2000 – it's now up to 175bhp – but the emphasis here is on quiet, relaxed, peaceful cruising. Older buyers on a budget love it.

The Regal is the dark horse in the Buick line-up; a car that should have brought a few more younger, performance-seeking buyers into the Buick fold. Sadly, it hasn't. Yet the top-of-the-line Regal GSE comes with a supercharged 3.8-litre V6 that packs a 240bhp punch and streaks from zero to 60mph in just 6.5 secs. Hot stuff. The only problem here is that the Regal goes head to head with the likes of Honda's Accord and Toyota's Camry – America's top-selling sweethearts. Nevertheless, the front-drive Regal is spacious, well-equipped, fun-to-drive and whisper quiet at speed. It should be a winner.

Best All-Rounders: Century Custom and Regal LS

Buick LeSabre

Re-designed from the ground up for 2000, the best-selling LeSabre looks, er, exactly like the last LeSabre. Even though every body panel is changed. Buick says its LeSabre buyers – some of the most loyal in the business – were emphatic about keeping the car looking the same. Not wanting to risk losing them, Buick did what their owners asked. But the car's stiffer bodyshell and revised suspension at least make the LeSabre more inspiring to drive. And the long-serving 3.8-litre V6 – carried over unchanged for 2000 – is whisper-quiet yet surprisingly energetic. For All-American families wanting six-passenger comfort, the LeSabre has few rivals.

Best All-Rounder: LeSabre Limited

Body styles:
Saloon

Engine capacity:
3.8V6

Price from:
$23,000

Manufactured in:
United States

Buick Park Avenue

Flagship of the Buick line-up, the 'Park' is one of a dying breed of big, buxom-bodied, six-seat luxury sedans that were once the darling of America's cigar-chomping business tycoons. Yet the Park Avenue still woos buyers with an appealing blend of armchair-like seating, whisper-quiet refinement and a cabin as big as an aircraft hangar. Refinement is the word here. The big Buick's vault-like body isolates almost all the noise from its muted and surprisingly punchy 3.8-litre V6 - particularly in 240bhp supercharged form – while its creamy-smooth automatic is still one of the industry's standard-setters. Passengers just love it.

Best All-Rounder: Park Avenue Ultra

Body styles:
Saloon

Engine capacity:
3.8V6, 3.8V6 supercharged

Price from:
$31,000

Manufactured in:
United States

BRISTOL

Body styles:
Coupe

Engine capacity:
5.9V8

Price from:
£124,500

Manufactured in:
England

Bristol Blenheim

They don't come much rarer than a Bristol. Revised last year, the £118,000 model's boxy styling and unconventional proportions are at odds with just about every other modern luxury limo. The Blenheim is remarkably lively despite its size, thanks to a powerful 5.9-litre Chrysler V8 engine; tall gearing makes it the perfect cruiser, too.
The Bristol offers a high driving position in its leather and wood-trimmed cabin which offers plenty of room and old-fashioned styling. Novel packaging, including a spare wheel mounted inside the front wing, means there's enough luggage space in the boot for a trans-continental hack. Bristol argues that its car is of a higher quality than anything from Germany, but it remains a choice largely for those determined to be different.

Best All-Rounder: Blenheim

CADILLAC

The full might of GM's resources is seemingly being thrown into the make-or-break rejuvenation of Cadillac. Starting in 2002, there'll be a stream of hard-edged, aggressive-looking, new-generation Caddys, kicking-off with the dramatic Evoq luxury two-seater roadster. Every model will be re-designed and new, macho-looking sport-utility niche vehicles will be added, all with the single goal of pulling-in younger, cash-rich buyers. We've been given sneak peaks of what's in store, and it's going to knock your socks off. These will not be your gold-trimmed, pillowy-soft Cadillacs of old. We can hardly wait.

Body styles:	Saloon
Engine capacity:	4.6V8
Price from:	$40,000
Manufactured in:	United States

Cadillac Seville

British back sufferers will appreciate the latest Seville. Optional for 2000 are Cadillac's 'adaptive' front seats which have internal air bladders that continuously inflate and deflate to massage the driver and passenger's lower back. It's like having your own on-board masseur. While the 300bhp STS is a dynamic performer packed with luxury accoutrements, it would take a brave buyer – back-sufferer or not – to choose the Caddy over more-established and fashionable European marques. But for lovers of all-things American, or those wanting to drive something a little different, the big, front-drive Seville won't disappoint.

Best All-Rounder Seville STS

New!

Cadillac Catera

Catera gets a fresh face and a new interior for 2000 in the hope of repairing the damage caused by marketing gaffs at the car's launch – the ads featured cartoon ducks and Cindy Crawford in thigh-high leather boots. Not the image Caddy dealers were hoping for. Built in Germany and based closely on the Opel Omega, the Catera keeps its under-powered-for-the-US 3-litre V6, but offers a Sport package that firms-up the suspension and adds sexier alloys and grippier tyres. Catera's problems however, centre around super-strong competition from European imports, rather than its own shortcoming. Look for its US-built replacement in 2002.

Body styles:
Saloon

Engine capacity:
3.0V6

Price from:
$34,000

Manufactured in:
Germany

Best All-Rounder: Catera Sport

Cadillac DeVille

The last new 'traditional' Caddy before the new wave appears in a couple of years, the re-designed DeVille gets a new platform, fresh bodywork and an arsenal of high-tech gizmos worthy of a Star Wars spaceship. It's the first car, for example, to get GM's infrared 'Night Vision' system which helps drivers see better in the dark. Basing the new DeVille on the current Seville platform significantly improves the agility of this full-size Caddy. Also offering Cadillac's impressive Stabilitrak anti-skid system, traction control, four-wheel discs, plus the option of the 300bhp Northstar V8, turns the DeVille into a definite wolf in lounge-lizard clothing.

Body styles:
Saloon

Engine capacity:
4.6V8

Price from:
$40,000

Manufactured in:
United States

Best All-Rounder: DeVille DTS Touring Sedan

Cadillac Eldorado

The big Caddy Eldorado hangs on – barely – as the sole remaining XXL-sized American-built luxury coupe. Its future? Uncertain. So, for the time being, it's an interesting niche player; the last of a breed that still has lots of sporty appeal to the golf club retiree set. Think of it as Viagra on wheels. Powered by the potent Northstar V8, with 300bhp on tap in ETC form, the 'Eldo' is a lively performer with strong mid-range punch. Cadillac's hokey-named 'Road-Sensing' suspension and 'Stabilitrak' anti-skid system – they work better than they sound – make the Seville a surprisingly nimble handler. Despite the coupe body, its a spacious four-seater.

Body styles:
Coupe

Engine capacity:
4.6V8

Price from:
$39,000

Manufactured in:
United States

Best All-Rounder: Eldorado Touring Coupe

Cadillac Escalade

Call it the Rambo Caddy; a tough, rough-riding 4x4 with a stump-pulling 5.7-litre V8, yet with an interior dressed in wall-to-wall leather and polished walnut. Cadillac execs would have preferred to have waited until they could have designed their own 4x4 in-house, but US customers wanted a sport-utility, and they wanted it NOW! So the Escalade is little more than a spiffed-up Chevrolet Tahoe. An all-new, smoother-riding, more sophisticated Escalade is a year away. Until then, buyers make do with finger-light steering, mushy brakes and a ragged ride, particularly over the golf club fairway.

Body styles:
Estate

Engine capacity:
5.7V8

Price from:
$44,000

Manufactured in:
United States

Best All-Rounder: Cadillac Escalade

CHRYSLER

The merger with Mercedes-Benz in 1998 should give Chrysler a firm basis for future development, with access to a level of expertise it perhaps only dreamt about. But for now the company remains focused on its wide range of distinctive models, and what a broad range it is. Compact family saloons, large luxury cars, the Viper supercar, the Voyager MPV and of course, its charismatic off-roaders. There are issues to be faced by the company though, not least that for much of its product range there is newer competition around. That might not matter as much in the States, but in Europe it is starting to hurt.

New!

Body styles:	Saloon
Engine capacity:	2.0
Price from:	£11,000
Manufactured in:	United States

Chrysler Neon

The car with the bug-eyed headlights and cute smile has grown-up and become more sophisticated for 2000. Redesigned for the first time since its 1995 debut, this new Neon is longer, wider and more spacious than before, with full-frame doors replacing the previous frameless side glass. Carried over is the punchy but rather vocal 2-litre engine, which makes this four-door Chrysler a lively, spirited performer. Plusher suspension means a softer ride, though with its tight, responsive steering, the car is just as much fun to drive as the original. Impressive standard equipment and a competitive price tag ensure the Neon loses none of its appeal.

Best All-rounder: Neon LE

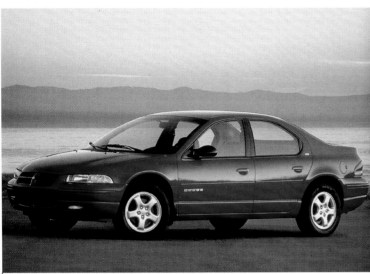

Chrysler Stratus

Chrysler's Mondeo-sized four-door offers striking looks, spacious accommodation and nimble road manners at a cut-throat price. Sold throughout Europe, but not in right-hand drive for the UK. Pity. Powered by a choice of 2.0 and 2.4-litre four-cylinders, and a smooth-spinning Mitsubishi-built 2.5V6, the Stratus is an agile performer. And with the optional Autostick automatic that allows the driver to make manual gear changes, the car feels surprisingly nimble. But the Stratus's big strength is its roomy interior, with particularly generous rear seat space and vast boot. Trim quality in the cabin is patchy, but overall, the well-equipped Stratus is a sound buy.

Best All-rounder: Stratus ES2.4

Body styles:
Saloon

Engine capacity:
2.0, 2.5V6

Price from:
$15,500

Manufactured in:
United States

Chrysler Concorde

Here is the world's first 'paperless' car, designed from ground-up on the screen of a computer. Pretty impressive. It's one of Chrysler's ground-breaking LH series of saloons that features so-called cab-forward design that pushes the wheels out to the far corners, and the base of the windscreen almost over the front wheels. The reason? Cavernous accommodation. On the road, there's no missing the Concorde's dramatic, concept car styling. And it drives as good as it looks, particularly with the larger 225bhp 3.2-litre V6. Suspension changes for 2000 smooth out the ride and reduce road noise.

Best All-Rounder: Concorde 3.2

Body styles:
Saloon

Engine capacity:
2.7V6, 3.2V6

Price from:
$22,000

Manufactured in:
United States

Chrysler 300M

Chrysler's first serious attempt at designing a car that's equally at home in Stuttgart as it is in Seattle. Even at the Euro-required five metres in length, the 300M is a big car. Yet its dramatic cab-forward design, athletic performance and nimble handling somehow make it manageable on tight European back roads. You can't fault its mechanical credentials either. A new 3.5-litre V6 packs a healthy 253bhp punch, allowing the 300M to hold its head high in the performance saloon pack. And Chrysler's Porsche Tiptronic-style AutoStick transmission adds manual control to the four-speed auto. Lots of dash for the cash

Best All-Rounder: 300M 3.5

Body styles:
Saloon

Engine capacity:
2.7V6, 3.5V6

Price from:
$29,000

Manufactured in:
United States

Chrysler Voyager

Chrysler makes the biggest people carrier available in Europe in the Grand Voyager, while the slightly shorter Voyager fulfils the same people carrying requirements with less luggage space. Criticised recently for its poor occupant protection in an accident, the Voyager otherwise offers an attractive combination of features and comfort. European models are assembled in Austria from panels shipped in from the States. Engine options comprise a rather wheezy 2.0-litre which only just copes with the weight, a delightful but thirsty 3.3 V6, and a turbo-diesel. The Voyager's suspension is taut enough to provide genuinely car-like handling, but parking can be awe-inspiring in the longer version.

Best All-Rounder: Grand Voyager 3.3

Body styles:
MPV

Engine capacity:
2.0, 2.5, 3.3V6, 3.8V6, 2.5TD

Price from:
£18,400

Manufactured in:
United States, Austria

Chrysler Viper

If you think the Viper looks outrageous, just wait until you lift the bonnet. Underneath lies the biggest engine currently fitted to any production car, an 8.0-litre V10. As you might expect the power is awesome, but its real beauty is the pulling power in any gear. Left-hand-drive means its not the most practical of supercars for British roads, and its handling can be lethal in the wet, but few cars offer the pose potential or the straight-line speed of the Viper at such a "reasonable" price. The coupe is more practical but the Targa-topped RT10 roadster is the only choice for real summer thrills. Either make a Porsche 911 look like a practical family car.

Body styles:
Coupe, convertible

Engine capacity:
8.0V10

Price from:
£69,000

Manufactured in:
United States

Best All-Rounder: Viper RT10

Jeep Wrangler

The archetypal Jeep has come a long way since World War 2 days. Steadily upgraded over the years, the most recent modifications have given it a smart interior, a standard heater and independent, coil sprung suspension. It's still a Jeep though, which means a torquey 2.5-litre or a 4.0-litre straight-six which sounds like a NASCAR racer. It burns fuel like one too. The off-road ability hasn't been compromised either, and the Jeep can still cut it with the best in the rough, where, in truth, the suspension is at its most impressive. But as an everyday car you have to be determined to live with its peculiarities.

Body styles:
Estate, convertible

Engine capacity:
2.5, 4.0

Price from:
£14,200

Manufactured in:
United States

Best All-Rounder: Wrangler 4.0 Sport

Jeep Cherokee

The car which relaunched the famous Jeep brand back in the UK is now looking a bit long in the tooth – it has been around in much the same form in the States for 16 years. Its main drawbacks are the poor interior space and dated appearance. The 2.5-litre Sport Cherokee looks great value, with air bags, electric windows and ABS as standard, but the performance is sluggish. Conversely the 4.0-litre straight six in the Limited model makes it one of the fastest off-roaders around but its thirst for fuel is from a different era. On balance the 2.5 turbo-diesel makes the most sense and is an economical tow car.

Body styles:
Estate

Engine capacity:
2.5, 4.0, 2.5TD

Price from:
£18,200

Manufactured in:
United States

Best All-Rounder: Cherokee 2.5TD Limited

Chrysler Jeep Grand Cherokee

Although the new Grand Cherokee doesn't look too different from the old one, it retains only a handful of components. There is now a choice of two petrol engines – the 4.0-litre is a revised version of the old one, and there is an all-new 4.7-litre V8 with a 3.1 turbo-diesel to follow soon. On the road the Chrysler is much improved, steering, stopping and cornering with reassuring skill. The ride is supple enough to absorb town bumps and ensure motorway jaunts aren't a pain. The V8 is highly impressive with the power and refinement to attack the Range Rover. Inside the facia also gets a major revision, but space remains an issue considering the car's size.

Body styles:
Estate

Engine capacity:
4.0, 4.7V8, 3.1TD

Price from:
£30,000

Manufactured in:
United States

Best All-Rounder: Grand Cherokee V8

CATERHAM

The specialist car manufacturer from Surrey has continued in the vein that has been the backbone of its success since the early 1970's – building the minimalist sports car, the Seven. Caterham Cars was Lotus's most loyal seller of the Lotus Seven so when Lotus stopped production, it seemed only right that Caterham should take it over. But while the company has remained true to the look and philosophy behind the Seven, it has been continually developed so that, almost every year, a new derivative offers more in the way of performance and, of course, excitement. The much newer 21 offers practicality and comfort the Seven so clearly lacks, though customers have been much harder to find.

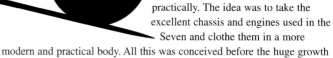

Body styles:	Convertible
Engine capacity:	1.6, 1.8
Price from:	£24,000
Manufactured in:	England

Caterham 21

The 21 is the car Caterham hoped the buyer of its popular Seven would move into when he needed a bit more practically. The idea was to take the excellent chassis and engines used in the Seven and clothe them in a more modern and practical body. All this was conceived before the huge growth of competition in the sports car market, not least from the Lotus Elise. As with the Seven, the 21 uses Rover's K-Series engines to deliver stunning performance, with the added advantage of a classier interior and a big boot. Against this is its price and the fact that the 21 retains most of the Seven's uncomfortable quirks and faults while removing some of its thrills.

Best All-Rounder: 21 VVC

Body styles:	Convertible
Engine capacity:	1.6, 1.8
Price from:	£13,400
Manufactured in:	England

Caterham Super Seven

Caterham has kept the Super Seven flag flying for 30 years or more, building a car that still retains most of the heritage of the Lotus from which it has developed. Today the car has modern Vauxhall or Rover power units, a far stiffer chassis and thoroughly re-worked suspension but the thrill and honesty of the Seven remains untouched. Indeed it is largely unchallenged too. The Seven is the most fun you can have on four wheels, with real race-car responses and supercar performance for a fraction of the cost. That means plenty of buyers use them for amateur motor sport events, although the Seven is a useable if uncompromising road car as well. The major problem is interior space – there isn't much.

Best All-Rounder: Seven VVC

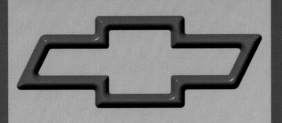

CHEVROLET

You name it, Chevy builds it. From a pint-sized Metro, to the thundering 175mph Corvette, to a rock-crushing, monster Silverado 4x4 'dualie' pick-up, Chevrolet is General Motors' high-volume division; the division they call the Heartbeat of America. While sales and loyalty remain strong, the heartbeat is getting a little weaker these days. The design of the latest crop of newcomers is dull and largely uninspiring, and the innovations few. But solid value-for-money and the convenience of a dealer on almost every street corner, keeps customers coming back. But for how long?

Body styles:	Coupe, targa, convertible
Engine capacity:	5.7V8
Price from:	£37,600
Manufactured in:	United States

Chevrolet Corvette

Nothing offers a more neck-snapping, adrenaline-pumping 'bang for the buck' than the latest 'Vette. Americans pay the equivalent of a paltry £24,000 for a 345bhp V8 six-speed supercar that scorches from zero to 60mph in just under five seconds, and tops out at around 175mph. And there's a choice of hardtop, Targa and convertible models. What's more, the Corvette is a sensation to drive. Performance is little short of explosive and road manners sensational, thanks to a girder-chassis and a computer-controlled 'active handling system'. Interior trim could be a little less flimsy, but the rest is hard to fault.

Best All-Rounder: Corvette Targa

Chevrolet Monte Carlo

Big coupe sales in the US have taken a dive, thanks to the sport-utility vehicle boom. But the Chevy Monte Carlo's strong presence in American NASCAR racing ensures strong owner loyalty. And the all-new for 2000 Monte Carlo, with its slightly retro two-door styling and more modern platform should ensure a continued, enthusiastic following. Two versions are on offer; the base LS with its workhorse 3.4-litre V6, and the more-punchy 200bhp 3.8 V6-engined SS. More the highway cruiser than country lane charger, the front-drive Monte Carlo combines safe, predictable handling with a smooth, unfussed ride. And like all Chevys, it's bargain-priced.

Best All-Rounder: Monte Carlo LS

Body styles:
Saloon

Engine capacity:
2.4, 3.1V6

Price from:
$18,500 (est)

Manufactured in:
United States

Chevrolet Impala

Chevy revived one of its most revered nameplates for its new-for-2000 mid-size family saloon. But it's a thin shadow of the 5.7-litre V8-engined muscle saloon that last wore the Impala badge. This new version features front wheel-drive, a 3.8-litre V6 and rather contrived styling. There's nothing special about the way it drives either; the V6 feels lively enough but suffers from a bad case of high-rev thrash 'n roar. But it's a competent handler, with precise steering and low-roll cornering, and its cabin offers generous accommodation for five. But apart from its bargain basement price tag, there's little to woo American buyers away from their Accords and Camrys.

Best All-Rounder: Impala Sedan

Body styles:
Saloon

Engine capacity:
3.4V6, 3.8V8

Price from:
$18,700

Manufactured in:
United States

Chevrolet Camaro

The Camaro highlights just what good value American cars are. How about a stylish looking coupe with a 285bhp V8 engine for the price of a large family saloon? Mechanically it may seem crude – there is a separate chassis, pushrod engine and live rear axle – and the interior is unbelievably tacky by European standards, but it delivers unbeatable performance for the price. The awesome six-speed Z28 is the cheapest way of getting to 170mph, but don't expect sophistication. The 200bhp 3.8-litre V6 auto is not as fast but better balanced and even cheaper, and the well-equipped convertible is good value too. The Camaro is sold in the UK, but only with left-hand drive.

Best All-Rounder: Camaro 3.8 Convertible

Body styles:
Coupe, convertible

Engine capacity:
3.8V6, 5.7V8

Price from:
£18,000

Manufactured in:
United States

Chevrolet Blazer

For those looking for the maximum amount of metal for their money, there is little to touch the Blazer. There's room for five large adults to travel in comfort, loads of stowage space and a sizeable boot. Power comes from a 4.3-litre V6. With all cylinders on full song the Blazer is capable of hauling itself around surprisingly swiftly. But – and it's a big but – once moving it requires every last ounce of concentration from the driver, mainly because the steering is so vague. Much of that is down to the crude suspension, but if that can be lived with, and the giant thirst for petrol is not an issue, the Blazer is a tempting proposition.

Best All-Rounder: Blazer 4.3 V6

Body styles:
Estate

Engine capacity:
4.3V6

Price from:
£23,000

Manufactured in:
United States

CITRÖEN

Part of the giant PSA group that also owns Peugeot, Citroen has much in common with cars of the same size from this family. That may be sound financial sense for PSA, but does mean that the individuality that used to be such a strong theme for Citroen is largely a thing of the past. The Saxo and Synergie are obvious examples, being almost identical to the Peugeot 106 and 806. But with the new Picasso Citroen does have an ace up its sleeve. This daring design is the latest in the Scenic/Zafira mould of mini-MPV that offers great versatility in a compact and affordable package.

New!

Body styles:	MPV
Engine capacity:	1.6, 1.8, 2.0TD
Price from:	£14,000 (est)
Manufactured in:	France

Citroen Xsara Picasso

The Picasso is Citroen's answer to the Renault Scenic and offers a very similar set of answers to the same issues. Thus it majors on convenience inside, with lots of storage areas, electrical outlets and individual seats for five occupants. The Picasso has the benefit of a dashboard-mounted gearlever that leaves the floor between the front seats free so that access to the rear is easy. Three engines are on offer: 1.6, 1.8 and the lower-powered version of Citroen's 2.0HDi diesel, with just one trim level. The biggest impression, however, is made by the swooping body lines, ensuring that the Picasso stands out in any crowd.

Body styles:	Estate
Engine capacity:	1.1, 1.4, 1.8, 1.8D, 1.9D
Price from:	£10,800
Manufactured in:	France

Berlingo Multispace

Based on the popular Berlingo van, the Multispace is supposed to appeal to the young as a practical lifestyle vehicle. Its happy nature is complemented by bright metallic paint, power steering and the world's largest electric sunroof. The engine choice has expanded to include a 1.4, a lively 1.8 and 1.9 (non-turbo) diesel though many others are offered in Europe. Performance is acceptable from all and the compliant ride can be enjoyed from five large seats which have excellent visibility. The cabin has plentiful oddments space and the big boot contains a washable rubber mat for convenience. If only it had five-doors and air-conditioning, the Multispace could really compete as a cheap alternative to some MPVs and estate cars.

Best All-Rounder: Berlingo 1.8

Body styles:	MPV
Engine capacity:	1.8, 2.0, 2.0turbo, 1.9TD, 2.1TD
Price from:	£16,900
Manufactured in:	France

Synergie/Evasion

VW and Ford have proven that two companies can agree an attractive design for an MPV, but Citroen, Peugeot, Fiat and Lancia seemed to have missed the boat. The van-like looks of the Synergie and its cousins hide a competent seven-seater which offers comfort and an easy drive – once you get used to the odd gearchange. Engine choice is petrol or turbo-diesel, both of which suit the Synergie well. Sliding rear side doors can be useful in a tight parking space, but access to the rear-most seats is never easy. Luggage space is worse than most with the rear seats in use.

Best All-Rounder: Synergie 1.9TD

Citroen Saxo

In the world of the enjoyable supermini, the French delight in market domination. Citroen's effort, the Saxo, is little more than a re-hashed Peugeot 106, though that needn't be a bad thing – its range of small engines drives one of the best chassis in the class.

Three and five-door hatchback body styles, with or without power steering, are enjoyable and comfortable to drive, despite a cramped driver's footwell. Space in the back isn't great for the class either, and the build quality doesn't have the perceived integrity of some rivals. But on the occasions that the roads get twisty or bumpy, that's easy to overlook.

Body styles:
Hatchback

Engine capacity:
1.0, 1.1, 1.4, 1.6, 1.5D

Price from:
£8,000

Manufactured in:
France

Best All-Rounder: Saxo 1.4 SX

Citroen Xsara

This smaller family car from Citroen has matured nicely. A new direct-injection turbo-diesel is the cream of the crop, giving the car all the performance a car like this might need, coupled to refinement and fabulous economy. As ever, the Xsara range comprises five-door hatchback and estate, and a three-door version of the hatch optimistically called a "coupe". The petrol engines are not exceptional, but are OK. Comfort and space are good for four, but the interior is functional rather than attractive. A pillowy smooth ride, crisp steering and fluid handling show that Citroen hasn't lost its talents.

Body styles:
Hatchback, estate, coupe

Engine capacity:
1.4, 1.6, 1.8, 2.0, 1.9D, 1.9TD

Price from:
£11,900

Manufactured in:
France

Best All-Rounder: Xsara 2.0 HDi LX

Citroen Xantia

Citroen has to try harder than most with the Xantia, for it is one of the longest running cars in its class. A recent facelift has kept the essential business market interested but of greater interest is the launch of two new diesels in 1999. Both the 90bhp and 110bhp 2.0-litre versions offer new-found levels of refinement coupled to excellent economy and ease of driving. There remains, of course, a good range of petrol models too, all in hatchback or estate body styles. Inside the Xantia remains one of the roomier family cars, but not all will like the soft seats. Hydractive suspension ensures a good (but not sporting) ride with standard self-levelling for those who tow or carry heavy loads.

Body styles:
Hatchback, estate

Engine capacity:
1.8, 2.0, 2.0 Turbo, 3.0V6, 1.9TD, 2.1TD

Price from:
£14,000

Manufactured in:
France

Best All-Rounder: Xantia 2.0 HDi 90 LX

Citroen XM

Citroen's large executive car was first sold in 1990, so as well as being long in the tooth, it still has all those quirks which used to make Citroens appealing and irritating at the same time. Most notable are the wedge styling, air suspension and strange brakes, but there is much more. The XM is not without qualities though, with a smooth ride and mile-munching motorway ability. Although the V6 Exclusive versions are fast and well equipped, it is the 2.1 and 2.5-litre turbo-diesels which are the stars of the range, with economy and reasonable performance. The interiors are fragile and take some getting used to, but estate versions are capable of carrying more than some vans.

Body styles:
Hatchback, estate

Engine capacity:
2.0, 2.0 Turbo, 3.0V6, 2.1TD, 2.5TD

Price from:
£24,000

Manufactured in:
France

Best All-Rounder: XM 2.5TD VSX Estate

DAIHATSU

Daihatsu bills itself as the Small Car Maker, a pretty accurate description if it weren't for the elderly Fourtrak. It might seem logical for Daihatsu to drop its sizeable off-roader, but it has established itself as a rugged machine that more-or-less sells itself. The real focus, however, is on the small cars, with Daihatsu' expertise in this area good enough for Toyota to take a controlling interest in the company in 1998. Much of the range is an acquired taste for European buyers, but the Sirion stands out as a world-class supermini.

Body styles:	Hatchback
Engine capacity:	700, 1.0
Price from:	£8,100
Manufactured in:	Japan

Daihatsu Sirion

Though Daihatsu would not say so at the time, the Sirion always was going to replace the supermini Charade, which has now finally bitten the dust. That's no great loss because the Sirion is Daihatsu's most promising car yet. Distinctive without being weird, it offers an impressive combination of virtues and its three-cylinder engine is remarkably economical. There is a fair degree of refinement for such a small car – the ride and noise levels are both good. Interior space and comfort are reasonable too and, in the UK at least, equipment levels are impressive, with power steering and twin airbags. The downsides are relatively minor. Performance is hardly lively, and the interior is drab, despite obvious attempts to liven it up.

Best All-Rounder: Sirion

Body styles:	Estate
Engine capacity:	1.5, 1.6
Price from:	£11,600
Manufactured in:	Japan

Daihatsu Grand Move

Daihatsu has aimed the Grand Move at the growing demand for recreational vehicles which answer a number of needs from family to fun. There's plenty of space inside, with real comfort for four or five, and a large boot. The Grand Move is easy to use in town too, with power steering and an incredibly tight turning circle. But despite an upgrade, where the engine size was increased to 1.6 litres, the suspension retuned and seats made better still, the Daihatsu does not compare well with Renault's Scenic. The rear bench seat lacks the versatility of the removable individual seats of the Scenic, while the interior is flooded with plastic which looks cheap and tacky.

Best All-Rounder: Grand Move

Daihatsu Cuore

Revised late in 1998, Daihatsu's smallest offering appeals to those needing reliable motoring on a budget. It comes with a 1.0-litre engine in most markets, but a 700cc three cylinder is still offered in its native Japan, with varying power outputs and a 4WD option. The 5-door body gives a healthy dose of practicality, as do split/fold rear seats. To drive, the Cuore is at its best in town. It's a doddle to park, even with unassisted steering. At higher speeds, the car's city intentions start to tell with a relative lack of refinement and power. For those where economy is high on the list of priorities, however, these is little to touch the Move.

Best all-rounder: Cuore

Body styles:
Hatchback

Engine capacity:
700, 1.0

Price from:
£6,500

Manufactured in:
Japan

Daihatsu Move

Daihatsu sold half a million Moves in the first three years of its production. Now there is an extensively revamped model that offers improved safety, performance and style. The core feature of the Move is the same however – the ability to sit four tall adults in relative comfort in a very short car. It is all achieved by making the Move TALL rather than long. The rear seats slide back and forth to give more luggage space if those in the back seats are not so long-legged. There is plenty of equipment on offer too, including air conditioning, airbags and power steering. The Move will never be great to drive, but the new 1.0-litre engine offers a healthy increase in power.

Best All-Rounder: Move 1.0

Body styles:
Estate

Engine capacity:
850

Price from:
£7,200

Manufactured in:
Japan

Daihatsu Terios

Daihatsu's Terios is undoubtedly one of life's oddballs, a cross between a four-wheel-drive off-roader and a city runabout. Shorter than a Seat Ibiza, narrower that a Ford Ka and higher than a Jeep Cherokee, the proportions of the Terios take some getting used to. The toy-town looks compromise the tough image, with the result that the Terios is more at home in the supermarket car park than off-roading through the mud, despite permanent four-wheel-drive and locking differential. The Terios drives well enough on the Tarmac, with pleasingly direct steering, but it doesn't take many bumps to get the car bouncing wildly. The 1.3-litre 16-valve engine is keen though it is buzzing away at motorway speeds.

Best All-Rounder: Terios 1.3

Body styles:
Estate

Engine capacity:
1.3

Price from:
£10,000

Manufactured in:
Japan

Daihatsu Fourtrak

Daihatsu's 'proper' off-roader has always appealed to buyers looking for a workhorse because of its no-nonsense attitude off the road and lack of refinement on it. Despite newer and more attractive looking competition, the Fourtrak will remain popular with farmers because of its ability in the mud, huge towing capacity, and faultless reliability in all weathers. The Fourtrak is only available with one engine option – a fine performing a 2.8-litre turbo-diesel. It has great pulling power for sticky situations or towing, and is also a relaxed motorway cruiser. Top models are well equipped but pricey, and there is no five-door model. Most buyers plump for the no-frills entry-level car.

Best All-Rounder: Fourtrak TDL

Body styles:
Estate

Engine capacity:
2.2, 2.8D, 2.8TD

Price from:
£16,100

Manufactured in:
Japan

DAEWOO

In Korea Daewoo is one of the largest industrial conglomerates, involved in everything from ship building to stock-broking to cars. 1999 saw the company go through a serious financial crisis, and as a consequence it seems that in future the core business will be built around the auto industry. Daewoo has been highly aggressive in this area, designing a whole raft of new models over a very short period of time. Until a year ago these were mainstream family cars, but in 1999 Daewoo bought struggling Ssangyong, so now it has added the Musso and Korando off-roaders to its fleet. In the UK its adventurous marketing style – cutting out the middle man – and comprehensive after-sales back-up has been highly successful.

Body styles:	Estate
Engine capacity:	2.0, 2.3, 3.2, 2.3D, 2.9D, 2.9TD
Price from:	£16,000
Manufactured in:	Korea

Daewoo Korando

The struggling Ssangyong car company was bought by Daewoo, enabling the Korean maker to instantly add two off-roaders to its range. The well constructed, medium sized Korando shows good engineering through and through, including two smooth engines from Mercedes-Benz. Daewoo has added a turbo-charger to the diesel, but it remains slow; the 2.3 petrol unit is a much better bet. Some of the cabin's ambience seems to have been inherited from the German marque too – there's an air of solidity throughout the interior. Space looks good but travel of the front seats is limited. The Korando is comfortable and drives well though.

Best All-Rounder: Korando 2.3

Body styles:	Estate
Engine capacity:	2.3, 3.2, 2.3D, 2.9D, 2.9TD
Price from:	£18,000
Manufactured in:	Korea

Daewoo Musso

The Musso first saw the light of day as a Ssangyong, but today Daewoo owns the company. The styling is not a very successful mixture of car and off-roader, but what is does offer is full four-wheel-drive ability for the price of a family estate with the benefit of Mercedes-Benz-designed engines. The turbo-diesel is refined and quiet, though slow. The petrol 2.3 is more pleasing, but neither has a decent manual gearchange. In terms of practicality the Musso beats most, with masses of room for passengers and a gigantic boot. Comfort levels are good, it rides well and steers with precision, but this bias towards road use means that off-road it falls behind the best.

Best All-Rounder: Musso 2.3

Daewoo Matiz

City cars tend to have many oddities, but as an increasing number of makers enter the fray, so the peculiarities lessen. The Matiz is Daewoo's first attempt and a fine effort it is too. From the perky styling to the mini-MPV interior, it shows the way to others who have been in this market for years. Powered by an 800cc three-cylinder engine, there's a throbby hum but not much in the way of performance. That aside, the interior will genuinely take four six-footers comfortably, the dashboard is as good as the best superminis and the Matiz is quite fun to drive. At the price it's outstanding value, and great fun too.

Body styles:
Hatchback

Engine capacity:
800

Price from:
£6,400

Manufactured in:
Korea

Best All-Rounder: Matiz SE

Daewoo Lanos

The Lanos replaced the Astra-based Nexia and certainly appears to offer a much more modern package. Available as a three or five-door hatchback and a neat saloon, the impressive specification includes two new engines, a 1.4-litre and 1.6-litre. The Lanos feels reasonably well put together, despite the cheap plastics inside. But it is neither refined enough for this class, nor is it good to drive, with a 1.4 engine that doesn't sparkle, and a coarse 1.6. It is an odd size too, bigger than a supermini like the Fiesta, but smaller than most Escort competitors. As before, the key factor in buying this Daewoo is the deal, but there are better budget buys around.

Body styles:
Hatchback, saloon

Engine capacity:
1.4, 1.5, 1.6

Price from:
£8,000

Manufactured in:
Korea

Best All-Rounder: Lanos 1.4 SE

Daewoo Nubira

In record time Daewoo has given its mid-range family car, the Nubira, a thorough reworking, now sporting a new "family" nose, revised engines, better seats and a little more space. As before the engines are either 1.6 or 2.0-litres, with a choice of saloon and estate body styles. The cosmetic changes largely pay off, with sleeker looks and a more solid facia, but the Nubira remains just another middle ground family model that does most things well yet will never grab your attention. The 1.6 performs well enough but performance from the 2.0-litre is disappointing while the ride comfort is rarely that good. As ever, equipment levels are very high and the back-up is brilliant.

Body styles:
Saloon, Hatchback, estate

Engine capacity:
1.5, 1.6, 1.8, 2.0

Price from:
£12,200

Manufactured in:
Korea

Best All-Rounder: Nubira 1.6 SE

Daewoo Leganza

Look at how long some Japanese makers have struggled to gain acceptance for their large cars and it becomes clear the enormity of the task that faces Daewoo with the Leganza. The Daewoo comes, as ever, armed with bags of equipment and the best after-sales package in the business. For the keen driver the Leganza falls a bit flat, with an engine too coarse when revved and soft handling. But others will appreciate the amount of space front and back, the comfort and the lack of noise when cruising. It is well finished as well, making it a Daewoo you don't need to justify to your friends.

Body styles:
Saloon

Engine capacity:
1.8, 2.0, 2.2

Price from:
£14,100

Manufactured in:
Korea

Best All-Rounder: Leganza 2.0 SX

FERRARI

The revitalisation of the Ferrari range has been completed with the introduction of the 360 Modena, the replacement for the much admired F355. Ferrari has taken a bold step here, deleting the traditional front grille for a look that owes more to the race track. But things move on and Ferrari of all manufacturers cannot afford to be left behind with the latest developments. That is particularly true now that Audi has bought Lamborghini, for there is sure to be some stronger competition for the prancing horse in the future.

Body styles:	Coupe
Engine capacity:	3.6V8
Price from:	£101,000
Manufactured in:	Italy

Ferrari F360 Modena

The F355 was always going to be a hard act to follow, but Ferrari seems to have done the business, even though few will admit that the new car looks as good as the old. Given that the new sports-car is a mid-engined 180mph-plus two-seater, the result is a real triumph of packaging, with a genuinely roomy cabin. Burnished aluminium in the interior is a departure from traditional Ferrari style, but overall, the interior design is simple and effective. The aluminium V8 pumps out 400bhp at 8,500rpm, so the 360 easily outperforms the F355. The gearshift action retains a mechanical feel, though if you want the car to do the work for you, an F1 paddle-operated transmission is available. And if the outright performance leaves you reeling, the Modena's depth of dynamic ability will knock you out.

Best All-Rounder: F360 Modena

Ferrari 550M

There were many who were shocked when Ferrari announced that it would be moving away from the theoretically superior mid-engined chassis to a front engine for its most powerful two-seater. Yet it makes some sense, for the 550M is a more practical machine that technological advances have ensured offers everything and more in terms of driving prowess. The huge power output helps.

The 485bhp on tap ensures the 550 Maranello brushes the magic 200 mph and hits 60mph in just over 4 seconds. State-of-the art traction control keeps things in check. Inside there's a new feeling of quality and luxury, though for many it will still be the howl of that V12 that is the most important aspect of any Ferrari.

Best All-Rounder: 550M

Body styles:
Coupe

Engine capacity:
5.5V12

Price from:
£150,000

Manufactured in:
Italy

Ferrari 456M GT

The 456GT came as the re-invention of a classic Ferrari formula, with a big V12 engine positioned up front and seating – notionally at least, for four. Thus designated Ferrari's Grand Tourer rather than an out and out sports car, there is no lack of performance – the 442 bhp motor can propel this projectile up to 186 mph. Designed by Pininfarina, it takes many of its styling themes from the classic

Daytona model of the late 1960s. The interior is just as mouth-watering, but despite its touring emphasis the 456 still shows race-bred responses when driven hard. A rear-mounted transaxle helps keep the weight evenly distributed and makes for an agility way out of keeping for its size.

Best All-Rounder: 456M GT

Body styles:
Coupe

Engine capacity:
5.5V12

Price from:
£168,000

Manufactured in:
Italy

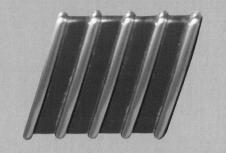

FIAT

1999 was Fiat's 100th birthday and it celebrated the event in Turin with a giant party to launch the new Punto. Punto Mark 1 was a milestone for Fiat, gaining the company acceptability throughout Europe even in places like the UK where a significant proportion of buyers used to greet the marque with a degree of suspicion. Now there is a new model to build upon that success, but of course Fiat has many other strings to its bow, with a broad range of family cars, the weird new Multipla and a cute sports car, the barchetta. Fiat also owns Alfa Romeo, Lancia, Ferrari and Maserati.

New!

Body styles:	Hatchback
Engine capacity:	1.2, 1.8, 1.9D
Price from:	£8,000 (est)
Manufactured in:	Italy

Fiat Punto

This all-new Punto brings some drama into the supermini arena. With the dramatic styling of the three-door model, and the slightly more conservative lines of the longer and roomier five-door, Fiat is striking out even though the old car was still selling well. The range of engines runs from 1.2-litre to the 1.8 from the barchetta roadster, as well as a couple of diesels. Manual gearboxes have five or six speeds, but there is a clever CVT automatic that offers a seven-speed sequential shift. Everything about the interior is better – more safety, higher quality, more stylish fascia, more storage. It is more refined to drive too. The key weakness is the rear vision in the five-door, obscured by the thick pillars.

Best All-Rounder: Punto 1.2-16v

Fiat Seicento

The Seicento replaces the Cinquecento as Fiat's city car with a blend of curves and nice detailing. The interior is a delight of Mickey Mouse switches and buttons, with plenty of stowage space. Room inside for people is tight, but the seats themselves are pretty comfortable, while noise is well suppressed. But is has some significant weaknesses too. The brakes are too heavy, the pedals – in right-hand-drive cars – are cramped and the performance of the 900cc model is pedestrian. The 1.1 Sporting overcomes this last problem, and with its tauter suspension, is the more pleasing car. New is the Citymatic, a half-way move to an automatic Seicento, with a normal gearlever but no clutch.

Body styles:
Hatchback

Engine capacity:
900,1.1

Price from:
£6,500

Manufactured in:
Poland

Best All-Rounder: Seicento Sporting

Fiat Palio

The Palio is Fiat's world car, built, or with plans to be built, in Brazil, Argentina, Poland, Turkey, India, China, Chile, Egypt, Morocco, South Africa and Venezuela. Shortly the production rate should reach a staggering million cars a year. Similar in size to the Fiat Punto, the Palio comes is six different body styles, three and five-door hatchbacks, saloon, estate, van and pick-up. Mechanically, it is simpler than cars for Western Europe, with fewer parts, a higher ground clearance to cope with worse roads and a design which is pitched towards more labour intensive factories. Only the estate is on sale in Europe.

Body styles:
Hatchback, estate

Engine capacity:
1.0, 1.2, 1.4, 1.5, 1.6, 1.7TD

Price from:
£na

Manufactured in:
Worldwide

Best All-Rounder: Palio 1.4

Fiat Bravo/Brava

The "Second Generation" Bravo and Brava were launched in 1999, though the changes are not easy to spot. But dig deep and there is much to shout about – not least a new common-rail turbo-diesel engine. Inside, the changes are more noticeable. The instruments are now round, air vents and speakers have been restyled, there's a soft-touch finish on door handles and window switches and new, attractive textiles. The new TD105 diesel offers big improvements in fuel consumption and performance. The 1.4-litre has been replaced by a 1.2 which, like all the petrol engines, is smooth and enthusiastic. The cars are easy to drive, with light steering and positive controls all round and, overall the revisions keep the Brava and Bravo a viable choice in its sector.

Body styles:
Hatchback,saloon, estate,

Engine capacity:
1.2, 1.4, 1.6, 1.8, 2.0, 2.0turbo, 1.9D, 1.9TD, 2.4TD

Price from:
£11,000

Manufactured in:
Italy

Best All-Rounder: Brava 1.6 SX

Fiat Marea

Bigger than a Focus yet smaller than a Mondeo, Fiat's Marea saloon and (Weekend) estate range falls into a grey area. Based upon the Bravo/Brava hatchbacks., it comes with an impressively broad range of engines, three petrol and three turbo-diesel. The 1.6 and 1.8 petrol units do the job well enough but it is the 2.0-litre five-cylinder unit from the Fiat Coupe that impresses the most. The top of the range diesel is the 2.4-litre five-cylinder which performs like no other car in its class. The Marea feels solid and well-made – indeed it drives like a Mondeo sized car – although the ride is rather firm. Legroom may not be that great in the back, but seat comfort all round is very good indeed.

Body styles:
Hatchback,saloon, estate,

Engine capacity:
1.2, 1.4, 1.6, 1.8, 2.0, 2.0turbo, 1.9D, 1.9TD, 2.4TD

Price from:
£12,800

Manufactured in:
Italy

Best All-Rounder: Marea 2.0 ELX

Fiat Multipla

Trust Fiat to attack the successful Renault Megane Scenic in a unique and bizarre manner. The Multipla looks even odder in the metal than in pictures, and you are in for a surprise when you climb inside too. Still, the important thing is that it all works well. The wide body and upright sides give sufficient space for three occupants to sit side-by-side in the rear and the front. The seats can be removed to give more luggage space and, importantly, the Multipla drives very well, hardly surprising as it uses the Bravo hatchback range as its base. The engine range initially comprises 1.6-litre petrol or 1.9-litre turbo-diesel.

Body styles:
MPV

Engine capacity:
1.6, 1.9TD

Price from:
£14,000 (est)

Manufactured in:
Italy

Best All-Rounder: Multipla 1.9TD.

Fiat Ulysse

Fiat got together with Citroen and Peugeot to design and build this MPV which appeals with its practical seating arrangements and good value. Its sliding rear doors are useful in tight spaces, but the downside is that rear seat passengers can't open their windows. If you haven't guessed already, the Ulysse is based on a van, something the dashboard-mounted gearlever and odd handbrake confirm. The engine choices are limited in the UK to a 2.0-litre petrol or a 1.9-litre turbo-diesel and both have a hard time of it when the Ulysse is fully laden. As a seven seater it's comfortable and reasonably spacious, but not as easy to drive or car-like on the road as rivals from Ford, VW and Seat.

Body styles:
MPV

Engine capacity:
1.8, 2.0, 2.0turbo, 1.9TD, 2.1TD

Price from:
£17,200

Manufactured in:
France

Best All-Rounder: Ulysse 2.0 EL

Fiat Coupe

In a market where style counts, the distinctive Fiat was bound to win friends. And even a few years on it still turns heads, with an interior that is equally distinctive. The front-wheel drive chassis will appeal to those promoted from hot-hatches, and the reasonably-sized boot and rear seats mean they won't have to give up all the practicality, though this is no hatchback. Both Coupe models are now fitted with five-cylinder 20-valve engines. The non-turbo produces 147bhp and is a pleasant and well-balanced car to drive, but the turbo is a real stormer, with 220bhp and shattering mid-range punch for overtaking. The chassis can struggle to cope though, and is a handful in the wet.

Body styles:
Coupe

Engine capacity:
1.8, 2.0, 2.0turbo

Price from:
£20,200

Manufactured in:
Italy

Best All-Rounder: Coupe 20-valve

Fiat barchetta

Fiat's answer to the sports car boom started by the Mazda MX5 is the barchetta, unique in this market in having front rather than rear-wheel-drive. While sports car traditionalists may scorn, to less demanding owners the barchetta can be lots of fun, not least because its noisy, eager 130 bhp 16-valve twin-cam engine gives the right sort of performance. The barchetta scores most strongly on its stylish detail touches; the retro-style chrome door handles which pop out at the press of a button and the cute dashboard, for example. This sort of style, but with modern mechanicals and a hood that's easy to operate, lie at the heart of the car's appeal. Shame, then, that it is available only in left hand drive.

Body styles:
Convertible

Engine capacity:
1.8

Price from:
£15,900

Manufactured in:
Italy

Best All-Rounder: barchetta 1.8

FORD

Ford has been the best selling brand in the UK for decades, a position it has held onto with increasing difficulty in recent years. That is not because the cars have become undesirable or that competitors are significantly better, it is just that there are so many more models for buyers to choose from. In reality Ford's European range is in better shape than ever. The Focus and Puma are genuine class leaders, while the Ka, Mondeo and Galaxy are very strong contenders too. More recently Ford has brought cars over from the states to fill gaps in the range – the Cougar and Explorer are two.

Ford Focus

The Focus is not only a real head-turner, it's practical too. By locating the tail-lights high up, the loading sill is wide, while the squared off back end means the boot is big. The interior design effectively blends curves and powerful diagonal lines, with the gently sloping dash giving an airy and spacious feel. On the road, the Focus is nothing short of a revelation, striking a sublime balance between ride and handling. The gearshift has a terrific action while the brakes have a meaty feel and are flawless in use. The engines are quiet and have a decent spread of power. Refined, practical and terrific fun to drive, it's everything the Escort wasn't.

Best All-Rounder: Focus 1.6 LX

Body styles:	Hatchback, saloon, estate
Engine capacity:	1.4, 1.6, 1.8, 2.0, 1.8TD
Price from:	£13,000
Manufactured in:	England, Germany

Ford Ka

Bold and distinctive inside and out, the Ka adds some real panache to the city car market. It comes in three variants: Ka, Ka2 and Ka3, each adding a few worthwhile options. The 1.3 engine is the same in all though, one of oldest in Ford's armoury, but reasonably refined nonetheless. Space in the front is fine, but room for rear passengers and luggage is restricted. The bold, clutter free facia is easy to use and the whole car exudes an air of purpose and fun. It's just as good on the road too, where sharp steering and handling help justify the fairly steep asking price.

Body styles:
Hatchback

Engine capacity:
1.3

Price from:
£7,500

Manufactured in:
Spain

Best All-Rounder: Ka

Ford Fiesta

Ford has to be congratulated for its work on the Fiesta. Three years ago it took what was at best a middle-ability supermini and, with some radical engineering and interior changes, improved it to be one of the best cars in its class to drive. Now for 2000, the Fiesta gets the Ford family face, improved safety equipment, an automatic transmission option and a new 1.6-litre Sports model, the Zetec-S. But the rest of the Fiesta story is largely unchanged, which has its good and bad points. The existing 1.25 and 1.4-litre 16-valve engines are terrific, and there is comfort for those in the front. The Fiesta's weakness is its rear space and boot - poor in comparison with most superminis.

Body styles:
Hatchback

Engine capacity:
1.25, 1.3, 1.4, 1.8D

Price from:
£7,700 (est)

Manufactured in:
England, Spain

Best All-Rounder: Fiesta 1.25 LX

Ford Escort

The Focus may have won countless awards, but the Escort remains in production until the new millennium for conservative buyers. The range is now limited to hatchback and estate body styles and just a (good) 1.6 petrol engine or an (outdated) 1.8 turbo-diesel. While the Escort long held the mantle of Britain's best selling car, only in the last years did it shape up to better opposition. It has a good feeling of quality and comfort, as well as room for four adults. These Escorts are good to drive too, with power steering and suspension that is sharp enough to provide an enjoyable yet comfortable drive. But the Focus is much, much better.

Body styles:
Hatchback, estate

Engine capacity:
1.3, 1.4, 1.6, 1.8, 1.8TD

Price from:
£10,500

Manufactured in:
England, Germany, India

Best All-Rounder: Escort 1.6 Finesse

Ford Mondeo

Ford's Mondeo is having trouble hanging onto its mantle as Britain's favourite family car but there are strong reasons for any buyer to choose one. Sit in the driver's seat and everything falls to hand. There's plenty of head and legroom in the front, while space is now better in the back thanks to a redesign of both front and rear seats. On the road everything feels just as good. The four-cylinder engines have been recently redesigned, there's a terrific new sporting model, the ST200, the controls are reassuringly positive, there is good visibility, a slick gearchange and a crisp throttle response. A very well-rounded package indeed.

Body styles:
Hatchback, saloon, estate

Engine capacity:
1.6, 1.8, 2.0, 2.5V6, 1.8TD

Price from:
£14,400

Manufactured in:
Belgium

Best All-Rounder: Mondeo 1.8 GLX

Ford Galaxy

The Galaxy is the result of a joint venture with the Volkswagen Group which has resulted in three MPVs built alongside each other in Portugal. In the UK the Ford consistently outsells both the VW Sharan and Seat Alhambra, though there is little to choose between them. The main differences are down to the engines – Ford uses its own 2.0 and 2.3 petrol units, but borrows a 2.8 V6 and excellent turbo diesels from VW. Since its launch in '95, the Galaxy has been heralded as one of the nicest MPVs to drive and that's still true. The airline-like cabin seats are upright but comfortable, space is commodious and performance is fine.

Body styles:
MPV

Engine capacity:
2.0, 2.3, 2.8V6, 1.9TD

Price from:
£18,200

Manufactured in:
Portugal

Best All-Rounder: Galaxy TDi 110

Ford Puma

The striking Ford Puma is the simple result of taking a competent supermini (the Fiesta) and turning it into a great coupe. The exterior cues are carried through to the interior, and the good news doesn't stop there. The Puma is roomier up front than a Fiesta, with fine head and legroom, though in the back even children will find it cramped. But it's driving enjoyment that is the Puma's primary concern. The 1.4-litre engine lacks much of the punch of the 1.7, but retains the same smooth and eager nature. And it wants for little when it comes to driving dynamics, displaying a balance and poise that would shame many a far more expensive sports car.

Body styles:
Coupe

Engine capacity:
1.4, 1.7

Price from:
£14,000

Manufactured in:
Germany

Best All-Rounder: Puma 1.7

Ford Cougar

Ford learnt its lesson with the Probe, which offered neither the style nor the space demanded by European buyers. The Mondeo-based Cougar addresses both of those points and is a far better car as a result. Like the Probe it is built in the States, but the power units are familiar – 2.0-litre or 2.5 V6. In either form the Cougar is good to drive, with smooth engine response coupled to fabulous steering and handling. It is a big car overall, lacking the compact feel of a Fiat Coupe, but that helps rear space which, though tight, is passable for adults for a short while. There is also a massive boot beneath the hatchback body style.

Body styles:
Coupe

Engine capacity:
2.0, 2.5V6

Price from:
£20,000

Manufactured in:
United States

Best All-Rounder: Cougar V6

Ford Explorer

Offering real US muscle with its 4.0-litre, 206 bhp V6, it's not just the engine that is big – everything about the Explorer is huge, both inside and out. There's enough room for the largest occupants, but petite drivers fit too. Boot space is cavernous. The leather interior is comfortable, although the flat seats in the rear provide little support. Performance of the V6, coupled to 5-speed automatic transmission, is very strong for a 4x4, and the Explorer is an easy car to drive with great visibility. But despite the leather, the interior lacks class and the clang when the doors shut would disgrace a Fiesta, let alone £25,000-worth of Explorer.

Body styles:
Estate

Engine capacity:
4.0V6

Price from:
£26,000

Manufactured in:
United States

Best All-Rounder: Explorer 4.0

FORD USA

Ford is on a roll. The company has a tough new boss who is pulling-in some of the best management, design and operations talent in the business – even if it means poaching from other car-makers; its products are a hit with buyers; and its quality is first rate. As a measure of its success, you have to look no further than the American sales chart where Ford has five of the top 10 best sellers, including the number one. While Ford pick-ups and 4x4 sport-utilities are the back-bone of its US success, its passenger cars are still the weak link.

New!

Body styles:	Saloon, estate
Engine capacity:	3.0V6, 3.4V8
Price from:	$18,900
Manufactured in:	United States

Ford Taurus

If at first you don't succeed, try again. That could be Ford's motto with its unloved Taurus saloon. Introduced originally with a controversial 'ovoid' styling theme – everything, apart from the wheels seemed to be oval-shaped – the Taurus was judged to be too oddball for a mainstream market. Now, for the 2000 model year, Ford is shedding some of the Taurus's ovoid design cues and giving the car more conventional looks. The two 3-litre V6s on offer also get more power, while the suspension becomes slightly softer. A casualty of the re-design is the sporty but slow-selling V8-engined Taurus SHO, which gets axed for 2000.

Best All-Rounder: Taurus SE

Ford Escort

Ignore the name; this Escort that has nothing remotely in common with the European version. Built south of the border in Mexico, it features bland, 'lose-it-in-the-car-park' styling, a buzzy 2-litre engine and saloon-only body styles. So no hatchbacks. But no one will complain about the prices, which start at the equivalent of £7,100. Despite the dull shape, the US Escort is a lot of fun to drive, particularly in two-door ZX2 form, which uses a punchy 130bhp twin-cam version of the 2-litre 'four'. How sales will be effected by the recent introduction of the new Focus, which will be sold alongside the Escort, will be anyone's guess.

Body styles:
Saloon, Coupe

Engine capacity:
2.0

Price from:
$11,500

Manufactured in:
United States

Best All-Rounder: Escort SE 4-door

Ford Mustang

Tough to believe that in the States you can drive away in a brand new Ford Mustang coupe, powered by a punchy 3.8-litre V6, for the equivalent of just £10,000. Even the high-octane 4.6-litre V8 GT version costs only £3-grand more. No wonder the 'Stang is still America's best-selling muscle car. There's nothing too sophisticated about the car: the suspension gets easily upset on bumpy roads, both V6 and V8 sound asthmatic as the revs rise and the interior trim is on a par with a 1973 Yugo's. But pumping iron doesn't come much cheaper than this.

Body styles:
Coupe, convertible

Engine capacity:
3.8V6, 4.6V8

Price from:
$16,500

Manufactured in:
United States

Best All-Rounder: Mustang V6

Ford Windstar

Ford's best-selling Windstar people-carrier got a major facelift a year ago, with the addition of an extra sliding side door, and a redesigned body that was 30 per cent stiffer. Now it's the minivan of choice among so-called 'minivan moms' saddled with the responsibility of daily school runs. Some of the Windstar's many features make life a little easier for the harassed mother, like the power-operated sliding side doors, which open at the push of a button. And the sonar sensors in the rear bumper, which sound a warning if there's an obstacle in the way while reversing.

Body styles:
MPV

Engine capacity:
3.0V6, 3.8V6

Price from:
$18,400

Manufactured in:
United States

Best All-Rounder: Windstar SE

Ford Excursion

Ford's new-for-2000 Excursion has the dubious honour of being the world's biggest and heaviest sport-utility vehicle, with fuel consumption that struggles to make it into double figures. Will it fit the average domestic garage? Not a chance. But sport ute-loving American's are queuing-up to buy one. The appeal? It can carry nine people and tow a boat roughly the size of the QE2. Take your pick on power; the choice is either 5.4 V8, 6.8 V10, or stump-pulling 7.3 V8 turbo-diesel. And Ford says each engine meets the toughest emissions standards, and the whole vehicle makes extensive use of recycled materials. Who said size doesn't matter?

Body styles:
Estate

Engine capacity:
4.6V8, 5.4V8, 6.8V10

Price from:
$34,000

Manufactured in:
United States

Best All-Rounder: Excursion XLT

FORD AUSTRALIA

The Falcon, Ford Australia's only locally assembled model, was launched in the all-new AU guise late in 1998 to a mixed reception. Minor revisions including a lower ride height, have been incorporated for 2000. Ford enthusiasts are excited by the news of three T-series Fairmont/Fairlane models developed by Tickford and designed to emulate Holden's Special Vehicle range. Short and long-wheelbase versions with 268bhp 5.0-litre V8 engines were joined by a 295bhp short-wheelbase rocket ship, to match the power output of Holden's new Chevrolet-sourced alloy V8, in an October 1999 launch through selected Ford Tickford Experience (FTE) dealerships. The Cougar coupe from the States was introduced at the same time. Ford's other local models include the Korean-sourced Festiva, the Mazda-based Laser, the European Mondeo and the US Explorer. The Ka and three-door Focus are likely to join the line-up early in 2000.

Body styles:	Saloon, estate
Engine capacity:	4.0, 5.0V8
Price from:	$30,000
Manufactured in:	Australia

Ford Falcon

The now completed AU Falcon line-up ranges from the base model, badged Forte, through the Futura and more luxurious Fairmont, the sporty Falcon S and Tickford developed XR6 and XR8 saloons. Estate versions and luxury Fairlane and LTD models share the same long-wheelbase platform. A 4.0-litre six cylinder engine is the standard power unit with the option of a 5.0V8 sourced from the US on some versions. Most models have a rigid rear axle and rear wheel drive to contain costs and to appeal to fleet buyers; only the luxury and sports models get full independent rear suspension.

Best All-Rounder: Falcon Futura

HOLDEN

General Motor's Holden enters the new millennium with a range of cars covering the mainstream market, a mix of locally built and imported models. The Series II Commodore, launched in June 99, is little changed inside and out – the availability of side airbags, standard on some models, and a powerful new V8 option is the main news. The long wheelbase Statesman and Caprice versions of the Commodore were also launched in mid-99, the Statesman with the choice of standard or supercharged V6 and V8, the luxury Caprice with the V8 as standard. Local Vectra production commenced late in 1998 in both saloon and estate versions using the same twin-cam four assembled in Australia and exported to Europe for Vectras and Astras. Holden's other passenger cars are sourced from the Opel range – the Barina (Corsa) and Astra, plus the Jackaroo (Monterey).

Body styles:	Saloon
Engine capacity:	3.8V6, 3.8V6 supercharged, 5.7V8
Price from:	$30,000
Manufactured in:	Australia

Holden Commodore

The VT Commodore has comfortably maintained its position as Australia's best-selling car. Starting with the base Executive model for the fleet market, the short-wheelbase range also consists of the well-equipped Acclaim, more luxurious Berlina and luxury Calais models, plus the sporty S and SS derivatives. The cavernous estate and luxury Statesman and Caprice models all share the long-wheelbase platform. Independent rear suspension is standard, unlike the Ford rival, with power coming from either the 3.8-litre V6, in standard or supercharged form, or a new Chevrolet-sourced aluminium alloy 5.7-litre V8, which though not much heavier than the V6, produces a massive 295bhp. Holden's Special Vehicles Division produces a heady range of enhanced models, the majority featuring the new V8 with in excess of 335bhp. Early in 2000, a limited run HSV GTS model is planned with around 400bhp to rival the BMW M5 and Mercedes E55.

Best All-Rounder: Commodore 5.7 V8

HONDA

Honda may make a great number of mainstream family cars, but the attention is inevitably drawn to its prowess with high technology. The NSX supercar is the pinnacle, but recently that has been overshadowed by the new S2000 sports car, with which Honda has grabbed the limelight once again. The S2000 may have only a 2.0-litre engine, and may cost "only" £28,000, but it produces more power than the much bigger engines in the Porsche Boxster, Mercedes SLK and BMW Z3. Honda's aim is for buyers to be impressed enough by such feats as to buy the ordinary cars – they too genuinely do offer that little bit extra over their rivals.

Body styles:	Cabriolet
Engine capacity:	2.0
Price from:	£28,000
Manufactured in:	Japan

Honda S2000

Every year there is a sports car of the moment – this time it is the turn of Honda. The S2000 might not look particularly exciting, with an exterior that is rather unimaginative and an interior that is just plain, but it is the driving experience that is the attraction. The 2.0-litre VTEC engine produces an astonishing 240bhp, and that is without turbo-charging. Clever engine design means that if 6,000rpm is never exceeded, the S2000 drives like a sprightly MX-5. But the engine is designed to rev to 9,000rpm, and once this range is exploited, the howl from beneath the bonnet and the thrust at the rear wheels produces the widest grin from the driver. There is steering, handling and a gearchange to match, coupled with a price that knocks the competition.

Best All-Rounder: S2000

Body styles:	Coupe
Engine capacity:	1.8
Price from:	£20,500
Manufactured in:	Japan

Honda Integra

Throughout the world the Integra appears in a number of forms, the core models being a sleek four-door saloon and stylish two-door coupe. Engine power can be a 1.8-litre 16v unit producing a healthy 144bhp, but it is the scorching 1.8-litre Integra R which raises the game and is the only version sold in the UK. This is a staggering machine. A kitten to drive around town, it transforms into a tiger as the revs rise, the 190 bhp producing breathtaking acceleration. There is a great chassis and excellent steering to complement the performance, though this is a totally no compromise machine. Noise, fuel consumption and the ride are all horrifying.

Best All-Rounder: Integra Type-R

Body styles:	Coupe, Targa
Engine capacity:	3.0V6, 3.2V6
Price from:	£69,600
Manufactured in:	Japan

Honda NSX

The NSX was built to show that Honda could design a supercar as good as a Ferrari. A showcase for Honda's renowned engineering prowess, the NSX boasts an aluminium body and suspension and a 276bhp V6 24-valve engine; a six-speed gearbox is standard, but a semi-automatic is offered too. The coupe is complemented by the removable roof on the NSX-T version. It is a stunning car to drive, with enormous depths to its performance and a sound like a muted Grand Prix car. Yet the NSX is child's play to drive around town, just like any other Honda. But it has never managed to gain the acceptance of a Ferrari – the styling is a little unbalanced and the interior just too plain.

Best All-Rounder: NSX Coupe

Honda Logo

The Logo has been around for some time in Asian markets, but this new model is the first car of its size to be sold by Honda in Europe for ten years. Much the same size as the average supermini, but taller than most, the Logo is claimed to offer more space than competitors. The engine is a 1.3-litre unit designed to give good acceleration at low revs rather than the usual Honda blast of performance at high speeds. There is a choice of 5-speed manual transmission or an electronically controlled continuously variable automatic. The Logo went on sale in Europe in early 1999 with power steering and twin airbags as standard, with UK sales starting later that year.

Best All-Rounder: Too soon to say

Body styles:
Hatchback

Engine capacity:
1.3

Price from:
£8,000 (est)

Manufactured in:
Japan

Honda Civic

Honda's Escort-class competitor is a confusing range of machines that are only loosely related. The British-built five-door hatchback and estate are kissing cousins to Rover's 400 hatch. The saloon is derived from the Japanese-built three-door hatchback, both from a newer, sixth generation of Civic. So is the Coupe, but this is built in the States. The Civic's appeal, however, runs across the range, with models to charm the mature driver looking for a reliable, refined cruiser as well as those demanding an understated performance machine. For the latter, smooth VTEC power is coupled with race-car like double-wishbone suspension, and it's this which allows near class leading refinement and pace.

Best All-Rounder: Civic 1.5 LSi 5dr

Body styles:
Hatchback, saloon, estate

Engine capacity:
1.3, 1.4, 1.5, 1.6, 1.8, 2.0TD

Price from:
£12,500

Manufactured in:
Japan, England, United States

Honda Accord

Honda has chosen to make its latest Accord a more middle-of-the-road design. Initially a saloon, a hatchback has been recently launched, but as ever, it is the mechanical package which receives a strong emphasis. Three engine choices are offered in the British-built family cars – 1.8, 2.0 and 2.2 (but no diesel) while the American-built coupe gets a 2.0 or 3.0 V6. The 1.8-litre engine impresses, more so in fact than the 2.0-litre, while the 2.2 Type R provides the thrills of a high-revving engine for those who like living closer to the edge. Inside the Accord there is comfort and much attention to detail, even if the cabin isn't the most spacious in the class.

Best All-Rounder: Accord 1.8

Body styles:
Hatchback, saloon, coupe

Engine capacity:
1.6, 1.8, 2.0, 2.2, 3.0V6, 2.0TD

Price from:
£15,600

Manufactured in:
Japan, England, United States

Honda Legend

Honda has proved it can compete in most sectors, so it's a surprise that its attempt at taking on BMW's 5-Series has failed. You may wonder why – £32,000 seems reasonable for a car of the Legend's size loaded with every conceivable extra, but besides not being entertaining to drive, the Honda lacks the prestige badge so essential in this class. There is only one Legend derivative available, powered by the 200bhp, 3.5-litre V6. There are few extras available as almost everything is standard, from leather upholstery to CD player. Honda's reliability is good too, but you are offered more choice, and a better drive, in other manufacturer's ranges.

Best All-Rounder: Legend 3.5 V6

Body styles:
Saloon

Engine capacity:
3.5V6

Price from:
£32,000

Manufactured in:
Japan

Honda Shuttle/Odyssey

Honda took a slightly different approach with its MPV, aiming a bit more towards luxury and refinement than most competitors. Available with either six 'captains' chairs or seven normal seats, all versions have automatic transmission and air conditioning as standard. There's an excellent, car-like driving position and a panoramic all-round view, but overall accommodation isn't particularly generous and seating arrangements aren't as versatile as those on other people carriers. A big plus is a rear bench seat that folds away neatly beneath the floor when not needed. The 150 bhp engine is smooth and superbly refined, but there's too little low-down pulling power when laden.

Best All-Rounder: Shuttle 2.3i LS

Body styles:
MPV

Engine capacity:
2.3, 3.0V6

Price from:
£18,300

Manufactured in:
Japan

Honda Prelude

Honda's latest version of the Prelude offers more in the way of practicality at the loss of the avant-garde style of the previous car. Some will mourn that loss of character, but Honda feels it knows its customers. What is in no doubt is that this Prelude retains all its previous dynamic ability. Two engines are offered, a 2.0-litre and a higher performance 2.2 with Honda's VTEC and 185bhp. The latter is exceptional, howling enthusiastically to high revs whenever required. It comes with four-wheel steering as standard, with handling beyond reproach. Inside there is noticeably more room, but it remains a tight fit for adults in the rear seats.

Best All-Rounder: Prelude 2.2 VTi

Body styles:
Coupe

Engine capacity:
2.0, 2.2

Price from:
£19,100

Manufactured in:
Japan

Honda HR-V

Based on the Logo supermini, the HR-V looks like a car on steroids, all pumped up with lots of ground clearance and, in some models, four wheel drive. It is a wacky, highly distinctive package, though in reality little more than a jacked-up supermini estate with funny headlamps. Performance from the 1.6-litre unit is lively and smooth, with the obligatory Honda growl at high revs, and a bit too buzzy at motorway speeds. Inside there is lots of blue – dials, switch gear and seats. It looks good, and front seat comfort is fine, but legroom is mediocre in the rear. But the HR-V is a good car, fun to drive and with unusually good driving characteristics for something so high off the ground.

Best All-Rounder: HR-V 1.6

Body styles:
Estate

Engine capacity:
1.6

Price from:
£14,000

Manufactured in:
Japan

Honda CR-V

Honda's mid-range 4x4 is more car-like than most of the competition which, as most buyers of this type of vehicle rarely use in the really rough stuff, gives it a useful edge. One advantage is its practicality and Honda's CR-V offers lots of thoughtful touches. The floor is completely flat allowing the seating positions to be changed and there's a concealed luggage area under the floor. The 2.0-litre engine gives performance which is usefully brisk, though it's hardly the GTi in 4x4 clothing that has made the Toyota RAV4 such a hit. Similarly, handling and ride are acceptable rather than inspiring. But it is a solid, roomy, well-built machine that is actually rather enjoyable to own and drive.

Best All-Rounder: CR-V 2.0 ES

Body styles:
Estate

Engine capacity:
2.0

Price from:
£16,900

Manufactured in:
Japan

ISUZU

ISUZU

Isuzu has, to an extent, been swamped by the General Motors influence in the last few years, so now there is little left that it can really call its own. The Trooper is sold in Europe as an Opel Monterey (but no longer in the UK as a Vauxhall – the Isuzu brand name proved too powerful a hurdle). The Isuzu Rodeo and Amigo are essentially the same as the Frontera 5 and 3-door models – Isuzu may have designed them originally but for European buyers they are built in Luton. The Oasis sold in the States is little more than a rebadged Honda Shuttle. But despite all this Isuzu has a strong brand image for its off-roaders, helped no end by the futuristic VehiCross.

Body styles:	Estate
Engine capacity:	3.0TD, 3.5V6
Price from:	£19,100
Manufactured in:	Japan

Isuzu Trooper

After some interesting battles with the giant General Motors in the UK – Vauxhall were selling the same vehicle as the Monterey – Isuzu has stayed the course while Vauxhall has given up. The Trooper is a particularly large off-roader that, while it does its job well enough, fails to really match the charm of some more stylish competitors. Despite a facelift, the interior still looks dated, though it has the advantage of seven seats in some versions. The revamp brought two new engines, a refined but thirsty 3.5-litre V6 petrol and an impressive turbo-diesel. The latter suits the Trooper better, with more low-down torque. The three door is better off-road, but the long wheelbase is more practical.

Best All-Rounder: Trooper 3.0TD Duty

Body styles:	Estate
Engine capacity:	3.2V6
Price from:	£na
Manufactured in:	Japan

VehiCross

Do all off-roaders really need to look the same? Isuzu doesn't think so, and there is little that draws more attention than its VehiCross. Only around 10 a day are built, and they are all swallowed up by eager buyers in Japan. Based upon the running gear of the Trooper, with a 212bhp V6 engine and sports suspension, the VehiCross goes and handles like no other off-roader – though it is probably worse than most in the rough stuff. Inside there's barely room for four, but then this is as much a style statement as practical transport.

HYUNDAI

Korean manufacturer Hyundai finds itself in the position that many Japanese car manufacturers were in a decade or two ago. It makes solid cars that answer most of the basic needs, but they lack any real charisma or status. That may be fine for many markets, where value for money is the key driving factor, but many European buyers want more. So it is disappointing to note that the image boost Hyundai achieved with its Coupe will be knocked on the head by an ugly facelift for 2000.

Body styles:	Saloon
Engine capacity:	2.5V6, 3.0V6
Price from:	£25,000 (est)
Manufactured in:	Korea

Hyundai XG

Hyundai has traditionally kept its biggest cars for the domestic buyers, but with the XG it feels that it has something worthy of mainstream world markets. Thus sales started in Europe in 1999 with a choice of 2.5V6 or 3.0V6 petrol engines coupled to a high-tech five-speed automatic transmission. Longer than most executive saloon competitors like the BMW 5 Series and Mercedes E-Class, the XG promises generous interior space coupled to luxury features by the bucket load. That may make the £25,000 price tag seem reasonable, but the lack of a prestige brand name will not help at all. In the UK Hyundai has enough trouble selling reasonable quantities of the smaller Sonata, so a car costing up to £10,000 more is not yet considered a viable proposition.

Best All-Rounder: XG 3.0V6

Body styles:	Saloon
Engine capacity:	2.0, 2.4, 2.5V6
Price from:	£14,000
Manufactured in:	Korea

Hyundai Sonata

This new Hyundai is now firmly pitched against mainstream family rivals rather than big executive models, offering in the place of a familiar name, an abundance of passenger space, heaps of equipment and a great warranty. The Sonata has just one body style – the saloon – and the choice of a 2.0-litre four cylinder engine, or a 2.5 V6 coupled to an automatic transmission. It is the sort of car that does almost everything at least adequately, but stands out in no area. So the performance is OK, the comfort satisfactory and the refinement reasonable. The overall selling package – and the space – remain the outstanding features.

Best All-Rounder: Sonata 2.0 CDX

Hyundai Atoz

It seems like the enthusiasm Far Eastern countries have for very small city cars is at last gaining acceptance within Europe. Hyundai's Atoz is, unarguably, one of the ugliest you can buy – quite why it has to look so extreme is something of a mystery. But the pricing is right and, importantly, it is one of the most appealing cars to drive and travel in. The Atoz uses a new, specially developed 1.0-litre engine which is refined and economical and, unlike so much of the competition, provides a decent turn of performance. The high roof may look odd, but it means the interior is comfortable even for tall passengers.

Body styles:
Estate

Engine capacity:
1.0

Price from:
£6,900

Manufactured in:
Korea

Best All-Rounder: Atoz +

Hyundai Accent

The Accent wins few prizes for style, but its budget pricing and no-nonsense finish keep it competitive, at least until the new model appears early in 2000. Inside there is generous headroom, terrific all-round visibility and an excellent driving position. For a small family car it is roomy, though it takes a bit of a squeeze to carry three adults in the rear. There's not much difference in the power output of the 1.3 and 1.5-litre engines, but the larger capacity unit does offer better flexibility. Both units are smooth but sound strained at higher revs under acceleration. Corners are taken with enthusiasm and the power steering is reasonably accurate. Ride comfort is good for such a small car.

Body styles:
Saloon, coupe

Engine capacity:
1.3, 1.5

Price from:
£7,000

Manufactured in:
Korea

Best All-Rounder: Accent 1.5 Luxe

Hyundai Lantra

The recent facelift has improved the Lantra's appeal, with a new nose, improvements in engine refinement and a better quality interior. The basic value remains built into the car though, with Hyundai aiming it at the Focus and cheaper Ford Mondeos, though it fails to match the space in either. Both engine options, 1.6 or 2.0-litre petrol units, are smooth, powerful, and fuel economy is good for this size of car too. Equipment levels are high, and even the supermini-priced Si has electric windows and sunroof as standard. The estate makes a stylish and practical no-nonsense workhorse.

Body styles:
Saloon, estate

Engine capacity:
1.5, 1.6, 1.8, 2.0

Price from:
£10,600

Manufactured in:
Korea

Best All-Rounder: Lantra 1.6 GSi Estate

Hyundai Coupe

Hyundai showed the world that it could design and build a classy looking car when it launched the Coupe back in 1996. Now things look more worrying with a major facelift due soon that shows Hyundai's designers are losing the plot. But underneath it remains largely the same competent coupe offering an attractive combination of performance and equipment at a lower price than the competition. The Lantra's fine 1.6 and 2.0-litre engines endow it with perky performance, and there is reasonable practicality. Only the interior quality doesn't stand comparison to rivals, though this is due to receive attention too. Space in the back is strictly for youngsters.

Body styles:
Coupe

Engine capacity:
1.6, 1.8, 2.0

Price from:
£14,000

Manufactured in:
Korea

Best All-Rounder: Coupe 2.0 SE

JAGUAR

Jaguar is riding on the crest of a wave, with sales stronger than ever, and an increasing number of new markets opening up. Key to the current success is the S-Type, combining traditional British styling with driving and comfort attributes that are strictly of the new Millennium. Within a couple of years Jaguar will launch a new sports car based upon the S-Type, but with two seats and folding roof. The current sporting model, the XK8, should not be overlooked in the meantime, a world class machine indeed. XJ8 saloon sales have been knocked a bit by the S-Type, but there is still no denying its desirability.

Body styles:	Saloon
Engine capacity:	3.0V6, 4.0V8
Price from:	£28,300
Manufactured in:	England

Jaguar S-Type

Jaguar's newest and smallest car offers a style harking back to the successful saloon of the 1960s in a package that rivals the BMW 5 Series and Mercedes-Benz E-Class. The heart of these cars is the 4.0 V8 automatic from the XJ8 which provides effortless performance coupled with high levels of refinement. With the optional semi-active suspension it a highly responsive machine on twisty roads.

The alternative 3.0 V6 also complements the car well too, and certainly provides more than adequate performance. Inside the car is a delight of wood and leather, offering high levels of comfort, though not the space of the Mercedes. But that is the only weak point in an otherwise fabulous machine.

Best All-Rounder: S-Type 3.0 SE

Jaguar XJ8

Ford's money has, at last, enabled Jaguar to move away from its rather tarnished image for quality control and has produced a luxury car that can stand up to the competition of its German rivals. As always there is a sumptuously appointed cabin that no-one else has managed to match in terms of its luxury and warmth. There is a terrific range of V8 engines. Even the base 3.2-litre model gives pleasing performance, but the supercharged XJR is mind-blowingly fast. So charisma still counts highly in this Jaguar's attributes, outweighing for many buyers the fact that neither the interior nor boot space is particularly generous.

Best All-Rounder: XJ8 4.0 Sovereign

Body styles:
Saloon

Engine capacity:
3.2, 4.0

Price from:
£35,200

Manufactured in:
England

Jaguar XK8

Offered in coupe or convertible forms, this 2+2 grand tourer has set the luxury car world alight, combining traditional Jaguar virtues with new standards of quality and with the sort of value that makes the competition – notably Mercedes-Benz – look absurdly over-priced. At the heart of the XK8 is a 4.0-litre V8, either in standard or supercharged (XKR) form. Even the standard XK8 is a peach to drive, smooth yet with a high level of sporting accomplishment. The XKR is phenomenal, providing performance unmatched at the price. The detail work inside the XK8 is delightful, with plenty of leather, wood and thick carpeting giving it real class, and comfort for hours on end.

Best All-Rounder: XK8 Coupe

Body styles:
Coupe, convertible

Engine capacity:
4.0 V8

Price from:
£50,700

Manufactured in:
England

KIA

Kia was taken over by the Hyundai corporation in 1999, giving the Korean manufacturer new stability after some worrying times. Future plans are that these two companies will share basic designs which will potentially have considerable economic advantages, but such developments are still a few years away. For the present Kia continues with its range of small to medium-sized family cars, selling more on value than any strong appeal. The Sedona MPV with V6 or 2.9TD arrives late in 1999 and Kia also has the rights to build the Lotus Elan, though the future of that car looks in increasing doubt.

New!

Body styles:	Hatchback, saloon
Engine capacity:	1.5, 1.8
Price from:	£8,500
Manufactured in:	Korea

Kia Mentor II/Sephia/Shuma

This is the all-new version of a car that failed to thrill anyone but those motoring on a firm budget. Offering Escort space for Fiesta money, the big attraction is still the pricing. To give the range a bit more zest, however, Kia offers two distinct bodies. The saloon continues in its ultra-conservative style, and is known as the Mentor II or Sephia, depending upon where it is sold. The Shuma five-door hatchback has been more radically restyled and offers the 1.5 engine from the saloon as well as a 1.8. Both have twin overhead camshafts to give lively performance, with automatic transmission an option. Redesigned seats improve comfort and larger rear doors give easier access.

Best All-Rounder: Mentor II SX

Kia Pride

A rebadged version of a long extinct Mazda 121 supermini, the Kia is way past its sell-by date. On paper it looks cheap and is surprisingly spacious inside, but it feels its age on the road. Build quality is reasonable, but the rest of the package struggles to match up to present day standards. There is now just one engine on offer, a petrol 1.3 which needs to be worked hard despite the car's small dimensions. A five-door adds a little practicality for the family driver, though the price comes up against some tough new opposition – all of which have the driver airbag.

Body styles:
Hatchback, estate

Engine capacity:
1.2, 1.3

Price from:
£5,500

Manufactured in:
Korea

Best All-Rounder: Pride 1.3 SX

Kia Clarus

Kia has kept its bigger models to itself for some time, but now the new Clarus is offered in right-hand drive form, a year after going on sale in Europe. Designed to compete head on with the mainstream family car sector, Kia will, like Hyundai, undoubtedly have a tough time on their hands in a segment where a "big name" counts. To counter this Kia is offering a high specification package at remarkable prices, and makes great claims about the high technological content of the 1.8 and 2.0-litre engines. There certainly seems to be plenty of room on offer, though the lack of a definitive style will not please everyone.

Body styles:
Saloon, estate

Engine capacity:
1.8, 2.0

Price from:
£11,000

Manufactured in:
Korea

Best All-Rounder: Too early to tell.

Kia Sedona/Carnival

Kia has offered an MPV – the Carnival – in Germany, Italy and Spain as well as at home for over a year, but now the Sedona, as it will be called here, has been launched in the UK. It is a traditional seven seater, but longer than most with an unusually powerful choice of engines – 2.5-litre V6 or 2.9-litre turbo-diesel with double overhead camshafts and 16 valves! Access to the rear is through sliding doors popular in the US, making entrance easy in tight spaces. The versatile seating slides, rotates and folds for maximum versatility. As with all current Kia products, the pricing has been set to undercut all its main rivals.

Body styles:
MPV

Engine capacity:
2.5V6, 2.9TD

Price from:
£na

Manufactured in:
Korea

Best All-Rounder: Too soon to say

Kia Sportage

Kia's offering in the trendy sport off-roader market is more credible than its other models thanks to cheeky good looks and the fact that for Europe the cars are built in Germany, not Korea. Inside there is a reasonable amount of room, and although the trim is not the best quality it should last well. A 2.0-litre engine helps the Sportage perform reasonably on and off the road, but the car is let down by a choppy ride and lifeless steering on the tarmac and low ground clearance off it. A 2.0-litre turbo-diesel and three-door versions are also available in some markets. All models are well equipped and it makes a viable alternative if you can't afford a Freelander.

Body styles:
Estate

Engine capacity:
2.0, 2.0TD

Price from:
£13,000

Manufactured in:
Korea, Germany

Best All-Rounder: Sportage S

LADA

Lada pulled out of the UK in the late 90's. Designs had moved on while Lada stood still, plus there was the problem of making the current range comply with increasingly tough European legislation. But the company continues to build cars for the home market, and exports to other countries still take place. Much hope must be pinned on the 110 range, though its more modern look is not carried through to engineering design. Lada also has several other new models on the books, including an all-new Niva, a Scenic rival call the Nadeschda and a VW Polo sized car – all assuming that it can find the money.

110

Body styles:	Hatchback, saloon
Engine capacity:	1.5, 2.0
Price from:	£na
Manufactured in:	Russia

Niva

Body styles:	Estate
Engine capacity:	1.7, 1.8, 1.5TD, 1.9D
Price from:	£na
Manufactured in:	Russia

Samara

Body styles:	Saloon, estate
Engine capacity:	1.1, 1.3, 1.5
Price from:	£na
Manufactured in:	Russia

Lada Nova, Samara, Niva and 110

The Nova is Lada's oldest model, introduced in 1970 when the design had already been cast-off by Fiat. A saloon or estate, the Nova offers all the attributes of a 1960's design, which means a big boot, and room for five. It is also very heavy to drive and, like all Ladas, not at all well built. Engines range from 1.5, 1.6 to 1.7 as well as a 1.7 diesel. In the UK it was known as the Riva.

The Samara was Lada's 1980s attempt to produce a modern car; it failed miserably. Power is almost acceptable in 1.5 form, barely so with the 1.3 and lethargic in 1.1 guise. None is quiet, especially when worked hard, as each model needs to be. As expected, the chassis is soggy and ill-controlled; the equipment and safety specification minimal.

The Niva was originally developed for the Russian army, with a simple selectable four-wheel drive system. As a road car, the Niva remains pretty basic transport. Even with the later 1.7-litre engine with fuel injection, performance is modest in the extreme and there's no power steering to ease the high parking loads required. Inside, there's plenty of room for four hefty adults, but not much boot space behind the seats. Given a long enough straight, it will work its way noisily up to about 80mph. Show it a muddy track and the Niva feels far more confident.

Lada's newest model is the 110. It may look more modern than the others but the reality is that this car also feels like it was designed 30 years ago. The quality is very poor by today's standards with cheap plastics used throughout the interior. The handling is acceptable though the body rolls a lot when cornering. There is a choice of five engines, all of which are reasonably responsive.

LAMBORGHINI

Now under Audi ownership, things are looking up for Lamborghini. It is difficult for any company to survive with just one hugely expensive model in the range, and Audi money will help broaden the base in the future. The first evidence will be in early 2000 when Lamborghini will introduce a face-lifted Diablo with improvements to both the interior and exterior. Then later in the year the Super Diablo, code-named the L147, will be launched, complete with 6.0-litre V12. As for the frequently mentioned new baby-Diablo, which will compete with the Ferrari 360M, that is still at least two years away.

Body styles:	Coupe, convertible
Engine capacity:	5.7 V12
Price from:	£136,000
Manufactured in:	Italy

Lamborghini Diablo

The Diablo has been around for a good few years now, taking on the position of the Grandfather of all the current supercar generation. It remains, however, a stunning piece of automotive design, with an impossibly loud and thrilling bark to the mid-mounted 5.7-litre V12 coupled to a chassis with extraordinarily high cornering limits. Four-wheel-drive is an option and so too is a roadster body with a removable roof. But the interest for late 1999 centres around the new GT version. With the aluminium bodywork being replaced by carbon-fibre composite, the weight has been cut by 90kg, and the power pushed up to 585bhp, ensuring a maximum speed of 211mph. Just 80 will be built – all for Europe – so get your order in now!

Best All-Rounder: Diablo GT

LANCIA

The big news for Lancia is the launch of its brand new Lybra saloon, a replacement for the somewhat unloved Dedra. That superseded model was hyped as an Italian alternative to the BMW 3 Series when it was launched, a position it never lived up to, but since then the Fiat Group, which owns Lancia, has repositioned the company as the luxury arm of its many brands, leaving Alfa Romeo to tackle the Germans. But Lancia's identity is muddled even today, with the Y supermini and Z people carrier hardly falling within most people's perceptions of a luxury vehicle. Lancia has not built right-hand-drive cars for the past five years.

New!

Body styles:	Saloon, estate
Engine capacity:	1.6, 1.8, 2.0, 1.9TD, 2.4TD
Price from:	£na
Manufactured in:	Italy

Lancia Lybra

The Lybra is Lancia's new medium-sized car, replacing the Dedra and once again available as either a saloon or estate. To distance this from the sporty cars of Alfa Romeo and the everyday virtues of Fiats, much emphasis is being placed on the luxury aspects of the Lybra – very low noise levels, advanced air conditioning system and a sophisticated Bose hi-fi. The centre console, designed to reflect the Lancia grille, is purposely big and imposing to house the large number of controls deemed necessary in a small luxury car. Five engines are offered, the smallest 1.6-litre producing 103bhp, rising to a 2.0-litre five-cylinder 20-valve unit with 155 bhp; two common rail turbo-diesels are also available.

Best All-Rounder: Too soon to say.

Lancia Y

Using the Fiat Punto's chassis, the Y was always going to be reasonable to drive, but Lancia has added a dash of style and luxury to the supermini class. The exterior's wacky styling is continued through to the luxuriously-appointed interior, with centrally mounted instruments and suede-look trim for the seats and dashboard. Three engine options are available, using the Punto's 1.1-litre or the 1.2 in 60 bhp or 86bhp versions. It's reasonably cheap in Italy too, but will never be engineered with right-hand drive. There are two trim levels, LS and LX, but more impressively the Y is available in a choice of 112 different colours.

Best All-Rounder: Y 1.2 86bhp

Body styles:
Hatchback

Engine capacity:
1.1, 1.2

Price from:
£na

Manufactured in:
Italy

Lancia Delta

The Delta should really be the epitome of a small Lancia, combining luxury with a degree of sporting prowess that others cannot match. But it has never really managed to approach this level of achievement. Inside there just is not enough room for a car of this class, while the chassis has neither the refinement nor handling ability expected. There is, however, no doubt that the Delta remains a stylish car, not least in HPE form. The sporting derivative of the Delta has always been available with an impressive 193bhp 2.0-litre turbo-charged engine. Now all the other engines – 1.6, 1.8 and turbo-diesel can be bought with the HPE style as well as the standard body.

Best All-Rounder: Delta 2.0 HPE

Body styles:
Hatchback

Engine capacity:
1.6, 1.8, 2.0 turbo, 1.9TD

Price from:
£na

Manufactured in:
Italy

Lancia Kappa

Lancia's entry into the executive market does well in its home market of Italy, but few other markets can see its appeal. That's a shame because the distinctive slab-sided styling hides a competent car with tidy handling and great refinement. The coupe is weird looking, but the estate can offer luxury and space. The Kappa formed the basis of the new big Alfa – the 166 – so it shares engines with the sporty marque, including the fabulous 3.0-litre V6. The 2.0-litre engines, even the turbo, don't have enough refinement for a Lancia, but the turbo-diesel is a remarkably good all-rounder. While the station wagon is practical, the odd coupe is for enthusiasts only.

Best All-Rounder: Kappa 3.0 V6

Body styles:
Saloon, estate, coupe

Engine capacity:
2.0, 2.0turbo, 2.4, 3.0V6, 2.4TD

Price from:
£na

Manufactured in:
Italy

Lancia Z

If ever there was an example of the confused direction Fiat has chosen for Lancia, it is the Z. Quite what a company with Lancia's heritage is doing producing a people carrier is a difficult question to answer. But you can guess the way the thinking went – Lancia has the right image, and Fiat has an MPV, so why not combine them to produce a really upmarket luxury six-seater? The trouble is, it looks like a van and is the car that, in Fiat form, is seen bashing around Italy's streets as a taxi. It is, of course, the same as the Peugeot 806 and Citroen Synergy too, and to top it all, built in France.

Best All-Rounder: Z 2.0 Turbo

Body styles:
MPV

Engine capacity:
2.0, 2.0turbo, 2.1TD

Price from:
£na

Manufactured in:
France

LAND ROVER

Still the name that most people think of first when it comes to four-wheel-drive vehicles, Land Rover has moved from a three-car range to a four, with the Freelander now solidly established at the lower end. Like the other Land Rovers, the Freelander does more than look the part. Land Rover acknowledges that while few people make much of the off-road capability, all welcome the fact that, should they choose, the ability is there in bucket loads. Land Rover is also good at disguising the technical developments. The Defender, Discover and Range Rover may look like they always have, but the sophistication built into today's vehicles is at the very forefront of off-road engineering.

Body styles:	Estate, convertible
Engine capacity:	1.8, 2.0TD
Price from:	£17,000
Manufactured in:	England

Land Rover Freelander

Smaller, cheaper and trendier than any previous Land Rover, the Freelander is another of the increasingly popular "lifestyle" 4x4s. Yet it is a credible off-roader, despite lacking the ground clearance of other Land Rovers. To compensate, there is a clever patented hill descent system that helps even novices tackle treacherous descents. The Freelander is roomy and comfortable inside, and it drives more like a car than most 4x4s, though the gearchange is notchy. The turbo-diesel engine provides good performance, but it is too noisy except when cruising. The 1.8 petrol engine is the better all-rounder, more fun but not as good on the hills. The fabric roof system on the Softback is also a real chore to use.

Best All-Rounder: Freelander 1.8i Station Wagon

Land Rover Discovery

So popular was the style of the original Discovery that the 1998 redesign retained the style while changing everything else. It has a new engine, state of the art suspension and a revamped interior. Most important for most owners will be the increase in interior space and an improvement in quality. Land Rover's new Active Cornering Enhancement suspension system stiffens the suspension on the road and softens the ride off it, with impressive results. The steering and brakes have been beefed up, and on the road the Discovery feels more stable than any other serious off-roader. You could almost forget that there's a new turbo-diesel, which is refined and economical enough to question the V8.

Best All-Rounder: Discovery TDi

Body styles:
Estate

Engine capacity:
4.0 V8, 2.5TD

Price from:
£25,500

Manufactured in:
England

Land Rover Range Rover

The Range Rover gets some mid-term revisions for 2000, though most are hard to spot. The V8 engines get more torque to improve their response, there is traction control to help in slippery situations, side airbags are standard and a whole raft of interior and exterior finishes are available through the "Autobiography" programme. Fundamentally though, it is the same impressive machine, with outstanding off-road ability coupled to an interior that has the ambience and comfort of a Jaguar. The Range Rover has become a very expensive machine, however, and while the cachet is undoubtedly strong, there's a strong argument that says the significantly cheaper Discovery does everything just as well.

Best All-Rounder: Range Rover 4.0

Body styles:
Estate

Engine capacity:
4.0V8, 4.6V8, 2.5TD

Price from:
£39,600

Manufactured in:
England

Land Rover Defender

The Land Rover Defender is one of a tiny group of vehicles that has reached immortality. Like the Mini and Volkswagen's Beetle, it has remained the definitive four-wheel-drive off-roader, despite the attempts of every Japanese manufacturer to oust it. Key to its success is the tough, rugged, no-nonsense design. Available in two basic forms, with either a 90 or 110 inch wheelbase, dozens of derivatives have been developed from this basic steel girder chassis/ aluminium panelled platform. Perhaps the most unlikely derivative is the "civilised" County, which just goes to show that even the Defender has its limits. Best to think of it as a workhorse, and by picking the turbo-diesel, there is still little to better it.

Best All-Rounder: Defender TDi

Body styles:
Estate

Engine capacity:
4.0 V8, 2.5TD

Price from:
£19,900

Manufactured in:
England

LEXUS

Toyota has achieved what many thought impossible ten years ago – to sell a car that can be compared in terms of ability and prestige against the likes of Mercedes-Benz and Jaguar. It did it by inventing a new brand, Lexus, and making the original car – the LS400 – so sophisticated that it could not be ignored. Until 1999 the Lexus range was always big and expensive, but now the company is attacking the mass "compact executive" market with the IS200 (a car also sold in Japan as the Toyota Altezza). Up against the Alfa Romeo 156, Audi A4 and BMW 3 Series, Lexus hopes for a massive increase in its overall sales, and if the pricing remains as competitive, it will undoubtedly succeed.

Body styles:	Saloon
Engine capacity:	2.0
Price from:	£20,500
Manufactured in:	Japan

Lexus IS200

The IS200 is the car that will move Lexus from the niche luxury car segment into a much larger area of the market. It is designed to compete head-on with BMW's new 3 Series, the Audi A4 and Alfa Romeo 156. It does not quite match any of those in terms of interior space, however, and the highly stylised interior will not be to everyone's taste either. But on the road the IS200 can match the best of the competition, with sharp, precise steering and a highly accomplished rear-wheel-drive chassis. There's just one engine, a 2.0-litre six cylinder which though not especially powerful, provides enthusiastic performance combined with a wonderful sound track. A six-speed manual gearbox is standard, but the four-speed automatic is an excellent sporting alternative.

Best All-Rounder: IS200 2.0 Sport

Lexus GS300

The original Lexus GS300 was too anonymous for its own good, hence the stronger looks of the latest model, now a much more stylish competitor for the BMW 5-Series and Mercedes E-Class than before. Performance from the 3.0-litre six-cylinder engine is impressive without being outstanding, helped by an all-new five-speed automatic gearbox. Inside, there are a few too many hints at the car's Toyota parentage, but the cabin design is sound and flawlessly built. On the road, the big Lexus feels solid and assured, with well-weighted steering and precise handling. The GS300 is hardly a sports saloon, but the quality and equipment make it an attractive proposition for those more interested in finer things.

Best All-Rounder: GS300 SE

Body styles:
Saloon

Engine capacity:
3.0, 4.0V8

Price from:
£31,200

Manufactured in:
Japan

Lexus LS400

Toyota's first real attempt to topple the might of the European prestige manufacturers is a mighty impressive effort, especially in this revised form. The LS400 is more refined inside than a Rolls Royce, with a whisper quiet 4.0-litre V8 matched to the smoothest-shifting automatic gearbox in the world.
The revisions to the range have made the single LS400 model even more comfortable, and there is enough standard equipment to make a Mercedes owner weep. Even satellite navigation is standard. But now this Lexus has to contend with a tough new competitor that has both the looks and badge the LS400 lacks – the new Mercedes-Benz S-Class.

Best All-Rounder: LS400

Body styles:
Saloon

Engine capacity:
4.0V8

Price from:
£50,000

Manufactured in:
Japan

Lexus SC300/400

Still a stunning-looking, two-door luxury coupe, despite its advancing years – it was introduced to the US way back in 1991 and has gone largely unchanged since. Sleek, elegant and wonderfully refined, the Lexus SC still manages to turn heads wherever it goes. In 3-litre in-line 'six' form, the SC is a little short on power. Much more appealing is the 400 with its potent yet creamy-smooth 4-litre 290bhp V8 from the LS400 flagship. In this form, the SC is near silent at speed, and made more athletic by its standard five-speed, seamless automatic. Could be a future classic.

Best All-Rounder: SC400

Body styles:
Coupe

Engine capacity:
3.0, 4.0V8

Price from:
$43,000

Manufactured in:
Japan

Lexus RX300

This is the hottest-selling mid-size sport-utility in America right now – which has been a surprise, even to Toyota-owned Lexus. Its combination of a car-like ride, an elevated, leather-lined cabin and the traditional Lexus reputation for quality and high re-sales has won it many fans. It will go on sale in the UK next year. Not that it's a traditional rough, tough, off-roader. It's platform is car-based – the old Celica 4x4 in fact. It doesn't have a low ratio 'crawler' gear, and its 3-litre V6 thrives on revs. But the US market doesn't mind. Luxury, a high-up driving position, and smooth performance are the requirements here.

Best All-Rounder: RX300 4x4

Body styles:
Estate

Engine capacity:
3.0V6

Price from:
$32,000

Manufactured in:
Japan

LINCOLN

Ford's luxury car division is currently going through a major product renaissance. The latest LS saloon – this is the car that's based on the S-type Jag – is finally bringing younger buyers into the fold, while the giant Navigator 4x4 is the vehicle of choice among America's golfing and country club set. Ford had planned to set-up Lincoln in Europe as a stepping stone between Ford and Jaguar. But following Ford's take-over of Volvo, it looks like the plans have been shelved, and Lincoln will stay put on the other side of the Pond.

New!

Body styles:	Saloon
Engine capacity:	3.0V6, 4.0V8
Price from:	$30,900
Manufactured in:	United States

Lincoln LS

The competition is still reeling at the prices posted for the new Lincoln LS; a well-equipped V6 version, for example, can be had for the equivalent of £19,300. The reviews are overwhelmingly positive for this remarkable-handling four-door, which even betters the new S-type Jag through the twisties. Based on the S-type's chassis and suspension, the LS features a version of Ford's 3-litre V6 used in the US Taurus, and a new 3.9-litre V8 based loosely on the Jag's 4-litre V8. The styling of this Lincoln could have been a little more adventurous – it looks like some big Mitsubishi – but the tactile, tingling feel of the car will quickly woo buyers.

Best All-Rounder: LSV6 5-sp

Lincoln Continental

When is techno-wizardry a turn-off to luxury car buyers? When you give the driver too many choices. Case in point; Lincoln's glitzy Continental. There are choices for the amount of power steering assistance, the firmness of the suspension, seat controls, even whether you want the horn to peep or honk. Talk about confusion. Pity, because the Continental is a fine driving car, and a delight to be passengered in. Ford's formidable 4.6-litre, 260bhp V8 provides muscular performance and whisper-quiet cruising. And for its bulk, the big Lincoln is an accomplished handler.

Best All-Rounder: Continental V8

Body styles:
Saloon

Engine capacity:
4.6V8

Price from:
£

Manufactured in:
United States

Lincoln Town Car

Take a trip to New York and it seems there's a Lincoln Town Car on every street corner – some of them 40 feet long. Since its redesign in '98, the sumptuous Town Car has become the car of choice for the Big Apple's limo companies. Makes sense, because of its six-passenger seating and leather-lined interior. Previous Town Cars used to roll around like freighters in a Force Five, but not this one. Air suspension keeps the car horizontal on corners, while the variable-assist steering – while still a little light to the touch – has precision and feel. A class act.

Body styles:
Saloon

Engine capacity:
4.6V8

Price from:
$38,500

Manufactured in:
United States

Best All-Rounder: Town Car Executive

Lincoln Navigator

Everything about the Navigator is gargantuan, from its whale-like body to its 5.4-litre V8. But this giant Lincoln has become one of America's sales sensations, and certainly a saviour for Ford's Lincoln division. Well-heeled buyers who previously snapped-up big luxury saloons now like the thought of more space for their golfing buddies, or grand-kids. While four-wheel drive is optional, don't expect to see Navigators in the rough – except on the golf course. This is a true luxury car, with leather trim, chrome wheels, deep-pile carpets and CD player. Its big V8 provides lively performance, though fuel consumption is embarrassing.

Body styles:
Estate

Engine capacity:
5.4V8

Price from:
$40,800

Manufactured in:
United States

Best All-Rounder: Navigator 4wd

LOTUS

Once upon a time Lotus was Britain's premier sports car manufacturer, but that mantle has arguably been taken on by Blackpool manufacturer TVR. But where TVR offers a combination of style and brute power, Lotus has always aimed at a more delicate engineering balance, producing highly sophisticated designs that appeal as much to the engineer and racer as to the general public. The latest design to hit production is the amazing 340R, based upon the Elise but aimed as much at track use as the road. Lotus is owned by Malaysian manufacturer Proton.

Body styles:	Coupe
Engine capacity:	3.5 V8
Price from:	£50,000
Manufactured in:	England

Lotus Esprit

What more can be said about the Esprit? For a car that has been around in the same form for a dozen years, with its mechanical roots going back another decade, it is remarkable that it still retains sufficient appeal. Certainly Lotus continually strives to improve the breed, and the last few years have seen a brand new V8 engine, a heavily revised interior and a Sport 350 model. It is the twin turbo-charged V8, producing 350bhp, that ensures the Esprit stays up there with the best supercars, and in true Lotus tradition, the steering and handling are perfectly matched to the performance. But it is a tough car to drive, with heavy clutch and gearchange and poor visibility – all a sign of the basic age of the design.

Best All-Rounder: Esprit V8 GT

Body styles:	Convertible
Engine capacity:	1.8
Price from:	£22,700
Manufactured in:	England

Lotus Elise

The Elise has come in for high acclaim from most who have driven it. But even before you move off there is the appreciation that this is one of the most technically fascinating cars you can buy, with its bonded aluminium chassis weighing just 70kg and a hundred and one other features designed to keep the weight down and performance up. Even with engines from the MGF it manages to perform like no other car at its price. A second derivative has now been added to the range, the 111S getting more power from the MG's VVC engine which adds an extra blistering edge to the driving experience. As ever, the stability at speed, steering precision and handling are exemplary, but the old problems still remain. The Elise is a great car only when driven hard; otherwise the noise, crashing suspension, awkward access and fiddly roof conspire to spoil the party.

Best All-Rounder: Elise 111S

MARCOS

No manufacturer apart from Morgan has kept a single design for so many years. The Marcos sports car has been running in the same form for decades, a highly individual two-seater for buyers who dare to be different. But appearances can be deceptive, for these cars have evolved continuously. The original had an intriguing chassis constructed of marine plywood. Today's use a full steel space frame. Marcos has used a wide variety of engines, but for 2000 the car is generally powered by a massive V8 providing performance never dreamt of when the car was conceived. And even the style has altered, subtly in the case of the sophisticated MantaRay, aggressively for the thundering Mantis.

Body styles:	Coupe, convertible
Engine capacity:	4.0V8, 4.6V8
Price from:	£35,000
Manufactured in:	England

Marcos MantaRay, LM and Mantis

Marcos has settled into a three model range for 2000, with the relatively new MantaRay now established as the entry to the range. The 'Ray was introduced in 1998 with a radical change for Marcos – a new rear end design, the first since the company began. It looks good too. The LM is a race-derived Marcos, all bulging biceps and not a hint of subtlety in sight. Both of these cars get Rover-derived V8 engines, while the top-of-range Mantis takes a 352bhp 4.6-litre US Ford V8. Performance of even the cheapest Marcos is breathtaking, but the Mantis is extraordinarily fast. All have a well-developed chassis and classy leather and Wilton interior.

Best All-Rounder: Mantis

MAZDA

Mazda is a manufacturer with two distinct personalities. One produces highly admired sports cars. The MX-5 was responsible for a world-wide revival in enthusiasm for reasonably-priced two-seaters, and the latest version still offers an an unbeatable combination of value and driving enjoyment. The rotary-engined RX-7 may no longer be imported into the UK but in Japan it continues to provide supercar performance in a unique package. In contrast, the host of family and luxury models rarely hit the mark. True all are competent and well engineered, but that is rarely enough when the competition is often inspired.

New!

Body styles:	Estate
Engine capacity:	1.8, 2.0TD
Price from:	£14,400
Manufactured in:	Japan

Mazda Premacy

This is Mazda's rival to the Renault Scenic, designed to offer a more enticing driving experience with all the versatility of the French car. Basing it on the latest 323 is a good start, and there is a choice of two 1.8 engines of either 100 or 115 bhp, with a 2.0-litre direct injection diesel to follow.

And drive well the Premacy does, with performance and road manners as good as the 323 hatchback. There is plenty of space inside, with a massive boot, rear seats that can be folded or completely removed, and strong equipment levels. But there is a downside too. The seats are hard and the air conditioning control is not versatile enough. More importantly, the Premacy lacks all those nice touches that make the Scenic such a delight – this is solid and sensible and rather unimaginative.

Best All-Rounder: Premacy 1.8 GSi

Mazda 121

In European countries Mazda sells Ford's UK-built Fiesta as the 121. Confusingly, elsewhere the 121 badge may be used on a completely different car, what Europeans refer to as the Mazda Demio. Like Ford's supermini the European Mazda 121 is an appealing car to drive, boasting taut handling and a pleasantly refined ride, allied to lively performance. Power is provided by the impressive 1.25-litre Zetec SE engine, as well as the older but still capable Ford 1.3 unit. This was never going to be one of the roomiest superminis, but the 121 offers a fair amount of space for those in the front, with good comfort levels. Its weak points are the accommodation for rear passengers and luggage.

Best All-Rounder 121 1.25-16v GSi

Body styles:
Hatchback

Engine capacity:
1.25, 1.3, 1.8D

Price from:
£8,200

Manufactured in:
England

Mazda Demio

The idea behind the Demio (121 in Australia) is to provide the space of a family car with the economy of a supermini. Its interior is certainly versatile, with a high driving position giving good visibility and rear seats that slide fore and aft to improve either legroom or luggage space. There's not a lot of headroom in the rear though. The 1.3-litre unit seems perky around town, but it's unwilling on the open road. The steering and controls are light and easy-to-use, but the Demio doesn't have the fun-to-drive factor of a Fiesta or Polo. It's a brave attempt to be different without being plain silly, but a conventional supermini still has more appeal.

Best All-Rounder: Demio 1.3

Body styles:
Estate

Engine capacity:
1.3, 1.5

Price from:
£10,600

Manufactured in:
Japan

Mazda 323

Mazda offers its latest 323 in three and five door hatchback form as well as a saloon, although the UK only takes the five-door. Less obviously stylish than the previous model, this time Mazda has aimed for much improved space and practicality. There is a choice of 1.3, 1.5 and 1.8-litre petrol engines, each having more than adequate power plus diesel and turbo-diesel variants. The new car handles even better than the fine 323 it supersedes. This is complemented by a ride comfort which, while slightly firm, takes the rough edges off poor roads. A smart yet unspectacular appearance masks a car which is practical, comfortable, has adequate performance and handles with dignity.

Best All-Rounder: 1.5 GXi

Body styles:
Hatchback, saloon

Engine capacity:
1.3, 1.5, 1.8, 2.0D, 2.0TD

Price from:
£11,700

Manufactured in:
Japan

Mazda 626

Mazda has produced the motoring equivalent of a microwave oven with the 626. It is a car that does all that might be expected yet could never be regarded as much more than a transportation device. That's fine for drivers who have little interest in cars, but may be a little too boring for the rest. The latest model offers a bit more space, a bit more refinement, a bit more equipment and a bit more economy for a bit less money than its predecessor, but it offers none of the flair of a Passat, 406 or Mondeo. The cabin is efficient and fuss free, space all-round is more than class competitive, the equipment is generous and it is painless to drive.

Best All-Rounder: 626 2.0 GXi

Body styles:
Saloon, hatchback, estate

Engine capacity:
1.8, 2.0, 2.5V6, 2.0TD

Price from:
£14,000

Manufactured in:
Japan

Mazda Xedos 6

Many makers have tried to muscle in on BMW's success with its 3 Series, but Mazda has had less success than most with its Xedos 6. This is a shame as the Xedos 6 is well built, refined and its silky smooth V6 engine performs well. And unusually for a Japanese car, even the styling is eye-catching and distinctive. The main bugbear of the small Xedos is the cramped interior, with the rear cabin especially tight for all but the smallest adults. As you would expect, even the entry V6 is equipped well, but the SE adds leather and air conditioning. All that's missing is a classy badge.

Body styles:
Saloon

Engine capacity:
1.6, 2.0V6

Price from:
£22,000

Manufactured in:
Japan

Best All-Rounder: Xedos 6 2.0 SE

Mazda Xedos 9

Mazda's luxury model has never quite had the kudos of a German brand or a Lexus. Perhaps that was partly down to the original 2.5 V6 engine which was smooth but not particularly lively. Now it has been supercharged and the resultant performance is both impressively lustful and particularly quiet. Low, sleek and good looking, the Xedos 9 is beautifully finished inside and out. The interior feels solid and classy, if a little dated. The seats and suspension are a little firm, making the Xedos 9 comfortable but not cosseting. Room in the rear is adequate, no more. But this top Mazda remains a highly agreeable package for those who dare to be different.

Body styles:
Saloon

Engine capacity:
2.0V6, 2.3V6, 2.5V6

Price from:
£28,700

Manufactured in:
Japan

Best All-Rounder: Xedos 9 2.5

Mazda MX-5

Mazda's new MX-5 has ably taken over where the hugely successful original model left off. Gone are the pop-up headlamps, with the new design a touch larger and a little more rounded. As ever, this two-seater is offered with a choice of 1.6 or 1.8-litre engines – Mazda wisely exercised caution when altering a near-legend, carrying over many parts and re-engineering rather than replacing. The new MX-5 is an even better driver's car as a result: the chassis is exploitable, the steering is fabulous and the switch-like gearbox is the best in the business. It remains the most enjoyable small sports car to drive, if not the classiest.

Body styles:
Convertible

Engine capacity:
1.6, 1.8

Price from:
£15,700

Manufactured in:
Japan

Best All-Rounder: MX-5 1.8i

Mazda RX-7

Introduced in this form in 1991, the RX-7 wowed the supercar world with its blend of slick style and twin-turbo Wankel rotary engines producing more power than had ever before been seen from this type of motor. But interest dropped and for the past three years the RX-7 has been confined to its home market. But that has not stopped development, with the latest RS version getting a power hike to 280bhp plus four-wheel-drive. It is a staggeringly quick proposition, not least because the RX-7 is relatively light-weight, but the RS needs a firm hand to keep things in rein. Pity it is not on sale in the UK, but then few people bought it when it was, anyway.

Body styles:
Coupe

Engine capacity:
2.6

Price from:
£na

Manufactured in:
Japan

Best All-Rounder: RX-7 RS

MASERATI

The company with the glorious heritage has been through some bad times, too little investment resulting in the range of Bi-Turbo cars hanging around for far longer than they should have without proper development. Now Fiat money and Ferrari expertise has gone into producing the beautiful 3200GT, a car that promises so much for the future – as long as the quality issues of the previous generation have been dealt with.

Body styles:	Coupe
Engine capacity:	3.2V8
Price from:	£60,600
Manufactured in:	Italy

Maserati 3200GT

With a new-found sense of style, Maserati has come back into the coupe market with a car that can, at last, do justice to this historic name. The 3200 GT offers the immediate promise of a luxury interior plus a tantalising hint that this car really does offer exceptional performance. Twin turbochargers on the V8 engine produce massive amounts of power, 370bhp to be precise, and, once you get used to the sudden rush of power when the revs reach 2,500rpm, the 3200 GT is a memorable drive indeed. Suspension settings are adjustable from inside, but in either the ride is very firm.

Maserati Quattroporte

This Quattroporte was never a great-looking car even when it was launched, but now it looks decidedly frumpy alongside the beautiful new Coupe. There are not many four-door saloons with supercar performance, however, and the Quattroporte offers powerful twin-turbo engines which delight and thrill. The choice falls between a 284bhp V6 or an even more entertaining 335bhp V8. It all sounds good, but the downsides are equally strong, not least the tricky handling, suspect quality and limited rear seat room. The four-door Maserati may be the answer for those wanting to please the family and satisfy their lust for exotic Italian sports cars. The trouble for Maserati is there are better built and equally rapid saloons from BMW, Jaguar and Mercedes.

Body styles:	Saloon
Engine capacity:	2.8V6, 3.2V8
Price from:	£60,600
Manufactured in:	Italy

MERCEDES

A comparison between what the German manufacturer was producing a dozen years ago and the range today shows how rapidly Mercedes has expanded. Then there were just three saloons and the SL two-seater. Now there is a range of ten models, ranging from city cars to a people carrier and an off-roader. Retaining those earlier levels of luxury and quality have not always been possible, however. While the traditional cars still maintain the kudos, there are signs that new factories (models are built in France, Spain and the US as well as Germany) and new types of vehicle have left buyers disappointed.

Body styles:	Hatchback
Engine capacity:	1.4, 1.6, 1.9, 1.6TD,1.7TD
Price from:	£14,500
Manufactured in:	Germany

Mercedes A-Class

The A-Class Mercedes is an inspired piece of design, combining genuine room for four adults to sit comfortably within a body shorter even than a Ford Ka. The key to A-Class is its height, which allows occupants to sit more upright and gain some legroom. It also gives a commanding driving position as well as allowing for impressively high safety levels to be designed into the double-floor package. The range of engines is all-new for the car, and comprises 1.4, 1.6 and 1.9 petrol units as well as three turbo-diesels. Surprisingly it is better on the open road than in towns, where its hard ride, inert steering, sharp clutch and poor de-misting spoil the story.

Best All-Rounder: A160 Elegance

Mercedes C-Class

The C-Class is due for replacement shortly, the forthcoming model carrying over the looks of the stylish E-Class. It is about time – the current model now looks dated alongside the other Mercedes saloons, though there is still appeal for conservative buyers who appreciate top-class levels of finish and safety. The range of saloons and estates now includes four, six and eight-cylinder petrol engines and two refined and economical turbo-diesels. All are long distance cruisers rather than sports cars, and even the awesome 306bhp C43 AMG is more at home on the autobahn than back road. The C-Class is not inspiring, but it offers most of the good-points of a Mercedes in a compact package.

Best All-Rounder: C240 saloon

Body styles:
Saloon, estate

Engine capacity:
1.8, 2.0, 2.0supercharged, 2.3supercharged, 2.4V6, 2.8V6, 4.3V8, 2.0TD, 2.2TD, 2.5TD

Price from:
£20,400

Manufactured in:
Germany

Mercedes E-Class

Mercedes launched a revised E-Class in the middle of 1999, with a new grille and lower front wings and bonnet to give a sportier look. More electronics make the car safer, with front, side and window airbags fitted as standard. To the already wide range of diesel and petrol engines is added a new six-cylinder 320 CDI diesel. Manual cars get a new six-speed gearbox, while the automatic is now a five-speed "Tipshift" system. Otherwise the E-Class still betters rivals from BMW and Jaguar in terms of space. It may not be as exciting to drive as these cars, but it still impresses on the road thanks to its range of V6 engines and refined and economical turbo-diesels.

Best All-Rounder: E280 saloon.

Body styles:
Saloon, estate

Engine capacity:
2.0, 2.4V6, 2.8V6, 3.2V6, 4.3V8, 5.4V8, 2.0TD, 2.2TD, 2.9TD, 3.0TD

Price from:
£26,400

Manufactured in:
Germany

Mercedes-Benz S-Class

In the last 12 months this new S-Class has received more acclaims as the 'best car in the world' than any other. The heavy style of the previous version has been replaced by an elegant exterior which is complemented by an exquisite interior. Edges, switches, door handles and instruments gel together cohesively to create an inviting environment. Space is plentiful, even with the hindrance of some of the most supportive and cosseting seats in the luxury class. Mechanically it is one of the most impressive and accomplished saloons ever, with pneumatic suspension which enables the big Mercedes to belie its size in an unbelievable fashion. The new S-Class coupe – the CL – is launched late in 1999.

Best All-Rounder: S430

Body styles:
Saloon, coupe

Engine capacity:
2.8V6, 3.2V6, 4.3V8, 5.0V8, 6.0V12

Price from:
£43,600

Manufactured in:
Germany

Mercedes V-Class

People-carriers are often derided as being nothing more than vans with windows but in this case the complaints are true. The Mercedes V-Class is based on the Spanish-built Vito van and it shows. The upside is that there is a huge amount of interior space, with six comfortable captain's chairs and sliding rear doors for easier access to the rear. The downside is that the V-Class is thirsty and uncompromising on the road due to its van roots and the quality can be disastrous compared with the German-built cars. It is offered with the choice of 2.3 or 2.8-litre petrol power or a 2.2 turbo-diesel, with prices high for an MPV, cheap for a Mercedes.

Best All-Rounder: V230

Body styles:
MPV

Engine capacity:
2.3, 2.8, 2.2TD

Price from:
£22,400

Manufactured in:
Spain

Mercedes SLK

The SLK has now established itself as the sensible £32,000 sports car. The steel roof that folds automatically into the boot at the touch of a button is still a brilliant concept, combining all the benefits of a full coupe with those of a proper convertible. The only downside is the significant loss of boot space with the roof stored away. As a serious sports car the SLK doesn't make the grade – there's only automatic transmission in the UK coupled to a 2.3-litre supercharged engine that gets coarse when extended. The manual gearbox available in Germany is awful anyway, and the 2.0-litre too slow. But for cruising rather than outright performance, it's a great car.

Best All-Rounder: SLK 230K

Body styles:
Convertible

Engine capacity:
2.0,
2.0supercharged,
2.3supercharged

Price from:
£31,600

Manufactured in:
Germany

Mercedes CLK

Although based on the C-Class, the CLK borrows the bug-eyed look of the larger E-Class and is offered in two body styles, coupe and convertible. The engine range has been extended to five, though not all are available in the UK, while the cheapest, the 2.0, will disappoint with its performance. But refinement is exceptional. In keeping with the car's role as a Grand Tourer, the interior is tastefully finished, with a first-class feel to all the switches and dials. The front seats are comfortable, look classy and will suit almost all shape and size of driver. In the back there is sufficient room for a pair of adults to get comfortable. For those who put that ahead of driving ability, the CLK is without equal.

Best All-Rounder: CLK 320

Body styles:
Coupe, convertible

Engine capacity:
2.0, 2.0
supercharged, 2.3
supercharged, 3.2
V6, 4.3V8, 5.5V8

Price from:
£27,400

Manufactured in:
Germany

Mercedes SL

It may no longer be the newest kid on the block and it may have had its halo stolen by the likes of the SLK and CLK, but the Mercedes SL remains the convertible at the top of most people's wish-lists. With a removable hard-top making the SL effectively a coupe for the winter months, it is available with a range of engines from 2.8 up to a whopping 6.0-litre V12. A 6.0-litre V8-engined AMG version is also on offer. It does not have the SLK's trick hood, but the SL's fully-electric folding canvas offering is still a head-turner and a wonder of modern engineering. The SL is in its autumn years, hence comes loaded with standard equipment to maintain interest.

Best All-Rounder: SL320

Body styles:
Convertible

Engine capacity:
2.8V6, 3.2V6,
5.0V8, 6.0V12

Price from:
£54,600

Manufactured in:
Germany

Mercedes M-Class

Unlike its much earlier G-Wagon, Mercedes' new M-Class has been tuned specifically for on-road driving, though it performs as well as most rivals off-road too. Built in the States in a purpose-designed factory, doubts have been raised over the quality of these vehicles. But there is no denying the amount of space on offer – the M-Class is a huge vehicle, and it is great to drive too. The original smooth and refined 3.2V6 has been joined by a 4.3V8 while some markets take a 2.3 as well; all get the option of an acclaimed five-speed automatic transmission. Overall, the M-Class is a well thought out piece of kit with something for everyone.

Best All-Rounder ML 320

Body styles:
Estate

Engine capacity:
2.3, 3.2V6, 4.3V8

Price from:
£31,800

Manufactured in:
Austria,
United States

MERCURY

Way back in the late 1930s, Ford planned to use its Mercury division to compete with GM's Buick and Oldsmobile line-ups. In recent times, however, it's lost its direction a little. Mercurys these days, tend to be little more than re-jigged Fords. That could change; Ford high-ups are starting to earmark Mercury as the company's sporty brand. It already badges the 'Edge Design' Cougar as a Mercury in the US, and a Toyota RAV4-like off-roader is in the pipeline. But it will need to jettison dullards like the geriatric Grand Marquis before perceptions can change.

Mercury Grand Marquis

Body styles:	Saloon
Engine capacity:	4.6V8
Price from:	$21,000
Manufactured in:	United States

Sable

Body styles:	Saloon, estate
Engine capacity:	3.0V6
Price from:	$22,400
Manufactured in:	United States

Villager

Body styles:	MPV
Engine capacity:	3.3V6
Price from:	$22,400
Manufactured in:	United States

Mercury Grand Marquis, Sable and Villager

One of the last of the great American rear-drive Yank Tanks, the Grand Marquis offers crude body-on-frame construction, six-passenger seating, big V8 power, and more chrome than a '60s Wurlitzer. But Americans just love 'em. Solid straight-line performance and a relaxed ride make 800-mile road trips a breeze in this cavernous four-door.

Not all America 4x4 fans want to drive the best-selling Ford Explorer, so they buy a Mountaineer instead; same body, same mechanical bits, same equipment. Just a different front grille and lights with a choice of 4-litre V6 or torquey 5-litre V8. To most Americans, it boils down to which dealer is the closest.

Twin to Ford's Taurus, the Sable's changes for 2000 are confined to a new front grille and bonnet, and rear lights that look like they were lifted from an XJ Jag. There's a choice of two 3-litre V6s, one delivering a weakish 153bhp, the other, a more muscley 215bhp. Providing a bench front seat and column gearchange – just like your dad's old Zephyr Six – tells you the kind of buyer the Sable is aimed at.

When is a Nissan not a Nissan? When it's a Mercury Villager. Nissan designed this versatile seven-seat minivan, and uses its V6 engine to power it. But Ford builds it, as well as the similar Nissan Quest version, at its plant in Ohio. Confused? Ford sells a longer version, the Windstar; consequently the Villager lacks both space and features to make it a winner.

Best All-Rounders: Grand Marquis LS, Mountaineer V6, Sable LS, Villager Sport

MITSUBISHI

Until recently Mitsubishi's sales presence in the UK has been dominated by a single model, the Shogun. That tended to obscure the fact that the Japanese company has an enormous range of models, a proportion of which do not make their way to Europe. In order to gain sales in the mainstream market therefore, Mitsubishi joined forces with Volvo to build the Carisma in Holland and this has lately been joined by the Space Star. The rest of the range covers everything from superminis to large family saloons to a run of coupes. And, stung by the number of grey imports coming to the UK, Mitsubishi has even started importing cars they were not planning to sell here, like the FTO, Evo VI and Galant VR4.

Mitsubishi Carisma

Mitsubishi addressed criticism of the Carisma by launching a facelifted version of the saloon and hatchback during the latter half of 1999. The revised model gets a new nose, lights and some very subtle changes to the interior and mechanical specification. All this adds up to........ not a great deal of difference. The Carisma remains a middle-of-the-road family car that does most things pretty well but excels at few. The 1.8-litre GDi engine may be one of the technological developments of the decade, highly economical if you want it to be, yet sporty too. But apart from that the Carisma is too anonymous. Volvo has showed, with the S40/V40 which is built alongside the Carisma in Holland, that this basic design can be given a lot of appeal.

Best All-Rounder: Carisma 1.8 GDi

Body styles:	Hatchback, saloon
Engine capacity:	1.6, 18, 1.9TD
Price from:	£13,000
Manufactured in:	Netherlands

Mitsubishi Colt

The Mitsubishi Colt is a difficult car to classify, bigger outside than most superminis yet those looks are deceptive. In the front it's comfortable and attractive but in the back space is very tight, with the lack of a five-door derivative a disadvantage. There's a limited choice of engines – 1.3 or 1.6 – neither of them performance-orientated. But the engines are sweet and refined and the Colt, like all Mitsubishis, is extremely well built. Light controls, decent steering and a slick gearbox make it a supremely easy car to drive in town, though it lacks any real handling prowess out on the open road.

Body styles:
Hatchback

Engine capacity:
1.3, 1.5, 1.6, 1.8, 1.8 Turbo, 2.0TD

Price from:
£10,800

Manufactured in:
Japan

Best All-Rounder: Colt 1.6 GLX

Mitsubishi Colt Space Star

The Space Star is Mitsubishi's contribution to the class established by the Renault Scenic. A five-door cross between a hatchback and an estate, it combines compact exterior dimensions with a versatile and roomy interior. The wide track and high roof give it well rounded proportions and plenty of room for driver and passengers, without compromising luggage space. Engines are 1.3 or 1.8 petrol units, but there's no diesel, a surprising omission. The suspension has been designed for comfort rather than speed, but the Space Star remains a good car to drive. It is built alongside the Carisma and Volvo S40 in the jointly owned factory in the Netherlands.

Body styles:
MPV

Engine capacity:
1.3, 1.8

Price from:
£11,200

Manufactured in:
Netherlands

Best All-Rounder: Space Star 1.8 GDi

Mitsubishi Galant

The Galant, available as a saloon or estate, has undergone a mild face-lift, the most obvious point being a new nose and lights. Mechanically a new 2.4-litre GDi engine is added to the existing 2.0-litre and 2.5 V6. Some countries also get the turbo-diesel and the astonishing VR4 with a 280 bhp twin-turbo V6. That last model is available in limited numbers in the UK with a "Tiptronic" style gearbox, a transmission that has also found its way into the GDi and standard V6. By any standards this is a fine-looking car. Comfort is good, the front seats are supportive, equipment is generous and there is a decent amount of room.

Body styles:
Saloon, estate

Engine capacity:
1.8, 2.0, 2.4V6, 2.5V6, 2.5V6turbo, 2.0TD

Price from:
£17,500

Manufactured in:
Japan

Best All-Rounder: Galant 2.5 V6

Mitsubishi Magna

Mitsubishi's contender in Australia's medium/large family car market is the Magna, manufactured locally in both saloon and estate versions and incorporating some minor exterior changes for 1999. The base Executive now comes with a 3.0 V6 as standard with the option of a 3.5V6. Advance, Altera and the top of the range Verada all get the bigger engine as standard, as does the Sports sedan which is available with either manual transmission or a competent Tiptronic shifter, lowered suspension and a body kit. The Magna's light weight compared with Ford's falcon and Holden's Commodore, combined with its responsive, fuel efficient engines, makes for a class-winning combination.

Body styles:
Saloon, Estate

Engine capacity:
3.0V6, 3.5V6

Price from:
Aus $29,000

Manufactured in:
Australia

Best All-Rounder: Magna 3.5V6 Altera

Mitsubishi Space Wagon and Runner

The all-new third generation Space Wagon MPV, introduced at the start of 1999, is noticeably bigger than its predecessor, putting it up against more mainstream competitors but losing the compact advantage of the earlier car – now taken on by the Vauxhall/Opel Zafira. It has several seat layouts, bags more space, extra safety features and loads of equipment, but only a 2.4-litre engine, which couples good performance with reasonable fuel economy. It is a comfortable, easy-going driving experience. The Space Runner is a shorter version of the Wagon, with just two rows of seats, a single sliding rear door on the nearside, and a 1.8-litre engine.

Body styles:
MPV

Engine capacity:
1.8, 2.0, 2.4, 2.0TD

Price from:
£17,800

Manufactured in:
Japan

Best All-Rounder: Space Wagon 2.4

Mitsubishi FTO

The FTO is at last making its way out of Japan onto other markets, and it is a good thing too. Look beneath that very stylish exterior, and the typically Japanese anodyne interior, and there's a sport cars that's eager to do your every bidding. There is a choice of engines, but it is the top-of-the-range 2.0 V6 that provides the real thrills. This engine has variable valve timing which gives it a Jekyll and Hyde character. Below 6,000rpm it feels pretty ordinary, but take it through to 8,000rpm and 200bhp is unleashed. There wouldn't be much point to all this power if the chassis couldn't cope, but it does, brilliantly well, though there is a downside in the very firm ride and hard seats.

Body styles:
Coupe

Engine capacity:
1.8, 2.0V6

Price from:
£na

Manufactured in:
Japan

Best All-Rounder: FTO 2.0 GPX

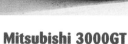

Mitsubishi Eclipse

The American design team that shaped the new-for-2000 Mitsubishi Eclipse describes the sexy lines of this new US-built coupe as 'geo-mechanical'. Translate the design-speak and it means lots of sharp edges and some softer, rounder bits. Simple. Powered by either a 154bhp 2.4-litre four-cylinder, or smooth-spinning 205bhp 3-litre V6, the new front-drive Eclipse is bags of fun to drive. It offers alert, chuckable handling; surgically-precise steering; and a surprisingly pliant, comfortable ride. The bad news? Mitsubishi only sells the Eclipse in the US where it's built. Worse news? There's going to be a soft top version next year.

Body styles:
Coupe, convertible

Engine capacity:
2.0, 2.0turbo, 2.4

Price from:
$18,000

Manufactured in:
Japan

Best All-Rounder: Eclipse GT

Mitsubishi 3000GT

As a showcase for automotive technology, the 3000GT is undeniably impressive. Four-wheel-drive, active speed-sensitive spoilers, a twin-turbo 24-valve V6 engine and six-speed gearbox all feature in this big, brash GT. They all work efficiently and the car is endowed with huge reserves of performance, grip and traction. On a wet road it will leave many a pure sports car a long way behind.

Yet there are those that criticise the 3000GT precisely because it is so competent, complaining that the challenge and excitement of driving a high performance car is lost. Perhaps it is too big and heavy to be a truly sporting machine – but as a GT it excels.

Body styles:
Coupe

Engine capacity:
3.0V6, 3.0V6turbo

Price from:
£45,800

Manufactured in:
Japan

Best All-Rounder: 3000GT

Mitsubishi Space Gear

People carriers are inevitably large, but the Space Gear is about as large as they get this side of a small bus. The floor is completely flat from front footwell to the tail end, allowing passengers to move around easily. Seven or eight seats are available, with the rearmost flipping up to the sides when not required. The Space Gear has an in-line front engine driving the rear wheels, with four-wheel-drive an option. This uses the system from the Shogun which, Mitsubishi claims, gives the Space Gear outstanding all-terrain performance. Top models get electronically controlled suspension. Popular in Europe and Japan, the Space Gear is not sold in the UK.

Body styles:
MPV

Engine capacity:
2.0, 2.4, 3.0V6, 2.5TD, 2.8TD

Price from:
£na

Manufactured in:
Japan

Best All-Rounder: Space Gear 2.8 TD

Mitsubishi Pinin

Mitsubishi, so successful with its full-sized 4x4, seemed to have overlooked the fact that everyone else was doing rather nicely with smaller "recreational" off-roaders like the Toyota RAV4 and Land Rover Freelander. But for 2000 the company is hitting back with the Pinin, built in Italy at a new Pininfarina factory, and fitted with the familiar Mitsubishi 1.8 GDI engine. Mitsubishi claims that it will have full off-road ability, although the four-wheel-drive system, unlike the permanent systems in the Toyota and Land Rover, needs to be switched in and out. Sadly, for those who thought that this would make a Mitsubishi off-roader easily attainable, entry prices are £15,000-plus.

Body styles:
Estate

Engine capacity:
1.8

Price from:
£15,000 (est)

Manufactured in:
Italy

Best All-Rounder: Too soon to say

Mitsubishi Shogun

One of the world best-selling off-roaders, the Shogun has acquired its reputation through extreme toughness and durability off-road. There's a choice of short-wheelbase three-door body or long-wheelbase five-door, as well as two tough turbo-diesels and two powerful petrol V6s. But as a road-going car it is less successful. The interior packaging is far from perfect, lacking the space or comfort of cheaper MPV's, despite seven seats in the five-door model. And it is questionable whether the myriad of adjustments available – seat springing, suspension softness, rear heating and so on – are of real value or merely covering up indifferent design.

Body styles:
Estate

Engine capacity:
2.4, 3.0V6, 3.5V6, 2.5TD, 2.8TD

Price from:
£20,400

Manufactured in:
Japan

Best All-Rounder: Shogun 2.8 TD GLX 5dr

Mitsubishi Challenger/Montero

The Challenger has been designed to offer a simple, cheaper 4x4 for buyers who have found the Shogun has moved out of reach. But though it may lack the sophistication of the more expensive vehicle, that would be to sell it short. There are few off-roaders that can be driven with such gusto; the ride is firm as a compromise, but for a large vehicle it's very controllable. It is the interior that is a bit of a let down. Although there is sufficient room for five people, a lack of storage space is disappointing. The good sized boot suffers from a high loading edge too. The dashboard is typically Japanese – extremely plain – but you can't complain about the way the Challenger is built.

Body styles:
Estate

Engine capacity:
3.0V6, 3.5V6, 2.5TD, 2.8TD

Price from:
£20,400

Manufactured in:
Japan

Best All-Rounder: Challenger 2.5 TD

MORGAN

With waiting lists down to a mere four and a half years, new-found production efficiencies at Morgan have upped the output to a staggering eleven cars every week. The delay is the price you have to pay for a car that is hand built and starts at the factory with pieces of wood and sheets of aluminium. The cars have looked the same for as long as time can remember, but for 2000 the four seater is re-introduced. The new model has more room, bucket seats in place of the rear bench and full safety belts. In Spring Morgan will launch a new sports model with an aluminium chassis and BMW V8 to sit above the current Plus 8 in the range.

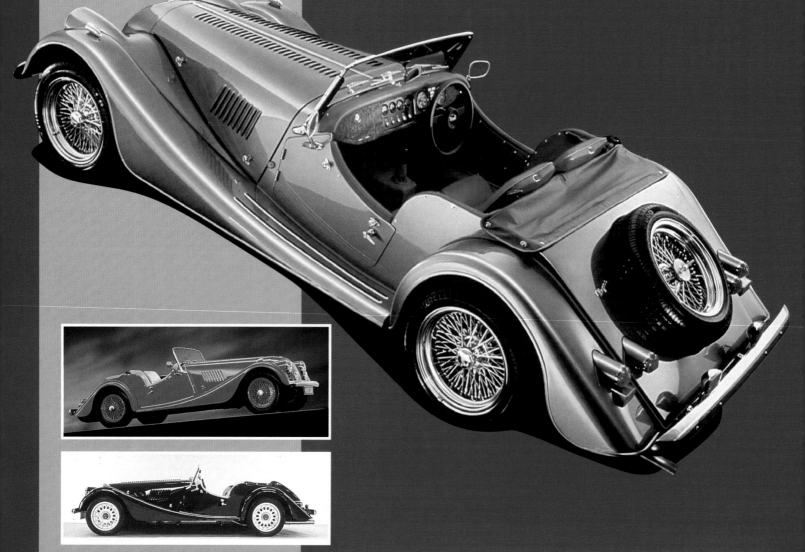

Body styles:	Convertible
Engine capacity:	1.8, 2.0, 4.0V8, 4.6V8
Price from:	£20,600
Manufactured in:	England

Morgan 4/4, Plus 8

A traditional English sports car built in a traditional English factory. The Morgan story ensures that a strong demand for the new cars continues, both at home and from all around the world. Four models are on offer – the 4/4 (in two and four seater form), Plus 4 and storming Rover V8-powered Plus 8 – although in practice it's a case of picking your engine and then the sky's the limit, the car being built to your exact requirements. Engine choice ranges from a Ford 1.8, Rover 2.0-litre right up to the 4.6-litre V8 from the Range Rover. Morgan has even embraced modern-day safety needs too as driver and passenger airbags are now available as options.

NISSAN

Of all the Japanese car manufacturers now involved, Nissan was the first to embrace the manufacture of its cars in Europe as a way to get around the quotas that limited imports from Japan. Nissan builds the revised Primera and Micra in the UK, and this will be joined by the new Almera in 2000. Nissan produces a blisteringly wide range of models in Japan, but some of these are kept for home consumption only. What the rest of the world sees is a well-developed range of family models and off-roaders, all of which are good but only in the form of the rarefied Skyline does Nissan really lead the way.

New!

Body styles:	Hatchback, saloon, estate
Engine capacity:	1.6, 1.8, 2.0, 2.0TD
Price from:	£14,000
Manufactured in:	England

Nissan Primera

Nissan's Primera has gone through a mid-life facelift, with a firm emphasis on the European buyer – the design and development took place in the EC and the car is built in Britain. A new front end and tail are the most obvious changes, but there is a revised interior, a new 1.8-litre engine and a clever CVT automatic transmission that offers the option of sequential manual control. Despite being a family car the Primera has always offered a rewarding drive. As well as the 1.8, Nissan offers 1.6 and 2.0 petrol engines as well as a 2.0-litre turbo diesel, though the high-performance 2.0-litre petrol model has been dropped. An all-round solid package then, but still without that final edge of desirability.

Best All-Rounder: Primera 1.8 SE

Nissan Micra

The Micra was the first Japanese car to win the coveted European Car of the Year award, and despite being around for seven years now, it remains a fundamentally sound machine. Its weakness is down to the age of the design. Newer competitors generally offer more space and have a wider range of engines – the Micra sticks to just a 1.0 and 1.3-litre, and no diesel. But it has been facelifted in the last couple of years and the basic concept has always been a solid one, with plenty of refinement, a very easy drive, good economy and first class reliability.

Body styles:
Hatchback

Engine capacity:
1.0, 1.3, 1.5D

Price from:
£7,900

Manufactured in:
England

Best All-Rounder: Micra 1.0 GX

Nissan Almera

A brand new Almera was shown late in 1999, but sales in the UK do not start until Spring 2000, so British buyers have to contend with the old model for a while yet. That's not really a bad thing, for despite its dubious style, it is a good package. Driving enjoyment is high up the scale of priorities and even the most basic model has positive, direct steering combined with sharp-handling. The 1.4 and 1.6-litre engines of the mainstream models (there is also a diesel) are both refined with a revvy, sporting nature. The 2.0 GTi uses these qualities to the full and is a serious hot-hatch, though with compromised luggage space.

Body styles:
Hatchback, saloon

Engine capacity:
1.4, 1.6, 2.0, 2.0TD

Price from:
£11,500

Manufactured in:
Japan

Best All-Rounder: Almera 1.6 GX

Nissan QX

The Nissan QX is one of a long list of Japanese executive saloons – the Honda Legend, Mazda Xedos 9 and Toyota Camry are others – that are highly capable but lacking that vital factor for success in the company car park status. As with those rivals, the QX is a big seller in other world-wide markets (notably the USA), but European buyers have yet to catch on. The big Nissan is offered with a choice of two smooth V6 engines, either 2.0 or 3.0-litre. The QX's on-road manners might not match the same high standards set by its refined engines, but they are good enough. Inside there is comfort, a vast amount of equipment and interior space.

Body styles:
Saloon

Engine capacity:
2.0V6, 2.5V6, 3.0V6

Price from:
£22,400

Manufactured in:
Japan

Best All-Rounder: QX 2.0 SE

Nissan Serena

The odd styling of the Serena sets it apart from other MPVs, the result of placing engine under the floor to serve its other persona as a commercial vehicle. That also means that the Serena is not nearly as good on the road as competitors, a factor which isn't helped by a couple of dismal engines – the 1.6 and 2.3 diesel; the only one with a bit of gusto is the 2.0-litre petrol version. The Serena does, however, have something of a bargain price tag and can, in some versions, offer seating for eight which is still unusual. Even so, this Nissan has little else to commend it.

Body styles:
MPV

Engine capacity:
1.6, 2.0, 2.3D

Price from:
£15,600

Manufactured in:
Spain

Best All-Rounder: Serena 2.0

New!

Nissan 200SX

Now in its final few months, Nissan's sporty coupe has already been superseded by the Silvia in Japan, but that car may not come to Europe. The 200SX boasts a front engine with rear wheel drive, superb performance from its 197bhp 2.0-litre turbocharged engine and a high level of equipment, especially with the optional Touring pack. The interior may be tight, particularly for those in the back, but the 200SX is entertaining all the same. If ever there has been an issue regarding the car it is that the looks and the driving experience fail to match those of some very competent competition, like the Alfa GTV, Fiat Coupe or Audi TT.

Body styles:
Coupe

Engine capacity:
2.0, 2.0turbo

Price from:
£22,000

Manufactured in:
Japan

Best All-Rounder: 200SX

Nissan Skyline

The Skyline is one of an elite bunch of Japanese supercars that most enthusiasts probably know more from their PlayStation than from real life. Nissan brought a few of the previous model into the UK in '97, and have now decided to export the latest R34 model, with Britain the only country in Europe to officially receive supplies. Changes to the new model have increased the grip and, being 75mm shorter, have made it lighter and stiffer, and consequently faster still. The performance is further enhanced by tweaks to the 2.6-litre twin-turbo straight six engine to improve the torque; power is a healthy 280bhp. A six-speed transmission and 18 inch alloy wheels round off a mouth-watering package.

Body styles:
Coupe, saloon

Engine capacity:
2.0, 2.5, 2.5turbo, 2.6twin turbo

Price from:
£54,000

Manufactured in:
Japan

Best All-Rounder: Skyline GT-R

Nissan Terrano II

Nissan now finds itself in a somewhat awkward situation with its Terrano II. Smaller than the "big" off-roaders, most other manufacturers producing cars at this price level have decided to build lifestyle 4x4s rather than down-scale version of their big cars. The result is that, now that Ford has dropped its sister car, the Maverick, Nissan is out on a limb. But the Terrano still has something to offer. Available in three and five-door forms, its on-road manners will come as a pleasant surprise to those moving to it from a normal car. As an off-roader it does reasonably well too, though its car-like styling doesn't win friends among serious mud-pluggers.

Body styles:
Estate

Engine capacity:
2.4, 2.7TD

Price from:
£18,000

Manufactured in:
Spain

Best All-Rounder: Terrano 2.7TD

Nissan Patrol

The latest Nissan Patrol has lost the Tonka toy looks of its predecessor, which is a blessing, but at the same time some of the appeal has gone too. But make no mistake, the Patrol is still big – even compared to most other 4x4s. Its off-road ability is certainly not in doubt, but with those more-rounded lines has come a change in character. That's mainly due to the lack of choice in the UK with only one engine available – a 2.8-litre turbo-diesel with 128bhp and dreadful performance – other world markets having the option of a 4.5-litre petrol unit too. Still, the Patrol has a fair amount of equipment and comes in three or five-door body styles, the latter with seven seats as standard.

Body styles:
Estate

Engine capacity:
4.5, 2.8TD, 4.2TD

Price from:
£21,500

Manufactured in:
Japan

Best All-Rounder: Patrol 5dr

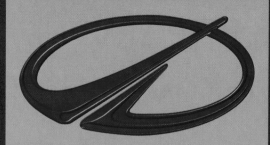

OLDSMOBILE

Rumours of the demise of General Motors' oldest division have, as the saying goes, been greatly exaggerated. Oldsmobile is alive and well, and cranking out new product. Like the swoopy Aurora executive express – due next spring – and a new hybrid 4x4, ready in a couple of years, that follows the current trend of being part sport-utility, part estate car. And, both the handsome Intrigue and stylish Alero models, seem to be doing a fine job of pulling-in buyers who would normally have picked Japanese. Long-term survival, it seems, is more assured.

Body styles:	Saloon
Engine capacity:	3.5V6, 3.8V6
Price from:	$21,600
Manufactured in:	United States

Oldsmobile Intrigue

Arguably the best-designed, best-built family saloon that General Motors builds. And, for 2000, the classy-looking Olds Intrigue gets a new anti-skid cornering system, designed to keep its owners on the straight and narrow. The so-called Precision Control System senses an impending skid and activates any of the four brakes independently to bring the car back in line. Powered by a smooth-spinning 3.5-litre twin cam V6 packing 215bhp, the Intrigue is an athletic performer. Its solid structure and tight suspension provide responsive handling and a comfortable ride. Where it really impresses is the high quality of the interior trim. Here is Lexus quality at Toyota pricing.

Best All-Rounder: Intrigue GL

Oldsmobile Alero

Oldsmobile's prime role at General Motors these days is to try and stop GM owners migrating to Accords and Camrys. As an import fighter, the latest Olds Alero does a fine job. Clean, handsome styling, punchy four-pot and V6 motors and sporty handling, is putting the Alero high on American's shopping list. It's even sold on the Continent as the Chevrolet Alero. In the US, it's offered as either a two-door coupe, or four-door saloon that looks like a coupe. On the engine front, there's a choice of a gutsy, but harsh-sounding 2.4-litre four-cylinder, or a smooth-revving 3.4 V6. Other advantages; lots of standard equipment, and competitive pricing.

Best All-Rounder: Alero Sedan V6

Body styles:
Saloon, coupe

Engine capacity:
2.4, 3.4V6

Price from:
$16,400

Manufactured in:
United States

Oldsmobile Aurora

The all-new Olds Aurora has a tough act to follow. The previous model was such a design knock-out that many feel the Aurora name should have died with it. But this new-for-2000 flagship has plenty to offer luxury car buyers; a 4-litre twin cam V8, space for five in leather-lined comfort, and a stiff, well-balanced chassis. No, it's not as visually stunning as the last car; the new Aurora's nose borders on being faceless, and the design of the rear looks like something Chrysler rejected for its 300M. But the cockpit design is striking, and the quality of the trim is first rate. Pricing, however, will be crucial.

Best All-Rounder: Aurora V8

Body styles:
Saloon

Engine capacity:
4.0V8

Price from:
$30,000

Manufactured in:
United States

Oldsmobile Bravada

Upscale version of Chevy's Blazer, the Olds Bravada is unique in that it features a different four-wheel drive set-up, called SmartTrak. Normally, it runs in rear-wheel drive, but when the system senses a front wheel slipping, it sends drive to the front axle for full four-wheel drive. Extremely well-equipped, the Bravada offers everything from leather trim, to power seats, to an upscale stereo with CD. GM's torquey 4.3 V6 coupled to a four-speed auto is the only drive-train option. Drawbacks include tight rear seat accommodation, mediocre fuel economy and a rather lofty price tag. Like the Blazer, the Bravada's design is also starting to show its age.

Best All-rounder: Bravada

Body styles:
Estate

Engine capacity:
4.3V6

Price from:
$31,000

Manufactured in:
United States

PEUGEOT

Among the mainstream car manufacturers Peugeot is in an enviable position. It produces cars with a unique edge to their performance – they combine excellent ride comfort with superb handling, maximising the appeal to both drivers interested in comfort and drivers interested in – well, just driving. The latest 206 supermini follows the usual formula and has proved very popular, while the 406 remains a strong contender as a family car with its recent facelift. Peugeot's weakness has for long been its executive model, so the brand new 607 that arrives in 2000 must do much better – the first details show a lot of promise.

Body styles:	Hatchback
Engine capacity:	1.1, 1.4, 1.6, 2.0, 1.9D
Price from:	£8,500
Manufactured in:	France, England

Peugeot 206

Building on a the warm feeling buyers had for the old 205, the 206 offers the promise the 106 never could, striking in appearance from every angle, with a look new to the Peugeot range. Inside there is distinctive 'elephant hide' finish to the fascia which is not to everyone's taste, but the 206 feels solid and well built. It does, of course, continue Peugeot's tradition of superb chassis design, and recently, with the launch of the 2.0-litre GTi, there is a car to exploit it fully. But the GTi is now too civilised while the standard engine range offers no more than adequate performance and refinement. With good looks, space and comfort, however, there is still much to admire.

Best All-Rounder: 206 1.6 GLX

Peugeot 106

The 106, Peugeot's smallest car, is now being eclipsed by the slightly larger and much newer 206 which before too long will replace it completely. Consequently the 106 range has been drastically cut back to mainly the budget models, though for those looking for a wider choice, Citroen's almost identical Saxo still offers great breadth. The 106 remains a good car to drive, with a comfortable seating position and a terrific chassis in the true Peugeot style. The latter is exploited to the full in the impressive 1.6 GTi, a truly enjoyable hot hatch. In the final analysis, however, the 106 does not have the space to compete with more modern offerings.

Best All-Rounder: 106 1.6 GTi

Body styles:
Hatchback

Engine capacity:
1.0, 1.1, 1.4, 1.6, 1.5D

Price from:
£7,100

Manufactured in:
France, Spain

Peugeot 306

Whilst its major European competitors have all been replaced since its launch, the 306 still competes with just a mild facelift made two years ago, plus cosmetic tweaks in 1999. Those modifications lifted the impression of quality while comfort, ride and handling have always been 306 strengths, making most versions a joy to drive. Peugeot makes great diesels, and the new 2.0 HDi offers even more in terms of performance, economy and refinement. All petrol engines are acceptable, providing adequate power and flexibility. The wide range of body styles comprises hatchback, saloon, estate and convertible. The weakness of the 306 is really confined to space – many rivals offer more.

Best All-Rounder: 306 2.0 XSi

Body styles:
Hatchback, saloon, convertible, estate

Engine capacity:
1.4, 1.6, 1.8, 2.0, 1.9D, 2.0TD

Price from:
£12,300

Manufactured in:
France, England

Peugeot 406

Four years after its launch, Peugeot's 406 has received a mid-life makeover. Visual changes include a more aggressive front grille with the cabin freshened up while engineers have been busy trying to put the 406 back on top where it is traditionally strongest – in the chassis department. Suspension adjustments have improved the low-speed ride, while handling remains smooth, if not as engaging as a Mondeo. In the cabin, better seats give improved support; space is as before – competitive, but no more. There are new engines – the 2.0-litre is disappointing, the turbo-diesels impressive. The beautiful coupe continues to offer a stylish alternative to a BMW.

Best All-Rounder: 406 2.0HDi GLX

Body styles:
Saloon, estate, coupe

Engine capacity:
1.8, 2.0, 3.0V6, 2.0TD

Price from:
£14,300

Manufactured in:
France

Peugeot 806

Peugeot joined forces with Fiat to produce its people carrier, with the result that it is available in many guises – Fiat Ulysse, Lancia Z, Citroen Synergie as well as the 806. And in theory making an MPV which could double as a van could have worked too, but the end result is styling that lacks appeal. Beyond the 806's awkward looks and those van-like sliding doors (which are a boon), it is an impressive package. Powered by a 2.0-litre petrol or a superb 1.9-litre turbo-diesel engine (a 2.0 petrol turbo is available in some markets), the 806 is not as roomy as the competition but there is a good deal of comfort. The unusual facia-mounted gearlever allows a step-through facility from front to back.

Best All-Rounder: 806 1.9TD

Body styles:
MPV

Engine capacity:
1.8, 2.0, 2.0Turbo, 1.9TD, 2.1TD

Price from:
£18,000

Manufactured in:
France

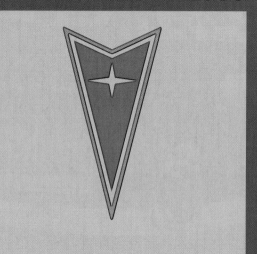

PONTIAC

If you're talking power, performance and punchy styling, you're talking Pontiac. This is General Motors' so-called 'Excitement' division. Its buyers are younger, more style-conscious and want their cars to look red hot. In fact, the vast majority of Pontiacs sold are red. And there's no subtlety when it comes to styling; flared bonnet nostrils, lots of bold body cladding, and big driving lights. To more restrained European tastes, the shapes look almost cartoonish. But young hip Americans love 'em – particularly when it's a fire-breathin' 5.7-litre Firebird packing 300-ponies.

New!

Body styles:	Saloon
Engine capacity:	3.8V6, 3.8V6 supercharged
Price from:	$23,500
Manufactured in:	United States

Pontiac Bonneville

Named after the legendary salt flats where countless speed records have been set, Pontiac's Bonneville saloon gets an all-new look for 2000. Again, nothing subtle here; big wheel arches, big air intakes, big driving lights, big, flashy wheels. But beneath all that flash, is a more rigid bodyshell, which tightens-up the previous model's sloppy handling, provides a smoother, less-turbulent ride, and reduces interior noise levels. As before, the 'Bonnie' uses GM's war-horse 3.8-litre V6, with a choice of either 205bhp regular, or 240bhp supercharged power. What is new is the car's anti-skid control system.

Best All-Rounder: Bonneville SE

Pontiac Grand Am

When you buy a new Pontiac Grand Am, there's no need to rush off to the customising shop for bolt-on spoilers, wings and big wheels; the Grand Am already has them fitted. With its swoopy lines, dramatic, corrugated side panelling and jokey rear wing, this is one car that's not best-suited for shy, retiring types. While there's lots of show, the Grand Am is a little short on 'go'. The standard 2.4-litre four-cylinder cranks out 150bhp, but dislikes being revved hard. The bigger 3.4 V6 packs more muscle at 175bhp and is smoother. Both come attached to automatic transmissions.

Body styles:
Hatchback, coupe

Engine capacity:
2.4, 3.4V6

Price from:
$16,100

Manufactured in:
United States

Best All-Rounder: Grand AM SE

Pontiac Grand Prix

Pontiac's catch-line for its sporty Grand Prix is 'Wider is Better'. That refers to the Grand Prix's trademark wide-track styling, which gives it a hunkered-down, ready-to-pounce look. And, at over six feet wide, the Grand Prix is w-i-d-e. This is one Pontiac that certainly goes as fast as it looks. The flagship GTP model comes with a 240bhp supercharged V6, while even the basic four-door saloon uses a 3.1-litre 'six'. A rigid body structure helps provide responsive handling, and despite all that power going through the front wheels, the steering is decently accurate.

Body styles:
Saloon, coupe

Engine capacity:
3.1V6, 3.8V6, 3.8V6 supercharged

Price from:
$19,600

Manufactured in:
United States

Best All-Rounder: Grand Prix GT 3.8

Pontiac Firebird

In the States, you can drive away in a fire-breathing, thundering 305bhp 5.7-litre V8 Firebird for the equivalent of a measly £14,500. For lovers of gen-u-ine American muscle, there is no better bang for the buck. But don't expect too much sophistication here. The Firebird is a heavyweight champ that delivers its V8 muscle in an explosion of raw, rumbling, roaring power. Standstill to 60mph comes up in 5.5 seconds, and with its long-legged six-speed 'box slotted into top, it'll run to 175-plus mph. Want more? The optional WS6 package offers 320bhp.

Body styles:
Coupe, convertible

Engine capacity:
3.8V6, 5.7V8

Price from:
$18,300

Manufactured in:
United States

Best All-Rounder: Firebird Formula V8

Pontiac Montana

If Pontiac stands for excitement, how does a minivan fit into the performance line-up? Easy; call it a Montana, after the once speed limit-free US state, and give it that over-stylised Pontiac look. Hence the flared-nostril nose, the corrugated panels along the side, and the big wheels. Similar in design to the now-departed Vauxhall Sintra MPV, the Montana features a gutsy 3.4-litre V6 that gains an extra 5bhp this year, taking it to 185. Inside, there's seating for seven, and a new feature is the optional rear-seat video system with its drop-down 5.5-in TV monitor and built-in VCR.

Body styles:
MPV

Engine capacity:
3.4V6

Price from:
S21,300

Manufactured in:
United States

Best All-Rounder: Montana 5dr

PORSCHE

Porsche has produced other cars that ran alongside the 911 in the past, but none has been so successful as the Boxster, cementing the company's future well into the next millennium. Porsche's attention to detail plus the continued introduction of new and improved versions of the existing models helps keep the interest at a high level. The recent 911 GT3 is the ultimate "limited edition" car, all examples snapped up by eager buyers well before it officially went on sale. Expect more soon – next up is the 911 Turbo.

Body styles: Coupe, convertible
Engine capacity: 3.4, 3.6
Price from: £60,300
Manufactured in: Germany

Porsche 911

The latest "996" version of the 911 range is being gradually extended with a cabriolet, limited edition GT3 and, soon, the return of the Turbo. The flat six-cylinder engine still hangs out behind the rear wheels, but now it is water rather than air cooled. The interior is a classy affair, helped no end by the facia borrowed from the Boxster. While it is still breathtakingly fast, the 911 is now more refined, easier to drive and much less likely to bite back than the earlier models. It still has its foibles, especially the small amount of luggage space, though this is helped if the tiny rear seats are folded forward.

Best All-Rounder: 911 Coupe

Body styles: Convertible
Engine capacity: 2.7, 3.2
Price from: £34,200
Manufactured in: Germany, Finland

Porsche Boxster

The Boxster has helped boost Porsche sales dramatically, its combination of the usual Porsche attributes and a comparatively affordable price enticing a new flock of buyers. If there could be one criticism of the original Boxster it was that the brilliant chassis was capable of handling much more power than its 2.5-litre flat six engine could provide. That issue is addressed by a bigger 2.7-litre engine in the basic model, plus the introduction of the new 3.2-litre Boxster S, with 252 bhp. It may cost 25 per cent more than the original, but the new S performs in a way that makes the 911 convertible seem redundant.

Best All-Rounder: Boxster S

PROTON

Malaysian manufacturer Proton may have been hit by the general problems in the Malaysian economy, but it remains the dominant supplier of cars in its home market. Cars exported to the UK are the Compact (Satria), Persona (Wira and Coupe (Putra) but there are others that do not make it here. The Perdana is Proton's luxury car, recently offered with a new V6 engine. The Wira is based on an old Mitsubishi Lancer, the original Proton sold in the UK. The Tiara is a reworked version of the Citroen AX. If this all sounds very family-car oriented, you may be surprised to know that Proton also owns Lotus.

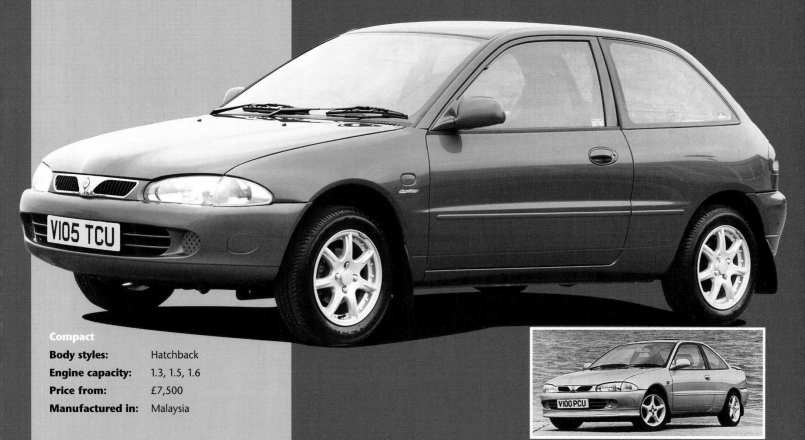

Compact

Body styles:	Hatchback
Engine capacity:	1.3, 1.5, 1.6
Price from:	£7,500
Manufactured in:	Malaysia

Persona

Body styles:	Hatchback, saloon, coupe
Engine capacity:	1.5, 1.6, 1.8, 2.0D, 2.0TD
Price from:	£8,500
Manufactured in:	Malaysia

Proton Compact and Persona

Basically a development of an earlier Mitsubishi Colt, the three-door Compact is one of the largest superminis around in terms of sheer dimensions, although the low roof means that interior space is smaller than most. With those good looks comes a quality interior, but the Compact's on the road manners are poor and it lacks refinement. But the new GTi version launched late in 1999 adds considerable appeal.

The Persona bears a family relationship, the main difference being that the Persona comes as a saloon, five-door hatchback and a pretty coupe. Engine choice ranges from a lowly 1.3-litre up to a 114bhp 1.8 and there is also a 2.0-litre turbo-diesel. The coupe gets its own uprated 1.8-litre engine with 133bhp. The Persona is effortless and easy to drive, which should be enough, but there is plenty of more recent competition around that makes this Malaysian-built car feel both a little dated and not of the highest quality.

Best All-Rounder: Compact 1.5 GLSi, Persona 1.8EXi

PLYMOUTH

Body styles:
Convertible

Engine capacity:
3.5 V6

Price from:
$39,300

Manufactured in:
United States

Plymouth Prowler

Slip on the Ray-Bans, turn-up your collar, put a little Beach Boys on the CD, and cruise, baby. Chrysler's Plymouth Prowler hot rod for the '90s is so c-o-o-l, it could chill an Eskimo. And for 2000, it gets just a little cooler with the availability of more-subtle Prowler Silver paintwork. Anything's subtle compared to the previous acid yellow. OK, so the 3.5-litre V6 under the 'hood' isn't a fire-breathin' Hemi V8, but it still packs 253bhp, and is muscular enough to chirp those 20-inch rear tyres. Standstill to 60 is a creditable 6.5 seconds. And new suspension re-tuning improves the quality of the ride and sharpens-up the handling.

Best All-Rounder: Prowler

PERODUA

Body styles:
Hatchback

Engine capacity:
850

Price from:
£5,100

Manufactured in:
Malaysia

Perodua Nippa

Britain's cheapest car, built in Malaysia, started out long ago as the Daihatsu Mira. Slightly revised last year, the Nippa continues with its 850cc three-cylinder engine, four passenger doors and pocket-money running costs: its economical motor returns 53mpg over the combined cycle. Even Perodua will happily admit that the car is basic motorised transport, with hard plastics and bare metal abound inside. Not that this detracts from the appeal too greatly though, with the Nippa displaying an endearing honesty about its intent. Maintaining progress outside town takes some effort, but city practicality and cash in the wallet more than compensate.

Best all-rounder: Nippa EX

RENAULT

Renault is a little bit braver than most major car manufacturers, prepared to move into unknown areas of car design but trusting their judgement that a new concept will come good. And largely they have – just look at the success of mould-breaking designs like the Espace, Twingo and Scenic – trends others have all been forced to imitate. Of course things do not always work out – the recent Spider was fun but a car without a roof, heater or door locks was always going to be rather too limiting. The mainstream family cars carry over some of panache, and there will be more to come in 2000 – the Clio V6 and the pumped up Scenic RX4.

Body styles:	Hatchback
Engine capacity:	1.2, 1.4, 1.6, 19D
Price from:	£8,400
Manufactured in:	France, Spain

Renault Clio

Introduced in 1998, the latest generation Clio had to build on the success of the well marketed previous version. Majoring on style and value for money, the new 1.2, 1.4 and 1.6 petrol powered Clio quickly went about continuing that theme, with a 1.9-litre diesel joining the range shortly afterwards. A 1.6, 16-valve warm-hatch with 110bhp also made its debut in summer 1999. Offered in 3 and 5-door body styles, the Clio gives reasonable accommodation, despite a surplus of hard grey plastic throughout the interior. Easy if not overly enjoyable to drive, competitive pricing and high equipment levels make for an attractive package.

Best all-rounder: Clio 1.2 RT

Renault Twingo

Renault is a great trend-setter, as the Scenic and Espace show, yet the competition has been a little slower following in its Twingo footsteps. The concept is a one-box car that maximises space on the inside while remaining a highly compact city car on the outside. There are lots of original ideas – sliding rear seats to offer a balance of space between passengers and luggage, delightfully cheeky exterior styling and the "one-model" policy. Under this, the options are kept to a minimum to keep costs in check. So there is just one engine on offer, a 1.2-litre, with trim changes largely confined to choosing your colour. A manual gearbox is standard but there is a clever semi-automatic too.

Best All-Rounder: Twingo 1.2

Body styles:
Hatchback

Engine capacity:
1.2

Price from:
£na

Manufactured in:
France, Spain, Colombia

Renault Kangoo

For less than £10,000 in the UK, Renault's Kangoo offers a massive amount of interior room thanks to its panel van origins. Introduced throughout Europe in autumn 1999 with twin sliding rear doors, 1.4 petrol and 1.9-litre diesel engines provide (some) power. Rear seat room is plentiful, there's bags of space in the front, the boot is huge and headroom is absurdly generous. If there is a downside, it's that noise has a large volume to boom around in. To drive, the Kangoo is fuss free, with a soft ride, good visibility and reasonable controls. A modern day Renault 4.

Best All-Rounder: Kangoo 1.4

Body styles:
Estate

Engine capacity:
1.1, 1.4, 1.9D

Price from:
£9,700

Manufactured in:
France

Renault Megane

Renault needed to raise its game with the Megane in the face of tough competition from newer rivals like the Astra, Focus and Golf. The answer is the 1999 revised model that, despite its conservative looks, boasts new and very economical 1.4 and 1.6-litre petrol engines, a revised 1.9-litre turbo-diesel, and a new instrument layout and steering wheel, although the big deal for many will be the highly impressive results in the NCAP crash test simulation. On the road, the Megane is competent and, even with the sportier suspension fitted to some models, the ride remains comfortable, the steering precise and the handling secure. Inside there is comfort but the cabin remains an uninspiring place to be.

Best All-Rounder: Megane 1.6 Alize

Body styles:
Hatchback, saloon, estate, convertible, coupe

Engine capacity:
1.4, 1.6, 2.0, 1.9D, 1.9TD

Price from:
£11,900

Manufactured in:
France, Spain

Renault Scenic

The Scenic was deservedly Europe's Car of the Year when it was launched, and such was the success of the concept that sales soared. Now that there is more in the way of competition Renault has revised the car with new engines, a redesigned nose with much bigger lamps and more interior stowage space. Otherwise the common-sense approach continues. The Scenic sits five adults comfortably with plenty of leg and foot room. The three back seats are independently mounted and can be moved back and forth or removed individually. While the Scenic is not a car for the enthusiastic driver, the new more powerful engines help. The forthcoming RX4 off-road version doubles the appeal.

Best All-Rounder: Scenic 1.6 Alize

Body styles:
MPV

Engine capacity:
1.4, 1.6, 2.0, 1.9TD

Price from:
£13,100

Manufactured in:
France, Spain

Renault Laguna

The Laguna remains as distinctive as when it was first launched in 1993, but its elegant lines still seem to meet with universal approval. A minor facelift in 1998 did little but tweak a few details to freshen the look and bring some good new 1.6 and 1.8-litre 16-valve engines. Now there are further changes including Renault's first "common-rail" diesel promising new levels of refinement and economy, and an improved 2.0-litre petrol unit. The Laguna's interior is pleasing to the eye and reasonably spacious, with the option of seven seats in the estate. Competitive pricing, a fine ride, reasonable (but not class leading) handling and good refinement and performance keep the Laguna in the lead pack.

Best All-Rounder: Laguna 2.0-16v RTi

Body styles:
Hatchback, estate

Engine capacity:
1.6, 1.8, 2.0, 3.0V6, 1.9TD, 2.2TD

Price from:
£14,000

Manufactured in:
France, Spain

Renault Safrane

For numerous reasons Renault's big executive cars, like their Citroen and Peugeot rivals, have never had much sales success outside of France. A hatchback body style on a big executive car has never caught on in the UK and the re-design with a Ferrari-style egg-crate front grille has only marginally helped sales. At the same time, the UK range has been slimmed down to just two engine choices – a 2.0-litre 16-valve and a 20-valve five-cylinder 2.5 from the Volvo S70; other markets still get the 3.0V6 and a turbo-diesel. Dynamically, the Safrane performs well with an excellent ride, comfortable seats and lots of room, but there's little driver involvement and the handling feels soggy – a shame given the performance of the 2.5.

Best All-Rounder: Safrane 2.5 Executive

Body styles:
Hatchback

Engine capacity:
2.0, 2.4, 3.0V6, 2.2TD

Price from:
£21,900

Manufactured in:
France

Renault Espace

Renault has moved its Espace upmarket, away from mainstream MPV competition and into the executive car price bracket. Inside, each of the seven occupants get an individual chair, with the rear five sliding back and forth in the top model. Space is impressive, with the longer Grand Espace offering that still rare MPV commodity – space for seven and their luggage. Those in the front are confronted by a majestic swooping facia incorporating a huge amount of storage space. The turbo diesel churns out the same power as the 2.0-litre petrol model, but the extra torque makes it an easy drive, although the manual gearbox can be a bit stubborn at times and Renault still hasn't fully cured the awkward pedal position of the old model. The 3.0 V6 provides the ultimate relaxing drive.

Best All-Rounder: Espace 2.2td RT

Body styles:
MPV

Engine capacity:
2.0, 3.0V6, 2.2TD

Price from:
£19,200

Manufactured in:
France

ROVER

BMW's ownership of Rover has been slow to offer any dramatic changes, at least in terms of new cars. The big news for 1999, however, was the replacement of two model ranges, the 600 and 800, with just one new car, the 75. Rover is building on its classic English image with the 75; expect more to come with the transformation of the 200 and 400 into the 25 and 45 for 2000. The new Mini, despite the prolific availability of pictures, will not be introduced until 2001, so the original soldiers on with regular special editions to liven it up. Rumours persist that a faster Supersport version of the MGF will appear before too long.

Body styles:	Saloon
Engine capacity:	1.8, 2.0V6, 2.5V6, 2.0TD
Price from:	£18,300
Manufactured in:	England

Rover 75

The 75 replaces both the 600 and 800 executive saloons, but in reality it is closer in size to the smaller model. It is a giant step upwards from either car however, with an exterior that nudges a few historical nerves and an interior that is masterpiece to behold; the genuinely classy facia wouldn't look out of place in a £60,000 Jaguar. There is a whole range of new or revised engines, including a new turbo-diesel from BMW. The 75 drives competently and though it is no sports car it is certainly a match for any of its rivals in terms of ride quality. Ultimately, the 75 is a thoroughly convincing package, marvellously refined and a competent handler.

Best All-Rounder: 75 2.5V6 Classic SE

Rover Mini

We have been hearing that there cannot be much life left in the Mini for years, but the 40-year-old trend-setter will be superseded by an all-new, and much more expensive, replacement within the next year. Meanwhile the charming original soldiers on, offering those with a stronger sense of nostalgia than reality a chance to drive a design classic. And yes, the Mini can still be great fun, especially in the Cooper form where it feels much faster than it really is. That impression is heightened by the firm ride, awkward driving position and tiny dimensions. Grab one now while you can – though the same money will already buy you a much better car elsewhere.

Best All-Rounder: Mini Cooper

Body styles:
Saloon

Engine capacity:
1.3

Price from:
£9,300

Manufactured in:
England

Rover 25

Late in 1999 Rover transformed the 200 into the 25. The key differences are a new nose with lights which mirror those of the bigger 75 and a revised interior to give the car a higher quality feel. The 200 was always one of the smaller family cars, and now, with the 100 well and truly buried, Rover has repositioned the 75 as a classy supermini to compete with the likes of the Punto and Polo. Mechanically, mildly re-worked and excellent K-Series engines sit alongside a good turbo-diesel. The driving experience is great too, with a composed ride which is the match of some cars in the class above. The 25 brims with showroom appeal.

Best All-Rounder: 25 1.4i

Body styles:
Hatchback

Engine capacity:
1.1, 1.4, 1.6, 1.8, 2.0TD

Price from:
£8,000

Manufactured in:
England

Rover 45

The 45 is the second Rover to be launched with the family nose first seen in the 75. Based on a mildly reworked 400, the new car has more emphasis on luxury and is pitched directly against smaller family models like the Focus and Astra. As before, saloon and five-door hatchback body styles are on offer, powered by a tweaked range of impressive K-Series petrol engines, the familiar 2.0 turbo-diesel plus the new 2.0-litre V6 from the 75. The 400 always succeeded by offering a bit more class than other vehicles at the same price level, with good comfort and a very pleasing interior. The 45 looks set to follow in its footsteps.

Best All-Rounder: 45 1.6i

Body styles:
Hatchback, saloon

Engine capacity:
1.4, 1.6, 2.0, 2.0TD

Price from:
£11,000

Manufactured in:
England

Rover MGF

The MGF gets a mid-term makeover though only the enthusiastic will spot the changes. Quality is said to be improved, and there is a body-coloured windscreen surround, improved centre console and new alloy wheels. The engines remains the sparkly 1.8 and the dynamic 1.8 VVC, either of which suit the car well. The really big news is the automatic transmission on the 1.8. This continuously variable Steptronic system offers standard and sport modes, plus the option of six manual ratios which can be selected by flicking the gearlever or via buttons on the steering wheel – it works very well. The MGF remains a great small sports car, even though drivers are forced to sit a little too high up.

Best All-Rounder: MGF 1.8i

Body styles:
Cabriolet

Engine capacity:
1.8

Price from:
£18,300

Manufactured in:
England

SAAB

Saab is owned by the giant General Motors but the cars are still manufactured in Sweden, with a two-model range. They are difficult vehicles to pigeonhole. Safe, yes, but doesn't Volvo do it better? Sporty, certainly now they are all turbocharged, but without the hard edge of a BMW. Luxurious, well the 9-5 certainly is, but it lacks the presence of a Mercedes. Perhaps Saabs should just be considered as individualistic cars, a mantle they carry rather well.

Body styles:	Hatchback, coupe, convertible
Engine capacity:	2.0 turbo, 2.2TD
Price from:	£16,800
Manufactured in:	Sweden, Finland

Saab 9-3

The 9-3 may have a relatively new name, but beneath the surface lays the 900 hatchback that was first seen in 1993. Still, there have been many changes made, with the grille from the 9-5, new seats and much development work on the chassis. The wide range of turbo-charged petrol engines can make the 9-3 a pleasure to drive, though the new Viggen has too much power for the chassis to cope with; there is also an impressive "sporting" turbo-diesel. But in any form the 9-3 lacks the hard sporting edge of the BMW 3-Series. Instead it offers more practicality, space and a high degree of comfort for four large adults combined with a massive luggage capacity.

Best All-Rounder: 9-3 2.0t SE

Saab 9-5

Conservative in appearance, the 9-5 will win few beauty contests but will quickly win over those who drive it. Every engine is turbo-charged, and even the 2.0-litre provides responsive performance in town and on the motorway. The steering and handling are biased towards comfort, but are none the worse for that. The interior of the higher specification models, all ruched leather and two-tone trim, has the ambience of a Jaguar, no mean feat in a car at this price. The 9-5 is spacious both for rear occupants and for luggage. The minor weaknesses are confined to the ride which is firm and the engine note of the four-cylinder cars.

Best All-Rounder: 9-5 2.3t SE

Body styles:	Hatchback, estate
Engine capacity:	2.0 turbo, 2.3 turbo, 3.0V6 t'rbo
Price from:	£22,800
Manufactured in:	Sweden

SATURN

Saturn execs like to call it the 'Different Kind of Car Company'. And back in 1990, when General Motors launched it, it was. One price, no-haggle pricing, friendly dealers and great service. Its cars too were a little different; they had plastic body panels, and looked vaguely Japanese. But, since then, Saturn gradually lost direction. No new models were added, and its line-up became old and tired. But things are looking up. A mid-size car based on a Vauxhall Vectra – called the LS – is new for 2000, and an all-important sport-utility has just been given the go-ahead for 2001.

Saturn LS, SC2

Body styles:	Hatchback, saloon, estate, coupe
Engine capacity:	1.9
Price from:	S15,500
Manufactured in:	United States

Saturn EV-1

Body styles:	Coupe
Engine capacity:	Electric motor
Price from:	$34,000
Manufactured in:	United States

Saturn LS, SC2 and EV-1

The long-awaited LS is Saturn's bright star for 2000. It's based loosely on an Opel/Vauxhall Vectra, but the body is all new and, in Saturn tradition, has ding-resistant plastic body panels. Opel's 3-litre V6 is offered as well as a brand new GM 2.2-litre four-cylinder. Available as either a saloon or estate, the Saturn LS is aimed at Saturn owners looking for an alternative to the best-selling Accords and Camrys.

Take one two-door coupe, and add a small, rear-hinged door on the driver's side. Makes it much easier for rear seat passengers to clamber in and out, and for the driver to pull out bags or a briefcase. Great idea. Powered by a twin cam 122bhp 1.9 four-cylinder, the Saturn SC2 has zippy performance, and for 2000, it's buzzy engine note has been quietened. There are changes too for the saloon and estate versions of the S-Series. New-look lower plastic body panels on the outside, and a fresh interior inside, with new controls and new instruments.

Plug-in, charge-up, drive-away. That's the theory behind GM's EV1, the world's first and only volume production electric car. With it's funky, two-seat coupe body, you could also describe it as the world's first electric sports coupe. It's quick off the line and will cruise at 70mph no trouble. But not for long; the juice runs out after 90 miles.

Best All-Rounders: LS 4dr, SL1, EV1

SEAT

Seat has had to become a master of niche marketing as the cars it builds in Spain owe a great deal of their origins to similar-sized Volkswagens. So Seat pitches itself as the "FUN" brand, aiming to capture buyers looking for cars with a degree of zest and excitement. Certainly the new Toledo saloon looks infinitely better than the model it replaced, and the heavily revised Ibiza and forthcoming Arosa take on the frontal treatment of the bigger car. What's is most interesting, however, is just around the corner. With the arrival of Lotus designer Julian Thompson, a prototype sports car has already been shown, with a production model promised soon.

Ibiza

Body styles:	Hatchback
Engine capacity:	1.0, 1.4, 1.6, 2.0, 1.9D, 1.9TD
Price from:	£9,000 (est)
Manufactured in:	Spain

Cordoba

Body styles:	Saloon, coupe, estate
Engine capacity:	1.4, 1.6, 2.0, 1.9D, 1.9TD
Price from:	£10,000 (est)
Manufactured in:	Spain

Seat Ibiza/Cordoba

The Ibiza hatchback and its saloon derivative, the Cordoba, are revised for 2000. The obvious external difference is the adoption of the nose from the latest Toledo, but inside everything has changed, from the dashboard to the seats. The engines are a mix of old and new – just look at the VW Polo and Golf to get an idea of the range – with, in time a choice of 11 engines available. Seat has always pitched the Ibiza as a supermini aimed at the young at heart and the range of high performance models – there is a now a 156bhp 1.8 Turbo – has helped the credibility. So too has a competent chassis, which makes this a good car not just for enthusiasts but for everyone.

Best All-Rounder: Too soon to say

Seat Toledo/León

Like the Toledo that preceded it, this new model is based upon the mechanical platform of the VW Golf, but that is about the only similarity. When the old car looked sensible and rather dull, the latest Toledo has all the swooping grace of a coupe. Seat has stuck to a sporty theme, with the smallest engine 1.6-litres, rising to the 2.3 V5 and a couple of turbo-diesels. It drives well too, though the steering lacks enough feel to make you feel entirely confident when going fast. The interior lacks the space of a full-sized family car, and boot access is limited through a narrow slot. The new León is a five-door hatchback based on the Toledo saloon.

Best All-Rounder: Toledo 1.8S-20v

Body styles:
Saloon, hatchback

Engine capacity:
1.6, 1.8, 2.3 V5, 1.9TD

Price from:
£14,300

Manufactured in:
Spain

Seat Arosa

The Arosa completed Seat's small car strategy by offering a budget hatchback with the design credentials of a Volkswagen. The first cars were even built in a VW factory in Germany, and the new VW Lupo is fundamentally an Arosa beneath the surface. The three-door body houses 1.0 and 1.4-litre petrol engines and an incredibly frugal 1.7-litre diesel. The Arosa feels a lot bigger inside than out, helped by the dashboard and switchgear straight out of the Ibiza. There's not a lot of room in the back or in the boot, but everything is fine in the front and the refinement is as good as most superminis.

Best All-Rounder: Arosa 1.0

Body styles:
Hatchback

Engine capacity:
1.0, 1.4, 1.7D

Price from:
£7,000

Manufactured in:
Germany

Seat Alhambra

The Alhambra is the final piece in the VW Sharan/Ford Galaxy jigsaw. In truth it is the same as the other two vehicles, but with an accent on fun, hence the jazzy seats. As the least well known of the brands, the Alhambra compensates with better equipment levels. It is all standard 7-seater fare, but good nonetheless. On the road the Alhambra offers a car-like driving position, while the stiff suspension prevents too much body roll. The 2.0-litre petrol engine is a refined and quiet cruiser, but not very lively. The turbo-diesels are more desirable, especially the 110bhp TDi, while the 1.8 petrol turbo adds some welcome performance.

Best All-Rounder: Alhambra TDi 110

Body styles:
MPV

Engine capacity:
1.8Turbo, 2.0, 1.9TD

Price from:
£17,400

Manufactured in:
Portugal

SKODA

No car company has been turned around like Skoda has. From a manufacturer of crude rear-engined saloons to one of a sophisticated family hatch and estate is quite a jump. Skoda itself made the first steps when it moved to front-wheel-drive, but Volkswagen now owns the company and has made the major difference. New for 2000 will be a small car that will eventually replace the Felicia.

Skoda Octavia

Body styles:	Saloon, estate
Engine capacity:	1.6, 1.8, 1.8Turbo,1.9D, 1.9TD
Price from:	£11,500
Manufactured in:	Czech Republic

Skoda Octavia

The Octavia shows that Skoda can tackle the full-sized car market with complete confidence. This full-sized family car has the quality and ability of a Volkswagen, as it should – mechanically it has much in common with the new VW Golf, with the same petrol and turbo-diesel engines. 1999 even sees a four-wheel-drive estate. That means it is a thoroughly pleasing car to drive – the 100bhp 1.6 is particularly well-suited (there is a slower 75bhp 1.6 too). Being something of a hybrid means that though there is plenty of width inside the car rear leg-room is more constrained than a Mondeo. But the massive boot makes up for this.

Best All-Rounder: Octavia 1.6 GLXi

Skoda Felicia

Body styles:	Hatchback, estate
Engine capacity:	1.3, 1.6,1.9D
Price from:	£7,000
Manufactured in:	Czech Republic

Skoda Felicia

The current Felicia will run until the end of 2000 alongside the new model, and for good reason. Both hatchback and estate versions offer great value by providing loads of space for supermini money. Today's cars feel well built and all give reasonable refinement. The 1.3 engine is Skoda's own, the 1.6 and diesel are from VW – better, but there's a cost penalty. Ride and handling are some way off the best cars of its size, but as budget workhorses go, the Felicia is probably the best in the business.

Best All-Rounder: Felicia 1.9D GLi

SHELBY

Body styles:
Convertible

Engine capacity:
4.0 V8

Price from:
$100,000

Manufactured in:
United States

Shelby Series 1

Production of Shelby's Series 1 is only now beginning to crank-up for this, the spiritual successor to the legendary AC Cobra. No worry; most of the 500 $100,000 carbon fibre-bodied two-seaters have already been snapped up by loyal Cobra fans. It may not be the prettiest sports car in the world, but it's one of the most-exciting. Bolting a 325bhp Oldsmobile V8 into a body that weighs about as much as a Tupperware container guarantees big performance. And the Series 1 doesn't disappoint. Race car suspension and brakes the size of dustbin lids add to the thrill.

Best All-Rounder: Shelby Series 1

SMART

Body styles:
Hatchback

Engine capacity:
600, 800TD

Price from:
£6,000

Manufactured in:
France

MCC Smart

The Smart is at long last in full production in France, after what seems like years of development. This two-seat city car has been jointly developed by Mercedes and Swatch, although the German manufacturer took over the whole show during the final stages. Available only in left-hand-drive, the rear-mounted 600cc turbo-charged engine is available in either 45bhp or 54bhp form. Neither is going to set the Tarmac alight, but there is sufficient power to provide lively performance. Amazingly there is a six-speed semi-automatic Tiptronic-style transmission – just like in a Porsche. For 2000 there will be an 800cc, 83mpg diesel as well as a convertible with a full-length removable roof.

Best All-Rounder: Smart Pulse

SUBARU

The ace up Subaru's sleeve is that everything it makes is four-wheel-drive. Well almost, for front wheel-drive Imprezas are available in Japan. No matter, for the image of a versatile, moderately rugged car that is as at home on the road as in the field has been established firmly in buyers' minds. That field may, of course, be a rally stage, for the Impreza Turbo in its many guises is a formidable performance machine that has helped built the company its strong reputation in the UK. Throughout 1999 the latest Legacy was offered in an ever-widening range, and the new Pleo city car was introduced in Japan to replace the Vivio.

Subaru Legacy

Subaru's latest Legacy was introduced as an estate in 1998, then as a saloon early in 1999. The Outback is a beefed-up estate, whilst the old Legacy – the Classic – also continues as a budget choice. Engines are all four-cylinder, of 2.0 or 2.5-litres and various power, though the range is restricted outside Japan. Subaru's latest offering to the compact executive market is a mixed bag. On the one hand, plentiful interior space, competent, enjoyable driving characteristics and keen pricing attract. On the other, a lack of engine choice and an absence of style detract from the appeal.

Best All-Rounder: Legacy 2.5 Estate

Body styles:	Saloon, estate
Engine capacity:	2.0, 2.5
Price from:	£15,600
Manufactured in:	Japan

Subaru Justy

The latest Justy is one of the cheapest 4x4s on the market. Part of that cost benefit is due to its construction – it is a clone of the Suzuki Swift, built in Hungary and fitted with four-wheel-drive. The four-wheel-drive system has the obvious benefits, though for less than enthusiastic drivers the extra traction will probably never be noticed until trying to accelerate up a steep, wet slope or drive on snow. Slack steering, a reluctant gearchange and a bouncy ride take the edge off the driving enjoyment. Inside, the cabin isn't as smart as a Ford Fiesta but rear seat legroom in the longer 5-door is generous.

Body styles:
Hatchback

Engine capacity:
1.3

Price from:
£9,500

Manufactured in:
Japan

Best All-Rounder: Justy 1.3 GX

Subaru Pleo

The replacement for the Vivio, and a direct competitor for the Daewoo Matiz, the Pleo has a less wacky design than most town cars but offers the expected combination of a compact exterior with an attempt to offer space for four adults. Performance should not be the usual desperately slow affair either - as well as offering an unexceptional 650cc motor with 44bhp, there are turbocharged and supercharged versions. Single or double overhead camshaft turbo models offer over 60bhp, while the 58bhp supercharged Pleo can be coupled with CVT automatic transmission with 7 sequential manual gears that can be changed at the steering wheel.

Body styles:
Hatchback

Engine capacity:
700

Price from:
£na

Manufactured in:
Japan

Best All-Rounder: Too soon to say

Subaru Impreza

The Impreza started life as a family car that offered a high-performance turbo-charged option. Now the performance derivatives have become the cars that dominate the attention, not just the straightforward 218bhp Impreza Turbo, but also the more mighty WRX and STi derivatives that offer 280bhp and more. It is hardly surprising, for they offer performance akin to a rally car for the price of a mid-range executive model. Front-wheel-drive is available in the lesser models in some countries, but most have four-wheel-drive and the option of saloon or hatchback-cum-estate body style. The Impreza is a likeable car to drive, even in standard 2.0-litre form; interior space and comfort are about average.

Body styles:
Hatchback, saloon

Engine capacity:
1.5, 1.6, 2.0, 2.0 turbo, 2.5

Price from:
£14,300

Manufactured in:
Japan

Best All-Rounder: Impreza Turbo

Subaru Forester

The sensible, estate-like styling of the Forester is based around a permanent four-wheel-drive platform from the Impreza. Power comes from the obligatory four-cylinder boxer engines, with anything from a reasonable 120bhp to a mammoth 250bhp. Even the base 2.0-litre engine powers the car well enough, the driving experience, aided by great ergonomics, is refined and relaxed. Impreza underpinnings give class leading handling and roadholding, whilst interior space is good all round – the large boot complemented by ample oddments space. It all helps make the Forester one of the better, if not the trendiest, sport utilities.

Body styles:
Estate

Engine capacity:
2.0, 2.0 turbo, 2.5

Price from:
£17,000

Manufactured in:
Japan

Best All-Rounder: Forester 2.0 Turbo

SUZUKI

Deep down Suzuki builds small cars – the Wagon R, Alto, Swift and Jimny all emphasise that point – and the success rate is good, with the unlikely Wagon R once again the best seller in Japan. The company has ventured into bigger cars with mixed success. The Baleno is Suzuki's small-to-medium-family car but it lacks the sophistication of European rivals. The four-wheel-drive Grand Vitara is a different matter, a highly competent lifestyle 4x4 that stands up well against the competition.

Suzuki Jimny

The Jimny is Suzuki's replacement for the SJ, its budget off-roader that ran for almost two decades. It has been designed to offer the practicality of a sport utility vehicle with the neat dimensions of a city car. Suzuki's new 1.3-litre, 16-valve engine takes some winding up to get the best results but then, unfortunately, it becomes irritatingly coarse. Nipping in and out of congested traffic is what the Jimny does best; with good all-round visibility it makes an excellent town car. A fidgety ride is the major handicap, otherwise four adults can be carried on short journeys provided they don't have any baggage. But if the value of its off-road ability is questionable, rivals like Ford's Ka can do everything else better.

Best All-Rounder: Jimny 1.3

Body styles:	Estate
Engine capacity:	1.3
Price from:	£10,000
Manufactured in:	Japan, Spain

Suzuki Vitara and Grand Vitara

Suzuki has sensibly moved upmarket with the Grand Vitara, with the first examples all long-wheelbase versions with a 2.5-litre V6. Now there is a shorter model, the GV 2.0-litre as well as a turbo-diesel. In its most expensive form the Grand Vitara is smooth and refined, pulling well at low speeds as well as when driven enthusiastically. The driving position and front seats give good support too, so this is quite a driver's car for a 4x4. But room in the back seats is tight and boot space is so-so. And that suspension can get too firm for comfort. Suzuki still makes the original Vitara which finds favour with those who love the 'pumped-up wheel-arch and tractor-tyre' look.

Best All-Rounder: Grand Vitara 2.5V6, Vitara 1.6

Body styles:	Estate, Convertible
Engine capacity:	1.6, 2.0, 2.5V6, 1.9D, 2.0TD
Price from:	£11,000, Grand V' £13,500
Manufactured in:	Japan, Canada, Spain

Suzuki Alto

Suzuki's Alto has more to offer other than anonymous looks and a low price. In this competitive sector, where the likes of the Ford Ka and Seat Arosa dominate, the cheap Alto can provide reliable, enjoyable transport. At its price it competes mainly with vehicles like the Perodua Nippa and Daihatsu Cuore and like these, it comes with a small capacity, relatively low-powered petrol engine. The cabin may not contain much equipment, but it's spacious, comfortable and well built. The cost has been kept down by minimising options and by building the car in India. Thankfully it feels well screwed together so the package isn't too unrefined on the road.

Body styles:
Hatchback

Engine capacity:
0.7, 1.0

Price from:
£6,300

Manufactured in:
India

Best All-Rounder: Alto 1.0

Suzuki Wagon R+

No matter what the qualities are of the Wagon R+ – and they must be reasonable for it is the best selling car in Japan yet again – it is impossible to overlook its appearance. Only those with a thick skin will drive around in something that looks this ugly. The tall body gives plenty of headroom, but otherwise space is ordinary, with the a commanding driving position offset by a lack of comfort for the driver. The Wagon R promises economical town driving and it is certainly easy to use in these conditions. Engine choice is a 1.0-litre or a 1.2 – the latter is a much better proposition.,

Body styles:
Estate

Engine capacity:
1.0, 1.0 turbo, 1.2

Price from:
£7,400

Manufactured in:
Japan

Best All-Rounder: Wagon R 1.2 GL

Suzuki Swift

The Suzuki Swift has been around in several forms since 1983, when it was sold as the Geo Metro in the States. A development of that car is still available in the US, though it is now known as the Chevrolet Metro. The original design is Suzuki's though and, several facelifts later, it is being built in Hungary for the Europeans. With either engine, 'Swift' is something of a contradiction. But interior space is good in the longer five-door version, it rides well and the car doesn't feel badly built. It's nothing like competitive with the best from Europe or Japan any more (if it ever was) but as a rock-bottom budget car, particularly in developing markets, it still has its place.

Body styles:
Hatchback

Engine capacity:
1.0, 1.3

Price from:
£6,800

Manufactured in:
Hungary

Best All-Rounder: Swift 1.3

Suzuki Baleno

Suzuki has always had a little difficulty convincing buyers that it makes proper family cars like the Baleno. Small hatchbacks and off-roaders, yes, but its credibility falls away in the mainstream market. But the Baleno is a reasonably good car, heavily revised in1999 with a new front end and interior, plus the addition of a diesel engine borrowed from Peugeot. Performance of the petrol-engined cars has always been a strong feature, though the chassis isn't sharp enough to maintain the sporty impression and when the performance is used to the full the engine becomes unrefined and unpleasantly noisy. Space inside isn't brilliant either but comfort levels are good.

Body styles:
Hatchback, saloon, estate

Engine capacity:
1.3, 1.6, 1.8, 1.9TD

Price from:
£10,400

Manufactured in:
Japan

Best All-Rounder: Baleno 1.6

TOYOTA

For a company the size of Toyota – Japan's biggest manufacturer and the world's number three – launching three new cars in one year is nothing new. But 2000 sees some rather special offerings, each a big change from what went before. The Celica coupe and MR2 sports car go in new directions, tighter, more compact packages that promise more nimble performance. The acclaimed Yaris comes in a new version, the Verso, a taller roomier hatchback which is to the Yaris what the Scenic is to the Renault Megane. And then, of course there is a wide range of other models covering, almost, every style you can think of.

Body styles:	Hatchback
Engine capacity:	1.0, 1.3
Price from:	£7,400
Manufactured in:	Japan

Yaris

Toyota's replacement for the long running but exceedingly dull Starlet is the Yaris. It is everything the Starlet wasn't – roomy, stylistically adventurous, technically advanced. The Yaris is truly roomy for a supermini in the front, while the rear can be altered via a sliding bench. Those heavy rear pillars restrict visibility however, and the cabin, with digital instruments, takes some getting used to, but it works. The 1.0-litre engine has been joined by a 1.3 – both are extremely capable, and there is a gearbox that is slick and easy to use as well. There's an impressive chassis with suspension tuned for comfort rather than thrills. All-in-all a highly impressive package.

Best All-Rounder: Yaris 1.0 GLS

Toyota Corolla

The smiling face of the current Corolla may be more distinctive than in the past, but beneath the surface it retains many of the previous model's components. That means 1.3 and 1.6-litre petrol engines, a 2.0-litre diesel and four body styles: three & five-door hatchbacks, a saloon and an estate. As you'd expect, the Corolla is competent in all areas. The airy but drably-trimmed cabin is effective, the engines are reliable, equipment levels are competitive and it's comfortable and easy to drive. In fact, there's nothing much wrong with the car, it's just that more recent competitors have moved the game on to another level.

Best All-Rounder: Corolla 1.3 GS

Body styles:
Hatchback, saloon, estate

Engine capacity:
1.3, 1.6, 1.8, 2.0D

Price from:
£10,000

Manufactured in:
Japan, England

Toyota Prius

Toyota's Prius is the world first production hybrid vehicle using the combination of a 1.5-litre petrol engine and an electric motor. It is a very sophisticated device, switching seamlessly between petrol and electric power and even combining the two when necessary – there's a delightful dashboard display which tells you exactly what's going on. The big deal is a massive reduction in emissions, but surprisingly the Prius also drives very well too. For some reason Toyota chose distinctly odd styling and it is a saloon too, so no hatchback versatility. The Prius is an admirable step in the right direction, but we have the feeling that in a few years it will seem very old fashioned.

Best All-Rounder: Prius 1.5

Body styles:
Saloon

Engine capacity:
1.5

Price from:
£na

Manufactured in:
Japan

Toyota Avensis

With the Avensis Toyota has at last managed to build a full-size family car that has some style to match its core attributes. The Avensis looks good and is calmly efficient. The engines are refined, offering good economy and power, and the chassis is tuned for smooth comfort, not overtly sporting dynamism. Equipment levels, interior space and build quality are as generously offered as ever too. It is just not a car to raise the pulse rate. There are cars that offer a more interesting drive, but the Avensis, with that legendary Toyota quality, does more than enough for a lot of buyers.

Best All-Rounder: Avensis 2.0 GLS

Body styles:
Hatchback, saloon, estate

Engine capacity:
1.6, 1.8, 2.0, 2.0TD

Price from:
£14,000

Manufactured in:
England

Toyota Camry

Toyota's executive saloon fulfils different roles in different continents. In Europe it is the company's top executive car, a role it struggles to handle effectively in the light of the more prestigious Lexus range. In the US, however, the Camry is just another reasonably-priced family car, but one that is respected so much that it became America's best selling model. From a European perspective this Toyota may not have the badge or upmarket interior of some of its rivals, but it boasts a roomy interior, a quality feel and much comfort. There's a long list of standard equipment too, plus a choice of two well-refined engines – a 2.2-litre 16v or 3.0-litre V6.

Best All-Rounder: Camry V6

Body styles:
Saloon

Engine capacity:
2.2, 3.0V6

Price from:
£20,200

Manufactured in:
Japan

Toyota Picnic

The Picnic has fallen into a void in the MPV world – smaller than full-size vehicles like the Ford Galaxy, and not as compact as the Renault Scenic. Yet Vauxhall has shown there is definitely a place for a compact seven-seater, and the Picnic is a thoroughly pleasing example – comfortable and very easy to drive, though not as sharp in the corners as the Zafira. Two engines are available, a 2.0-litre 126bhp petrol or a 2.2-litre turbo-diesel with 86bhp. In GL and GX forms, the petrol unit also offers the choice of a US-style steering column-mounted automatic like the Previa. In spite of new competition, the Picnic remains a good choice for those looking for a compact MPV.

Best All-Rounder: Picnic 2.0 GL

Body styles:
MPV

Engine capacity:
2.0, 2.2TD

Price from:
£16,000

Manufactured in:
Japan

New!

Toyota Previa

Toyota's huge Previa used to be one of the few people-carriers on the market that could accommodate seven or eight people and their luggage too, but no more. Buyers can choose from the Chrysler Grand Voyager and Renault's Grand Espace too, and there is no doubt that the Previa's age means it is less fashionable than it once was. Offered with just a single engine in the UK, the performance from the 2.4-litre 133bhp petrol hides the Previa's dimensions well, although its handling can't camouflage the fact that the Toyota is not a small car. That size is a bonus for carrying capacity though, and combined with the excellent build quality can make the Previa a practical and shrewd choice.

Best All-Rounder: Previa GL

Body styles:
MPV

Engine capacity:
2.4, 2.2TD

Price from:
£19,900

Manufactured in:
Japan

Toyota MR2 Roadster

The third generation MR2 hits the streets early in 2000 with a brand new look and a move back to the concept of the original. Once again the MR2 is a true sports car, rather than the Grand Touring guise taken on by the Mark 2 model. A full convertible with the option of a factory-fitted hard top, the MR2 Roadster gets a longer wheelbase and shorter overhangs in a much tauter chassis. Strictly a two-seater, the styling is unusual but distinctive, helped by a pop-up rear spoiler. The mid-engined 1.8 VVT-i engine is the same as in the lower-powered version of the new Celica, with 140bhp pitching it right up against the MGF and Mazda MX5.

Best All-Rounder: MR2 Roadster 1.8 VVT-i

Body styles:
Convertible

Engine capacity:
1.8

Price from:
£19,000

Manufactured in:
Japan

Toyota Celica

Toyota has moved firmly away from the touring coupes of the past into something much sportier with this new Celica. Shorter overall, yet with a longer wheelbase, the striking design is coupled to an equally radical change in specification. The first engine to be offered is a 1.8-litre coupled to a six-speed manual gearbox. With variable vale timing that might sound like an enticing proposition, although its 140bhp is quick rather than blistering. That need will be answered with a much more powerful 1.8 to be launched a few months later. Toyota aims to make the Celica a much more civilised machine than the Honda Integra, as well as being more fun to drive than ever.

Best All-Rounder: Celica 1.8 ST

Body styles:
Coupe, convertible

Engine capacity:
1.8, 2.0, 2.0 turbo

Price from:
£18,000 (est)

Manufactured in:
Japan

Toyota RAV4

Toyota's RAV4 single-handedly changed everyone's view of how an off-roader should drive. As enjoyable as a hot hatch, the RAV4, despite a recent refresh, now has some hot competition from the likes of the Freelander and Honda CR-V. Both offer more in the way of comfort, and the RAV4 cannot really handle tough off-roading like the Land Rover. The 2.0-litre engine is powerful if a little noisy when pushed. There is a choice of three and five-door body styles plus a newer Soft Top with a rather complicated folding roof. That and the three-door are a tight fit for four adults; the five-door is longer and consequently offers more space.

Best All-Rounder: RAV4 GX 3dr

Body styles:
Estate

Engine capacity:
2.0

Price from:
£15,000

Manufactured in:
Japan

Toyota Landcruiser Colorado

Toyota has a brilliant reputation for its tough off-roaders, but until the Colorado it never had anything to compete head-on with the hugely successful Mitsubishi Shogun and Land Rover Discovery. Available as a three or five-door, most of the models in the Colorado range are powered by a 3.0-litre turbo-diesel, although the flagship five-door VX also offers a thirsty 3.4-litre V6. The turbo-diesel five-door is the best of the bunch with two optional rear seats in the boot for further practicality, although the interior is disappointingly plain. A good level of equipment and permanent four-wheel-drive mean the Colorado is equally at home on road or mud-track.

Best All-Rounder: Colorado GX TD 5dr

Body styles:
Estate

Engine capacity:
2.7, 3.4V6, 3.0TD

Price from:
£21,000

Manufactured in:
Japan

Toyota Landcruiser Amazon

With the smaller Landcruiser suiting many owners' off-road requirements just fine, there was only one way for Toyota to go with its lead model – onwards and upwards. So everything about the Amazon is huge. Available as a seven seater, the boot-mounted seats may be cramped, but they fold up against the side when not in use. The tailgate is split, Range Rover-style. Engine choice is between a 232bhp 4.7-litre V8 petrol unit with crippling fuel consumption or a 4.2-litre turbo-diesel offering a marginally better 25mpg average. While lacking the Range Rover's image, the Amazon more than makes up with a huge list of standard equipment and, by comparison, a bargain price tag.

Best All-Rounder: Amazon VX TD

Body styles:
Estate

Engine capacity:
4.7V8, 4.2TD

Price from:
£36,8000

Manufactured in:
Japan

TVR

TVR has been on the crest of a wave for so many years that it seems that things cannot last like this for much longer. Yet the company seemingly produces a new model at every UK motor show, and buyers line up to place hefty deposits. The core of the range – Cerbera, Griffith and Chimaera – are joined for 2000 by the production version of the Tuscan Speed Six, first shown late in 1998. It still seems possible that the outrageous Speed 12 – £150,000, 7.7-litre V12 – will one day be sold to paying customers, but realistic eyes are looking out for what TVR unveils in London in October 1999.

New!

Body styles:	Convertible
Engine capacity:	4.0
Price from:	£39,000
Manufactured in:	England

TVR Tuscan Speed Six

The Tuscan Speed Six is TVR's latest two-seater. Based upon a shortened version of the Cerbera chassis and with the 4.0-litre, 350bhp straight six engine, the Tuscan offers the unusual combination of a rigid roof that can be removed in two sections to create – almost – a full convertible. What remains is the roll bar that doubles as the mounting for the LED rear lights. Such detail is, of course, a TVR trait, and there is plenty more – the curved aluminium top to the dashboard also stiffens the chassis and is a conduit for the cabin fresh air system. As ever, this TVR is powerful and light, so outrageous performance has not been neglected.

Best All-Rounder: Tuscan Speed Six 4.0

TVR Chimaera

The Chimaera is TVR's slightly softer, more practical offering, a traditional British sports car powered by Rover's V8 in various states of tune. The range starts with a 4.0-litre, but ultimately there's a 5.0-litre version churning out 320 bhp and enormous torque. When worked hard it bellows like a beast, yet it's quiet and refined on the motorway. Outright performance is brilliant, and thanks to the light weight of the glass-fibre body, 60 mph can be reached in five seconds or less. The cockpit comes close to the ideal romantic notion of what a sports car should be, with a wood-trimmed dashboard and beautiful leather seats. The Chimaera is brilliant fun, but it demands respect from the driver too.

Best All-Rounder: Chimaera 5.0 V8

Body styles:
Convertible

Engine capacity:
4.0V8, 4.6V8, 5.0V8

Price from:
£31,700

Manufactured in:
England

TVR Cerbera

The Cerbera was a departure for TVR when first shown in 1993 – a fixed roof grand tourer with 2+2 seating. It is a stunning piece of sculpture. No other car with four seats sits this low, which makes the Cerbera look even longer and wider than it already is. Being a TVR, performance is spectacular, with the company's own V8 producing enough power to out-accelerate a Porsche 911 Turbo. There is also the recent Cerbera Speed Six, offering a more traditional British feel with its straight six engine, softer suspension and (slightly) quieter nature. The chassis on either compliments the performance, but it takes a brave (or foolish) man to exploit the full envelope of the Cerbera's possibilities.

Best All-Rounder: Cerbera Speed Six

Body styles:
Coupe

Engine capacity:
4.0V8, 4.2V8, 4.5V8

Price from:
£41,100

Manufactured in:
England

TVR Griffith

Few would argue that the Griffith, TVR's oldest model, is still the most beautiful. It is also the least compromising, designed to give raw performance with little of the benign nature of the Chimaera. Powered by a 5.0-litre Rover V8, it produces 320 bhp, enough to place it in the serious supercar league. Inside there's luxury, with the tight-fitting cockpit trimmed in high quality leather. The controls are uniformly heavy but that's quickly forgotten when the throttle is pressed and the deep, evil rumble curls from the exhausts. The chassis may be good, but ultimately such power in a lightweight car, without traction control and in a relatively short wheelbase, is never going to be for the faint-hearted.

Best All-Rounder: Griffith 5.0 V8

Body styles:
Convertible

Engine capacity:
5.0V8

Price from:
£35,700

Manufactured in:
England

VAUXHALL/OPEL

Vauxhall and Opel make identical cars. Part of the giant General Motors, only the badges and grilles are different, with the UK being the only country where the Vauxhall name is used; in Australia a fair part of the range is exported to be sold as Holdens. The big success for Vauxhall/Opel in 1999 was the Zafira, but the rest of the range remains popular with business buyers and in Germany, Opel's home turf, comfortably outsells Ford, the reverse of the position in the UK. The excitement for 2000 is the launch of the Speedster, a reworked version of the Lotus Elise with a bigger, 2.2-litre engine and more in the way of comfort and refinement.

Body styles:	MPV
Engine capacity:	1.6, 1.8, 2.0TD
Price from:	£14,500
Manufactured in:	Germany

Vauxhall/Opel Zafira

The Zafira is General Motors answer to the Renault Scenic – a tall, versatile estate/MPV based upon a family hatchback. Renault choose the Megane as the base, Vauxhall/Opel the Astra, but the Zafira has one extra dimension – seven seats. While making little pretence at offering space for that number of adults, let alone much luggage, the Zafira does offer admirable flexibility for everyday use, particularly as the second and third row of seats fold away into the floor leaving a very spacious estate car. The Zafira's compact size means that it is less daunting to drive and park than a full-size MPV – in fact little different to the Astra. It is a concept many others are set to follow.

Best All-Rounder: Zafira 2.0Di Comfort

Vauxhall/Opel Corsa

The Corsa has been around a good few years now, with even its facelift now a memory. So it is a car that is going through the latter stages of its life, and Vauxhall/Opel has been unable to keep the pot boiling in the way Ford has so impressively with its Fiesta rival. But it is a practical car, with two body styles, the three-door being distinctive and fun while the five-door has a slightly more sober and practical design. Either way the shape results in a roomy interior boasting comfortable seats and a natural, easy driving position. If the Corsa was more refined and better to drive, things would look a lot more hopeful.

Best All-Rounder: Corsa 1.4-16v GLS

Body styles:
Hatchback

Engine capacity:
1.0, 1.2, 1.4, 1.6, 1.5TD, 1.7D

Price from:
£6,900

Manufactured in:
Portugal, Spain

Vauxhall /Opel Astra

The latest Astra is a big step forward for Vauxhall/Opel. Here for the first time in its small family car contender was a model that not only looked right, it offered the degree of driving pleasure that seemed to have eluded the company previously. The steering and handling are superb, with great feel and precision and excellent chassis control in corners. There is a fine range of engines too, from 1.2 to 2.0-litre plus turbo-diesels – the pick are the 1.4-16v and the 2.0TD. The ride is firm but smooth, and there is a surprising amount of space inside, though the unimaginative dashboard is the major weak point. Choose from saloon, hatchback or estate, with the coupe to come in 2000.

Best All-Rounder: Astra 2.0Di LS

Body styles:
Hatchback, saloon, estate, coupe

Engine capacity:
1.2, 1.4, 1.6, 1.8, 2.0, 1.7TD, 2.0TD

Price from:
£12,000

Manufactured in:
England

Vauxhall/Opel Vectra

The original Vectra sold well enough despite criticism of its on-the-road manners. Now there is a revised model with 2,500 changes. It does not look much different, just slimmer headlights and a new rear bumper, but inside there's a lighter facia and more rear knee-room. As ever there is a huge range of engines, with a new 1.8 and smoother 2.0-litre, plus some impressive diesels. The suspension changes work well and the Vectra is now a good car to drive, with reasonable steering feel and pleasing handling. Both the 1.8 and 2.0-litre drive well, but neither is as refined as some of the opposition. Still, as long as the driver is not too tall, the Vectra is now a comfortable family car.

Best All-rounder Vectra 1.8 GLS

Body styles:
Hatchback, saloon, estate

Engine capacity:
1.6, 1.8, 2.0, 2.5V6, 2.0TD

Price from:
£14,700

Manufactured in:
England

New!

Vauxhall/Opel Omega

The Omega gets a raft of 2000 revisions, notably a new grille similar to the Astra's, swoopier lights, a remodelled interior, improved safety equipment and a new engine. That engine is a 2.2-litre four-cylinder which is likely to replace the 2.0-litre before too long; the 2.5V6, 3.0V6 and BMW 2.5 turbo-diesel continue. Omegas have always performed well and have given reasonable economy for a car of this size. They are also good to drive. Smooth and refined, there is a superbly absorbent ride and an extremely well-balanced chassis that will indulge a keen driver without compromising comfort. An extremely roomy interior with excellent seating completes the picture.

Best All-Rounder: Omega 2.5 V6

Body styles:
Saloon, estate

Engine capacity:
2.0, 2.2, 2.5V6, 3.0V6, 2.0TD, 2.5TD

Price from:
£20,000 (est)

Manufactured in:
Germany

Vauxhall/Opel Tigra

Vauxhall's Tigra had the baby coupe market pretty much to itself until the Ford Puma and Renault Megane arrived to spoil the party. Though the Tigra has all the dramatic looks and style of a coupe, it was beaten hands-down for driver involvement by the model from Ford. Offered with either a 1.4 or 1.6 engine (the former available also as an auto), the Tigra's interior is cramped both for taller adults in the front seats and anyone but small children in the rear. It can be fun in a simple, undemanding sort of way, but there is no getting away from the fact that the Puma is by far the more competent all-rounder.

Best All-Rounder: Tigra 1.4

Body styles:
Coupe

Engine capacity:
1.4, 1.6

Price from:
£13,100

Manufactured in:
Spain

Vauxhall/Opel Frontera

The Frontera went through a metamorphosis for the 1999 model year, keeping its basic shape but with the rugged good looks subtly improved and a host of other changes. The engine choice was widened to 2.2-litre and 3.2 V6 petrol engines and a new 2.2-litre turbo-diesel. The TD is the pick of the bunch, only a little slower than the 2.2-litre petrol engine in everyday driving, it delivers superior economy and acceptable refinement. The 3.2-litre V6 is powerful and smooth, but thirsty. The road manners are now better but the Frontera is still far from being a class leader. Instead it offers large amounts of space and a fair degree of comfort at prices others find hard to approach.

Best All-Rounder: Frontera 2.2 TD Estate Limited

Body styles:
Estate, convertible

Engine capacity:
2.2, 3.2V6, 2.2TD

Price from:
£16,800

Manufactured in:
England

VENTURI

Body styles:
Coupe

Engine capacity:
3.0V6, 3.0 twin turbo

Price from:
£59,600

Manufactured in:
France

Venturi 300 Atlantique

Venturi builds France's fastest production car. In 1999 it gained twin turbo-chargers in place of the single unit, a mild cosmetic face-lift and the option of a non-turbo automatic transmission model. The Atlantique is a genuine supercar, rivalling Lotus in terms of performance. UK sales are slight, but markets in the Middle East seem to be absorbing the production. Underneath that composite bodywork is a complex semi-monocoque steel chassis which provides huge reserves of grip – the Venturi is a very forgiving car to drive fast. But it is surprisingly luxurious too – more so than most competitors – with deep carpets, walnut trim and leather. Do not dismiss the Venturi too quickly.

Best All-Rounder: Atlantique Twin Turbo

WESTFIELD

Body styles:
Convertible

Engine capacity:
1.6, 1.8, 4.0V8

Price from:
£12,900

Manufactured in:
England

Westfield SEi, FW400

Midlands based Westfield has been producing Caterham rivalling sports cars for several years, but its SEi models have generally remained in the shadow of more complete offerings from the Surrey based company. Now, Westfield seems keen to buck that trend around with the composite F(eather)W(eight) 400 (kg), which promises blinding responses from its no-compromise race-car-like construction and tuned Rover K Series engine. The SEi models also continue, selling in both kit and complete form. Power for these comes from 1.6 and 1.8 Ford units for accessible, brisk fun; as well as a thumping great Rover V8 for loud, scary thrills.

Best All-Rounder: SEi 1800

VOLKSWAGEN

VW has had its 12 months of new launches, with the Lupo, Beetle and Bora all hitting the streets in close succession. There is a replacement for the Polo on the horizon in 2000, but otherwise it is a case of settling down to doing what Volkswagen does best, selling family cars that offer that extra quality competitors cannot match. That, since the launch of the Beetle, has been the German manufacturer's strength, and though it sometimes produces exceptional cars too, that is not really the issue. Volkswagens are dependable, and for many car buyers that is enough.

Body styles:	Hatchback
Engine capacity:	1.0, 1.4, 1.6, 1.2TD, 1.7D
Price from:	£7,800
Manufactured in:	Germany

Volkswagen Lupo

The Lupo is Volkswagen's new city car – a simple, classless model which combines quality with low price and good fuel economy. Beneath the skin the Lupo is largely the same as the Seat Arosa, but the Lupo's nose is a cuter four-light affair and the dashboard design is far trendier. The engines are familiar – 1.0, 1.4 and a 1.7 diesel – and all work well in the undemanding circumstances of a small car. Inside the Lupo offers impressive space and comfort for those in the front seats though in the back, inevitably it's not such good news. The suspension soaks up the bumps well and though this is no sporting model, the Lupo offers a fine blend of attributes.

Best All-Rounder: Lupo 1.0

VW Golf

This Volkswagen may carry the hallmarks of previous Golfs, but the car is totally new, with the accent being on offering quality hitherto unavailable in this class of car. It feels like VW has done it too, with an all-new style inside that looks smart and is ergonomically exceptional. There's a fair amount room for four adults, with generally good levels of comfort though the ride is rather firm. There is a massive range of engines, including four for the GTi alone, yet while the Golf is a no-nonsense, evenly balanced and predictable car on the move it is not up to the standards of the Astra, Focus or the Peugeot 306 for driver enjoyment.

Best All-Rounder: Golf 1.6S

Body styles:
Hatchback, estate, convertible

Engine capacity:
1.4, 1.6, 1.8, 1.8 turbo, 2.0, 2.3VR5, 2.8V6,1.9D, 1.9TD

Price from:
£12,300

Manufactured in:
Germany

VW Polo

The most noticeable evidence of the parts sharing that is becoming increasingly common within the VW Group can be seen in the Polo, which has a great deal in common with Seat's Ibiza and Cordoba. While the hatchbacks have enough differences to look like separate models, the Polo estate and saloon are no more than re-badged versions of the equivalent Cordobas. That, of course, doesn't stop the Polo being a good car. Its interior has a solid (if sombre) feel lacking from rivals – particularly Oriental and French ones – and interior space is competitive. The range of engines is wide enough to please most and refinement is excellent too. The Polo may not be the most fun in its class, but its maturity provides good compensation.

Best All-Rounder: Polo 1.6 CL

Body styles:
Hatchback, saloon, estate

Engine capacity:
1.0, 1.4, 1.6, 1.7D, 1.9D, 1.9TD

Price from:
£8,200

Manufactured in:
Germany, Spain

VW Beetle

The Beetle is back, with that unmistakable style that has endeared so many over the years, from the impoverished looking for sensible budget transport to hippies for whom the Beetle was ultimately cool. But the new car is a completely different beast, thoroughly modern beneath the skin and priced well out of reach of the budget buyer. The Golf forms the basis, so there is a front engine with front-wheel-drive and a rear end with a small but quite normal hatchback boot. It drives like a Golf too, with a choice of 2.0-litre or 1.9TDi engines, with more to follow. Comfort is great in the front, but rear seat space is very tight.

Best All-Rounder: Beetle 1.9TDi

Body styles:
Hatchback

Engine capacity:
2.0, 1.9TD

Price from:
£15,800

Manufactured in:
Mexico

VW Bora

For years Volkswagen has built saloon versions of the Golf, with mixed sales success. The Jetta and Vento seemed just too worthy and ordinary to excite much attention, but this time around the latest attempt is aiming for a new buyer. The Bora is being sold as a sporting alternative to German rivals like the BMW 3 Series and Audi A4. The combination of a stiffer body and low-profile tyres means that the suspension isn't as refined as the Golf's but the Bora behaves well over uneven surfaces, and has a keener appetite for corners. There is a familiar but tempting range of engines too, from an eager 1.6 to a thumping 2.3 V5.

Best All-Rounder: Bora 2.3 V5

Body styles:
Saloon

Engine capacity:
1.6, 2.0, 2.3VR5, 1.9TD

Price from:
£14,400

Manufactured in:
Germany

VW Passat

This current design moved the Passat from being a solid but dull family car to a class leader. As ever, there is a feeling that this car is built to last, but the Passat now has a strong style that runs from the swooping curves of the exterior through to the solid interior. Offered as a four-door saloon or five-door estate, there is considerable legroom, and while that roof line cuts into the rear headroom a little, all-round space is still better than most rivals. Petrol engines run from 1.6 to 2.8V6 with the turbo-diesels the real headline attractions. Rounding it all off is excellent steering and handling that makes the Passat as enjoyable as it is competent.

Best All-Rounder: Passat TDi 110

Body styles:
Saloon, estate

Engine capacity:
1.6, 1.8, 2.3VR5, 2.8VR6, 1.9TD, 2.5TD

Price from:
£16,100

Manufactured in:
Germany

VW Sharan

The Sharan is the result of a joint venture with Ford that also results in the similar Galaxy and Seat Alhambra. It is among the most stylish and easy to drive of this type of car, with a good looking, well-thought-out interior, though like many it fails to provide sufficient luggage space with seven seats in use. The Sharan's engine range offers something for everybody, though the 2.0-litre petrol and quite noisy 1.9-litre 90bhp turbo-diesel have to work hard in this big vehicle. Better are the more powerful 110bhp turbo-diesel and the 1.8-litre petrol turbo – lively yet quiet and refined.

Best All-Rounder: Sharan TDi 110

Body styles:
MPV

Engine capacity:
1.8, 2.0, 2.8VR6, 1.9TD

Price from:
£17,600

Manufactured in:
Portugal

VW Beetle

A new Beetle may have arrived but that doesn't mean the end of the original. Still built in Mexico, this model can offer budget motoring that is totally outside the scope of its "replacement". With the new Beetle selling for the same amount as a European-built Golf, the original's cheap price keeps it popular, especially with taxi drivers. These days it has front disc brakes, a fuel-injected version of the famous flat four engine, a catalytic converter and even the option of a full-length electrically-operated fabric soft-top. In all other respects, it's very faithful to the evergreen Beetle of yore.

Best All-Rounder: Beetle 1.6i

Body styles:
Hatchback

Engine capacity:
1.6

Price from:
£na

Manufactured in:
Mexico

VW Gol

Gol means 'goal' in Portuguese and Volkswagen's Brazilian subsidiary has certainly scored with this car, not to be confused with the Golf. It's Brazil's best-selling car (the old model sold over 1.5 million) and a genuine answer to the imported European hatches which are starting to gain a hold in an increasingly open Brazilian economy. Although its styling cues are taken from Wolfsburg, the whole car is Brazilian designed and made. Four fuel-injected engines are offered (1.0, 1.6, 1.8 and 2.0), the top GTi version having no less than 145 bhp. There are three and five-door hatchbacks and an estate version called the Parati.

Best All-Rounder: 2.0 GTi 16V

Body styles:
Hatchback, estate

Engine capacity:
1.0, 1.6, 1.8, 2.0

Price from:
£na

Manufactured in:
Brazil

VW Citi Golf

The original Golf was something of a landmark in automotive history. Small family hatchbacks were not necessarily new, but the Golf somehow moved the whole game on, helped no little by its solid build and the development of the first real hot hatchback, the Golf GTi. And they are still built in South Africa at the rate of over 10,000 units each year. But with the attention now focused on the latest Golf, these Mark 1 models are cheap and cheerful. Engines are tried and tested 1.3 or 1.6 , neither particularly powerful but, like the rest of the car, dependable over big mileages.

Best All-Rounder: City Golf 1.6i

Body styles:
Hatchback, estate, convertible

Engine capacity:
1.4, 1.6, 1.8, 1.8 turbo, 2.0, 2.3VR5, 1.9D, 1.9TD

Price from:
£na

Manufactured in:
Germany

VOLVO

Volvo has reached the point where it needs to prove that it is going in the right direction. The model range has finally been completed with the late arrival of the C70 convertible and, with everything else in place, Volvo now has to sell enough cars to prove to its new owner, Ford, that the correct decisions have been made. In many ways Volvos in the year 2000 are the most enticing yet, combining the traditional strong safety attributes with good driving qualities and no small sense of style. But convincing buyers to move over from prestige German brands will never be an easy task.

Body styles:	Saloon
Engine capacity:	2.4, 2.0, 2.8, 2.9, 2.5TD
Price from:	£22,900
Manufactured in:	Sweden

Volvo S80

Volvo's finest car yet, the S80 is the company's attempt to topple the dominant German brands in the executive car area. With its own distinctive style and an interior that offers considerable room and comfort, there are many reasons why it should do well. But unlike BMW and Mercedes, the Volvo has front wheel drive, which is fine for safety and cornering ability but does not offer the fine precision of its competitors. Engines range from 2.4-litre to a twin-turbo 2.8 six; the 2.9-litre is likely to be a popular choice, producing a refined and willing performance, though the smoothness of the transmission is not perfect. Being the top Volvo it is unsurpassed when it comes to safety equipment.

Best All-Rounder: S80 2.9

Volvo S40/ V40

The S40/V40 range is built in Holland alongside the Mitsubishi Carisma yet Volvo has managed to set it well above its sister in terms of image. There is a range of good-looking saloons and estates, with the usual Volvo emphasis on safety. But there is a performance side to this Volvo too, with the T4 producing 200 bhp. A wide range of alternatives is on offer, including a new but disappointing turbo-diesel from Renault. Inside there is no shortage of space for passengers, but the estate is far from a real load carrier. A huge range of option packs, including sports or standard suspension, gives buyers a lot to think about.

Best All-Rounder: V40 2.0 Turbo

Body styles:
Saloon, estate

Engine capacity:
1.6, 1.8, 1.9 Turbo, 2.0, 2.0 Turbo, 1.9TD

Price from:
£14,500

Manufactured in:
Netherlands

Volvo S70/ V70

Volvo has firmly established the S70 saloon and V70 estate as its charismatic sporting-executive contenders. A facelifted version of the 850, as ever this Volvo is big on safety and refinement and there are plenty of those attributes in every version. There is a new range of 2.4-litre petrol engines plus the faithful, hugely powerful 2.3 T5 and a 2.5 turbo diesel. This car is now the oldest in Volvo's range but apart from the sombre cabin, it still stands up well. These cars are good to drive, with plenty of grip, and the interior is comfortable. Those used to the space of the old 940 will find the passenger and luggage space only average, however.

Best All-Rounder: V70 2.4T

Body styles:
Saloon, estate

Engine capacity:
2.0, 2.4, 2.0 turbo, 2.4 turbo, 2.3 turbo, 2.5TD

Price from:
£19,000

Manufactured in:
Sweden, Belgium

Volvo C70

Volvo has been pretty clever with its C70 coupe and convertible, pitching in with a roomy four-seater for the price of the smaller BMW 3 Series coupe. But despite the 240bhp turbo T5 model, this is not a real sporting car, more an elegant model that offers a strong blend of luxury and style. There is a great deal of comfort to be found in the front and though rear space is not as good as a saloon, it is about as good as it gets in a coupe. Not that the C70 is unenjoyable to drive. There is plenty of power from the two turbo-charged models and the suspension provides exceptional control, at the expense of a firm ride.

Best All-Rounder: C70 2.5T

Body styles:
Coupe, convertible

Engine capacity:
2.0, 2.0 Turbo, 2.4, 2.3 turbo

Price from:
£25,700

Manufactured in:
Sweden

CURIOS

Aro

Romanian 4x4 maker Aro is now tied up with Korean manufacturer Daewoo, and the big news this year is the availability of a 1.6-litre 106bhp Daewoo engine in the rugged Aro 10. The old Renault 12 engines offered since year dot remain available, though, as well as 1.9-litre diesel and turbo-diesel engines. This off-road utility machine is available in a variety of body styles, including soft-top, hard-top and Spartana, which is marketed as a beach/leisure vehicle. The Aro 10 was sold as the Dacia Duster in the UK 15 years ago. It has the same basic feel, dodgy build quality and utter simplicity.

Hindustan Ambassador

Solid, dependable, widespread. Despite the fact that Calcutta-based Hindustan is now making Mitsubishi Lancers under licence, it soldiers on with the Ambassador, otherwise known as the 1954 Morris Oxford. Really the only major changes are under the bonnet, where there's a 73bhp Isuzu 1.8-litre petrol engine or a choice of 1.5 or 2.0-litre diesels. When a company is proud to announce that radial tyres are now standard, you know this is a pure slice of the fifties! Pictured is a special-bodied Ambassador created by an Indian coach-builder called DC Design, which will convert the car for £3,250, with air conditioning, electric windows and leather upholstery extra.

Ligier Ambra

The Ligier name ought to be familiar to most people – it's the same as the Formula 1 team that was recently taken over by Alain Prost. While Ligier used to make sports cars in the 1970s, it's now doing rather well with its range of microcars. Anyone who has driven in France will probably have seen these little devices, which don't require a driving licence to run. The smart Ambra is a two-seater powered by a 505cc diesel engine that does 45mph and returns 85mpg. There is CVT automatic transmission and generous equipment. The Ligier looks set to arrive in Britain at £7000 if Reliant's plans to market it go ahead.

Mahindra

In Bombay they still make what is essentially a war-time Willys Jeep. Naturally its appeal is pretty rustic, which is why attempted marketing in the UK didn't last long. These days it's offered with Peugeot diesel engines. Four different wheelbase lengths are offered, ranging from 231cm to 268cm and there is a wide choice of open or closed bodywork, 2WD or 4WD and three, four and five-speed gearboxes. The base CJ model is painfully stark, noisy and slow, though the big five-door Armada estate is more comfortable. The Mahindra only really shines in road conditions like those in India – full of potholes, if there's a road at all.

Mitsuoka Galue

Having made its mark on Japanese culture with a Nissan Micra altered to look like a Jaguar Mk2, Japanese specialist manufacturer Mitsuoka is back with the Galue, a saloon that tries to look like a Bentley. Under the skin it's a Nissan Crew, a Japan-only saloon that is principally designed for the taxi market. Inside the Galue you have leather and wood trim, but there's no disguising the humble origins of the dials and switchgear. Mitsuoka also makes a Lotus 7 style sports car called the Type F, as well as two microcar designs using the company's very own 50cc engine.

Reliant Robin

In the UK the law allows the Reliant Robin three-wheeler to be driven on a motor cycle licence. That fact, plus its fabulous fuel economy, has been its major appeal, particularly to older motorist who never got around to passing the full car driving test. But today it is difficult to ignore the serious downsides of the Reliant, not least that it costs as much as a decent four-wheeled supermini. The Robin has recently been updated with a smoother glass-fibre reinforced plastic body but it remains a tight fit inside. Power comes from a lively 850cc all-aluminium four cylinder engine – the light weight of the Robin ensures at least that the performance is reasonable.

...a dozen oddball cars from around the World

San Storm / Streak

This Bangalore-based railway company has branched out into car production with a pair of delightfully styled small sports cars. Both were designed in France by Gerard Godfroy, the man behind the Venturi sports car. Part of a very modern specification is the 1149cc engine from the Renault Twingo. Two models are being made: the Storm, a two-door coupe, and a convertible called the Streak. Both have glassfibre bodywork, air conditioning, electric windows and alloy wheels. In Britain, Reliant showed them at the 1998 Motor Show and looks set to offer the 100mph miniature cars through its own franchises in Britain at bargain prices.

Tata Indica

No longer does India have to put up with cast-offs from other manufacturers. Tata's new Indica is as sophisticated as many Western small cars, and it aims to become India's best-selling car. Styled in Italy by IDEA, with a French-designed engine, the Tata is a little five-door hatchback with thoroughly up-to-date all-independent suspension and power steering. Its 1.4-litre engine is offered in petrol and diesel forms, and you get a five-speed transmission. Excellent packaging means this is a very spacious little car, and the interior is well presented and comfortably equipped. An impressive options list includes air conditioning and electric windows.

Tata Safari

Tata is one of India's biggest companies, and the name has become well-known among builders in the UK thanks to its Loadbeta range of budget pick-ups, vans and double-cabs. Now it has its sights set on higher ground with a Land-Rover Discovery style vehicle. It will, however, be priced very much more competitively when it comes to the UK. Shift-on-the-fly transmission switches electronically to 4x4 mode while on the move. Performance is respectable from either turbo-diesel or petrol engines and the suspension is relatively sophisticated, with wishbones up front and a multi-link rear. The attractive body design was created in Britain by IAD.

Dacia

The form of the Renault 12 is instantly recognisable in this Romanian time-warp. The company has recently been acquired by Renault, so the Dacia 1310 is unlikely to last much into the new millennium, as the new French owners will almost certainly produce newer models. The 1310 received a facelift in 1998, with a longer snout and new headlamps, but under the skin it's the 1969 Renault 12, produced in saloon and estate guises. Engines these days are 1.4 and 1.6-litre petrol units. Dacia produces another model called the Nova, which is actually a modified Peugeot 309!

Volga 3111

Economic crisis has decimated the Russian car industry but one of the strong survivors is Volga – Russia's favourite taxi. It now ranks as the second biggest car producer behind Lada, with an annual production of 125,000 cars. This has given it the cash to develop an all-new model, the 3111. Looking surprisingly modern, it's a rear-wheel drive saloon in the Vauxhall Omega class and can be powered by a 2.3-litre four-cylinder, 3.4-litre V8 or 2.1-litre turbo-diesel engine. A four-wheel drive version is also under development. Volga has a reputation for being the toughest car on sale in Russia, which it needs to be to cope with Siberian winters.

Zil 4104

It's lucky that the Muscovite ZIL company doesn't rely on its limousines for commercial success – fridges and trucks support the business – because only six were made in 1998. Relics of an age of Brezhnev, when they even had their own traffic lane, ZILs don't really fit into modern Russian life. The ZIL is also a relic of the past mechanically. It's very much Detroit circa 1976, which means a gargantuan 7.7-litre V8 engine and a live rear axle. You can have a standard model at a mere 5.75 metres long or a Pullman version that measures fully 6.33 metres stem to stern.

TECHNICAL DATA

The table on the next few pages outlines the technical background to cars listed in the Guide. With close to 1400 versions listed, it is the most comprehensive guide you'll find.

By and large we have used the car manufacturers' own figures, so in places where they are unable or unwilling to release the information we have placed a dash. Engine capacity is given in cubic centimetres, power in bhp, although the common metric power unit, PS, gives much the same result. Fuel type is denoted by P for petrol, D for diesel. Engine configuration is a combination of the layout and the number of cylinders – S equates to straight (or in-line), F for flat (or horizontally opposed) V is self explanatory; the number of cylinders follows. The driven wheels are noted, Front, Rear or 4 wheel drive. Top speed and acceleration from rest to 60 mph are the two universally popular measures of a car's performance. Just one fuel consumption figure is given, the combined cycle, as this is arguably the most realistic of the statutory tests. The insurance group is the standardised rating system used in the UK, on a scale of 1 to 20. Groups cannot be given for cars not sold in the UK, or the very latest models which have yet to be rated. Length and width are for the saloon or hatchback version, with two figures given where there is a discrepancy between models. Figures for estate cars are not included, and the weight, in kilograms, is for the lightest version in each range.

Finally, not all the cars listed will be available for sale in the UK. Check the new price tables later on for the definitive list of availability, then cross refer back to this list. Remember that some cars are sold only in a restricted model range in the UK, and different examples are available elsewhere – the data table is as complete as we can make it.

	Engine – CC	Power – bhp	Fuel	Engine config.	Driven wheels	Top speed – mph	0–60 mph – secs	mpg – average	Insurance group	Length – mm	Width – mm	Weight – Kg
AC												
Ace	4601	326	P	V8	R	155	5.7	23	20	4420	1870	1510
	4942	243	P	V8	R	135	6.9	23	20	4420	1870	1510
	4942	326	P	V8	R	155	5.5	23	20	4420	1870	1510
Aceca	4601	326	P	V8	R	155	5.7	23	20	4420	1870	1615
Superblower												
5.0 V8	4942	326	P	V8	R	165	4.2	22	20	4200	1746	1160
5.0 V8 CRS	4942	–	P	V8	R	145	5.3	–	20	4200	1746	–
ALFA ROMEO												
145												
1.4 Twin Spark	1370	103	P	S4	F	115	11.2	35	–	4060	1710	1135
1.6 Twin Spark	1598	120	P	S4	F	121	10.2	35	11	4060	1710	1165
1.8 Twin Spark	1747	144	P	S4	F	128	9.1	34	13	4060	1710	1195
2.0 Cloverleaf	1969	155	P	S4	F	131	8.3	32	14	4060	1710	1240
146												
1.4 Twin Spark	1370	103	P	S4	F	116	11.5	35	–	4235	1710	1160
1.6 Twin Spark	1598	120	P	S4	F	122	10.5	34	11	4235	1710	1190
1.8 Twin Spark	1747	144	P	S4	F	130	9.3	34	13	4235	1710	1215
2.0 ti	1969	155	P	S4	F	134	8.5	34	14	4235	1710	1275
156												
1.6 Twin Spark	1598	120	P	S4	F	124	10.5	34	–	4430	1745	1230
1.8 Twin Spark	1747	144	P	S4	F	130	9.3	34	13	4430	1745	1230
2.0 Twin Spark	1969	155	P	S4	F	134	8.6	33	14	4430	1745	1250
2.5	2492	190	P	V6	F	143	7.3	25	16	4430	1745	1320
1.9 JTD	1910	105	D	S4	F	117	10.5	48	–	4430	1745	1270
2.4 JTD	2387	136	D	S5	F	126	9.5	42	–	4430	1745	1350
166												
2.0 Twin Spark	1969	155	P	S4	F	132	9.6	29	15	4720	1815	1420
2.0 Turbo	1997	205	P	V6	F	147	8.1	24	–	4720	1815	1495
2.5	2492	190	P	V6	F	140	8.4	25	16	4720	1815	1490
3.0	2959	226	P	V6	F	151	7.8	23	17	4720	1815	1510
2.4 JTD	2387	136	D	S5	F	125	9.9	39	–	4720	1815	1490
Spider												
1.8 Twin Spark	1747	144	P	S4	F	128	9.3	32	–	4285	1780	1350
2.0 Twin Spark	1969	155	P	S4	F	131	8.4	31	17	4285	1780	1350
2.0 Turbo	1997	200	P	V6	F	141	7.7	26	–	4285	1780	1430
3.0	2959	192	P	V6	F	140	7.3	26	17	4285	1780	1420
GTV												
1.8 Twin Spark	1747	144	P	S4	F	130	9.2	32	–	4285	1780	1350
2.0 Twin Spark	1969	155	P	S4	F	134	8.4	31	17	4285	1780	1350
2.0 Turbo	1997	200	P	V6	F	146	7.4	26	–	4285	1780	1430
3.0	2959	220	P	V6	F	155	6.7	24	19	4285	1780	1415
ARO												
10												
1.4	1397	63	P	S4	4x4	75	–	28	–	3870	1645	1120
1.6	1557	91	P	S4	4x4	83	–	26	–	3870	1645	1120
1.6 16v	1598	106	P	S4	4x4	87	–	25	–	3835	1645	1120
1.9 D	1870	64	D	S4	4x4	80	–	28	–	3870	1645	1285
1.9 TD	1870	92	D	S4	4x4	97	–	25	–	3835	1645	1285
ASTON MARTIN												
DB7												
3.2	3239	340	P	S6	R	165	5.5	18	20	4645	1830	1725
6.0 V12	5935	420	P	V12	R	185	5.0	15	20	4666	1830	1780
V8 – 5.3 V8	5341	355	P	V8	R	149	5.9	14	20	4745	1945	1950
Vantage												
5.3 V8	5341	557	P	V8	R	186	4.6	13	20	4745	1944	1975
5.3 V8	5341	608	P	V8	R	198	3.9	13	20	4745	1944	1975
AUDI												
A3												
1.6	1595	101	P	S4	F	117	11.0	37	9	4150	1735	1090
1.8	1781	125	P	S4	F	125	9.6	34	11	4150	1735	1160
1.8 Turbo	1781	150	P	S4	F	135	8.2	36	14	4150	1735	1175
1.8 Turbo	1781	150	P	S4	4x4	133	8.2	33	–	4150	1735	1290
1.8 Turbo	1781	180	P	S4	F	141	7.5	36	–	4150	1735	1180
1.8 Turbo	1781	180	P	S4	4x4	140	7.5	32	–	4150	1735	1300
1.8 S3 Turbo	1781	209	P	S4	4x4	148	6.8	31	–	4150	1735	1375
1.9 TD	1896	90	D	S4	F	112	12.4	57	–	4150	1735	1185
1.9 TD	1896	110	D	S4	F	120	10.5	58	11	4150	1735	1190
A4												
1.6	1595	101	P	S4	F	118	12.4	35	10	4480	1735	1200
1.8	1781	125	P	S4	F	127	10.6	33	12	4480	1735	1235
1.8 quattro	1781	125	P	S4	4x4	125	11.0	31	–	4480	1735	1355
1.8 Turbo	1781	150	P	S4	F	137	8.4	35	15	4480	1735	1255
1.8 Turbo quattro	1781	150	P	S4	4x4	136	8.6	33	–	4480	1735	1375
1.8 Turbo quattro	1781	180	P	S4	4x4	144	7.6	32	–	4480	1735	1345
2.4 V6	2393	165	P	V6	F	140	8.4	30	15	4480	1735	1315
2.4 quattro V6	2393	165	P	V6	4x4	139	8.4	28	–	4480	1735	1430
2.8 V6	2771	193	P	V6	F	149	7.4	29	17	4480	1735	1320
2.8 quattro V6	2771	193	P	V6	4x4	148	7.3	27	17	4480	1735	1440
2.7 Turbo S4 V6	2671	265	P	V6	4x4	155	5.6	25	20	4485	1735	1510
1.9 TD	1896	90	D	S4	F	113	13.5	52	10	4480	1735	1265
1.9 TD 110	1896	110	D	S4	F	123	11.3	54	11	4480	1735	1275
1.9 TD 110 quattro	1896	110	D	S4	4x4	119	12.0	48	–	4480	1735	1395
2.5 TD V6	2496	150	D	V6	F	136	9.0	42	14	4480	1735	1385
2.5 TD quattro V6	2496	150	D	V6	4x4	134	9.4	37	15	4480	1735	1495
A6												
1.8	1781	125	P	S4	F	126	11.3	33	–	4795	1810	1320
1.8 Turbo	1781	150	P	S4	F	135	9.5	34	14	4795	1810	1390

Model	Engine – CC	Power – bhp	Fuel	Engine config.	Driven wheels	Top speed – mph	0–60 mph – secs	mpg – average	Insurance group	Length – mm	Width – mm	Weight – Kg
1.8 Turbo quattro	1781	150	P	S4	4x4	134	9.6	31	–	4795	1810	1540
2.4 V6	2393	165	P	V6	F	138	9.2	29	15	4795	1810	1430
2.4 quattro V6	2393	165	P	V6	4x4	136	9.3	26	–	4795	1810	1535
2.7 V6	2671	230	P	V6	F	153	7.5	27	–	4795	1810	1520
2.7 quattro V6	2671	230	P	V6	4x4	152	7.1	24	18	4795	1810	1610
2.8 V6	2771	193	P	V6	F	146	8.1	29	17	4795	1810	1430
2.8 quattro V6	2771	193	P	V6	4x4	143	8.0	26	17	4795	1810	1615
4.2 quattro V8	4172	300	P	V8	4x4	155	6.9	22	19	4795	1810	1730
4.2 quattro V8 S6	4172	340	P	V8	4x4	155	6.7	–	–	4795	1810	1730
1.9 TD 110	1896	110	D	S4	F	120	12.6	50	13	4795	1810	1415
2.5 TD V6	2496	150	D	V6	F	135	9.7	41	14	4795	1810	1520
2.5 TD quattro V6	2496	150	D	V6	4x4	134	9.9	36	14	4795	1810	1680
A8												
2.8 V6	2771	193	P	V6	F	146	8.4	26	18	5035	1880	1510
2.8 quattro V6	2771	193	P	V6	4x4	146	8.5	25	–	5035	1880	1580
3.7 V8	3697	260	P	V8	F	155	8.1	25	–	5035	1880	1645
3.7 quattro V8	3697	260	P	V8	4x4	155	8.6	23	19	5035	1880	1725
4.2 quattro V8	4172	310	P	V8	4x4	155	6.9	22	20	5035	1880	1750
2.5 TD V6	2496	150	D	V6	F	136	9.9	39	–	5035	1880	1595
2.5 TD quattro V6	2496	150	D	V6	4x4	132	11.1	32	–	5035	1880	1705
TT												
1.8 T	1781	180	P	S4	F	141	7.4	35	18	4040	1765	1205
1.8 T quattro	1781	180	P	S4	4x4	140	7.4	32	18	4040	1765	1320
1.8 T quattro	1781	225	P	S4	4x4	151	6.4	31	18	4040	1765	1395
1.8 T quattro Roadster	1781	180	P	S4	4x4	139	–	–	18	4040	1765	1310
1.8 T quattro Roadster	1781	225	P	S4	4x4	147	–	–	18	4040	1765	1310
Cabriolet												
1.8	1781	125	P	S4	F	121	11.5	31	16	4365	1715	1370
2.6 V6	2598	150	P	V6	F	130	10.2	27	17	4365	1715	1430
2.8 V6	2771	174	P	V6	F	135	9.8	26	17	4365	1715	1430
1.9 TD	1896	90	D	S4	F	109	14.7	47	–	4365	1715	1390
BENTLEY												
Arnage V8	4398	354	P	V8	R	149	6.5	17	20	5390	1930	2300
Continental R V8	6750	389	P	V8	R	154	6.3	16	20	5340	1880	2450
Continental SC V8	6750	408	P	V8	R	154	6.4	16	20	5240	1920	2610
Continental T V8	6750	426	P	V8	R	169	5.9	15	20	5220	1920	2450
Azure V8	6750	389	P	V8	R	149	6.7	16	20	5340	1880	2610
BMW												
3-Series												
316i	1596	102	P	S4	R	118	13.2	35	11	4430	1710	1280
316ti	1895	105	P	S4	R	118	11.9	37	11	4210	1700	1175
318i	1796	116	P	S4	R	122	11.7	35	11	4430	1710	1280
318ti	1895	140	P	S4	R	130	9.9	36	12	4210	1700	1200
320i	1991	150	P	S6	R	131	10.2	31	–	4430	1710	1345
323i	2494	170	P	S6	R	138	8.3	31	15	4430	1710	1365
328i	2793	193	P	S6	R	143	7.4	31	16	4430	1710	1365
M3	3201	321	P	S6	R	155	5.5	26	20	4430	1710	1325
318tds	1665	90	D	S4	R	111	14.5	44	12	4430	1710	1215
325tds	2497	143	D	S6	R	128	10.5	38	14	4430	1710	1410
New 3-Series												
316i	1895	105	P	S4	R	124	12.4	37	11	4470	1740	1285
318i	1895	118	P	S4	R	128	10.4	36	12	4470	1740	1285
320i	1991	150	P	S6	R	136	9.9	32	–	4470	1740	1365
323i	2494	170	P	S6	R	143	8.0	31	15	4470	1740	1370
328i	2793	193	P	S6	R	149	7.0	31	16	4470	1740	1395
320d	1951	136	D	S4	R	128	9.9	50	–	4470	1740	1375
5-Series												
520i	1991	150	P	S6	R	136	10.2	32	14	4775	1800	1470
523i	2494	170	P	S6	R	141	8.5	30	15	4775	1800	1475
528i	2793	193	P	S6	R	149	7.5	30	16	4775	1800	1440
535i V8	3498	235	P	V8	R	155	6.9	25	17	4775	1800	1610
540i V8	4398	286	P	V8	R	155	6.2	23	18	4775	1800	1630
M5 V8	4941	400	P	V8	R	155	5.3	20	–	4775	1800	1720
525td	2497	115	D	S6	R	123	11.9	36	–	4775	1800	1510
525tds	2497	143	D	S6	R	131	10.4	35	–	4775	1800	1510
530d	2926	184	D	S6	R	140	8.0	39	15	4775	1800	1575
7-Series												
728i	2793	193	P	S6	R	141	8.7	28	17	4985	1860	1710
735i V8	3498	235	P	V8	R	151	8.2	23	18	4985	1860	1810
740i V8	4398	286	P	V8	R	155	7.0	23	19	4985	1860	1850
750i V12	5379	326	P	V12	R	155	6.8	21	20	4985	1860	1980
725tds	2497	143	D	S6	R	128	11.5	35	–	4985	1860	1745
730d	2926	184	D	S6	R	136	9.2	32	–	4985	1860	1830
8-Series												
840Ci	4398	286	P	V8	R	155	6.6	22	20	4780	1855	1780
850Ci	5379	326	P	V12	R	155	6.3	20	–	4780	1855	1880
Z3												
1.8	1895	118	P	S4	R	120	10.4	36	–	4025	1690	1220
1.9	1895	140	P	S4	R	127	9.5	35	14	4025	1690	1200
2.0	1991	150	P	S6	R	130	9.0	32	–	4025	1690	1250
2.5	2494	170	P	S6	R	133	7.5	31	–	4025	1740	1285
2.8	2793	193	P	S6	R	140	6.9	30	16	4025	1740	1285
M	3201	321	P	S6	R	155	5.4	26	19	4025	1740	1350
X5												
2.8	2800	–	P	S6	4x4	–	–	–	–	4660	1720	–
3.2	3200	–	P	S6	4x4	–	–	–	–	4660	1720	–
3.5 V8	3500	–	P	V8	4x4	–	–	–	–	4660	1720	–
4.4 V8	4400	–	P	V8	4x4	–	–	–	–	4660	1720	–
2.9 TD	2900	–	P	S6	4x4	–	–	–	–	4660	1720	–

Model	Engine – CC	Power – bhp	Fuel	Engine config.	Driven wheels	Top speed – mph	0–60 mph – secs	mpg – average	Insurance group	Length – mm	Width – mm	Weight – Kg
BRISTOL Blenheim	5898	265	P	V8	R	156	6.6	22	20	4825	1765	1740
BUICK												
Century 3.1 V6	3100	175	P	V6	F	121	–	29	–	4940	1850	1520
Regal												
3.8 V6 S'charged	3791	203	P	V6	F	121	–	30	–	4980	1840	1560
3.8 V6 S'charged	3791	243	P	V6	F	136	–	28	–	4980	1840	1605
Le Sabre – 3.8 V6	3791	205	P	V6	F	124	–	30	–	5080	1865	1620
Park Avenue												
3.8 V6	3791	205	P	V6	F	121	–	28	–	5250	1900	1715
3.8 V6 S'charged	3791	243	P	V6	F	136	–	27	–	5250	1900	1760
Riviera 3.8 V6 S'charged	3791	243	P	V6	F	143	–	27	–	5260	1910	1685
CADILLAC												
Catera	2962	203	P	V6	R	124	8.5	26	–	4930	1790	1710
Seville												
4.6	4565	279	P	V8	F	127	7.8	21	–	4995	1900	1800
4.6 STS	4565	305	P	V8	F	149	7.8	20	19	4995	1900	1815
Escalade	5733	258	P	V8	4x4	110	10.5	18	–	5110	1955	2530
Eldorado												
4.6	4565	279	P	V8	F	112	7.4	26	–	5095	1920	1745
4.6	4565	305	P	V8	F	148	7.5	26	–	5095	1920	1760
Deville												
4.6	4565	279	P	V8	F	112	7.1	26	–	5330	1940	1820
4.6	4565	305	P	V8	F	130	7.0	26	–	5330	1940	1845
CATERHAM												
Seven												
1.6	1588	117	P	S4	R	112	6.4	36	–	3130	1580	540
1.6 Supersport	1588	133	P	S4	R	120	5.7	–	–	3130	1580	540
1.6 Superlight	1588	133	P	S4	R	129	4.6	–	–	3130	1580	460
1.8	1795	124	P	S4	R	118	6.0	32	–	3130	1580	540
1.8 Supersport	1795	140	P	S4	R	122	5.3	–	–	3130	1580	540
1.8 Superlight R	1796	190	P	S4	R	142	4.0	30	–	3130	1580	470
C21												
1.6	1588	117	P	S4	R	118	6.4	32	–	3800	1580	650
1.6 Supersport	1588	133	P	S4	R	124	6.0	–	–	3800	1580	650
1.8	1795	124	P	S4	R	124	6.3	34	–	3800	1580	650
1.8 VVC	1795	153	P	S4	R	130	5.3	–	–	3800	1580	650
1.8	1795	190	P	S4	R	136	5.0	26	–	3800	1580	650
CHEVROLET												
Camaro												
3.8	3791	203	P	V6	R	125	8.5	24	13	4910	1880	1500
5.7	5665	288	P	V8	R	158	5.5	22	18	4910	1880	1570
Corvette												
5.7	5665	345	P	V8	R	174	4.7	22	20	4565	1870	1470
Malibu												
2.4	2392	152	P	S4	F	112	9.5	34	–	4840	1760	1385
3.1 V6	3135	152	P	V6	R	112	9.0	28	–	4840	1760	1395
Impala												
3.4 V6	3350	182	P	V6	F	112	10.0	25	–	5080	1855	1540
3.8 V6	3791	203	P	V6	R	124	8.5	25	–	5080	1855	1560
Blazer												
4.3V6	4300	193	P	V6	R	112	10.1	21	–	4650	1830	1665
CHRYSLER												
Neon												
1.8	1796	122	P	S4	F	118	9.0	32	–	4390	1710	1200
2.0	1996	133	P	S4	R	124	9.5	31	–	4390	1710	1200
LHS – 3.5	3518	257	P	V6	F	130	9.0	27	–	5275	1890	1625
Stratus – 2.0	1996	133	P	S4	F	127	10.9	31	–	4750	1820	1350
Concorde												
2.7V6	2736	203	P	V6	F	124	10.5	26	–	5310	1900	1570
3.2V6	3231	228	P	V6	F	130	9.5	26	–	5310	1900	1570
300M												
2.7	2736	203	P	V6	F	130	10.5	28	–	5000	1920	1610
3.5	3518	254	P	V6	F	143	8.8	27	–	5000	1920	1660
Sebring												
2.0	1996	141	P	S4	F	124	11.0	29	–	4850	1770	1335
2.5	2497	166	P	V6	R	130	10.5	26	–	4850	1770	1450
Viper – 8.0	7990	455	P	V10	R	185	4.6	14	20	4490	1924	1590
Voyager												
2.0	1996	133	P	S4	R	109	12.6	29	12	4730	1950	1705
2.4	2429	150	P	S4	R	112	12.0	27	–	5070	1950	1720
3.3	3301	158	P	V6	R	109	11.7	23	14	5070	1950	1775
3.8	3778	178	P	V6	R	112	12.0	21	–	5070	1950	1940
2.5 TD	2500	116	D	S4	R	109	12.6	25	13	5070	1950	1810
Jeep Wrangler												
2.5	2464	122	P	S4	4x4	88	14.8	24	12	3860	1680	1405
4.0	3964	184	P	S6	4x4	108	9.4	22	14	3860	1680	1465
Jeep Cherokee												
2.5	2464	127	P	S4	4x4	102	13.0	25	13	4250	1790	1350
4.0	3964	193	P	S6	4x4	112	10.1	21	14	4250	1790	1430
2.5 TD	2500	116	D	S4	4x4	100	12.3	30	13	4250	1790	1470
Jeep Grand Cherokee												
4.0	3956	198	P	S6	4x4	112	10.0	19	16	4610	1840	1695
4.7	4701	220	P	V8	4x4	124	9.0	19	17	4610	1840	1800
3.1 TD	3124	140	D	S5	4x4	99	12.0	30	–	4610	1840	1900
CITROEN												
Saxo												
1.0	954	50	P	S4	F	92	19.1	46	–	3720	1595	805

Model	Engine – CC	Power – bhp	Fuel	Engine config.	Driven wheels	Top speed – mph	0–60 mph – secs	mpg – average	Insurance group	Length – mm	Width – mm	Weight – Kg
1.1	1124	60	P	S4	F	100	15.3	44	4	3720	1595	805
1.4	1361	75	P	S4	F	109	12.9	44	5	3720	1595	840
1.6 8v	1587	88	P	S4	F	116	11.4	39	7	3740	1620	920
1.6 16v	1587	118	P	S4	F	127	8.7	35	14	3740	1620	935
1.5 D	1527	57	D	S4	F	98	18.3	40	4	3720	1595	890
Xsara												
1.4	1361	75	P	S4	F	109	14.1	41	6	4170	1700	1020
1.6	1587	88	P	S4	F	113	13.1	39	7	4170	1700	1070
1.8 8v	1762	90	P	S4	F	113	13.1	36	–	4170	1700	1070
1.8 8v (auto only)	1762	101	P	S4	F	110	15.4	31	–	4170	1700	1100
1.8 16v	1762	110	P	S4	F	121	10.7	34	9	4170	1700	1100
2.0	1998	132	P	S4	F	127	9.9	32	–	4170	1700	1155
2.0	1998	163	P	S4	F	136	8.7	30	16	4170	1700	1190
1.9 Diesel	1868	71	D	S4	F	100	17.2	46	7	4170	1700	1100
2.0 HDi	1997	90	D	S4	F	112	11.4	54	7	4170	1700	1140
Xantia												
1.8 8v	1762	90	P	S4	F	112	14.5	34	–	4525	1755	1245
1.8 16v	1762	110	P	S4	F	120	11.9	34	12	4525	1755	1265
2.0 16v	1998	132	P	S4	F	126	11.0	31	13	4525	1755	1320
2.0 Turbo	1998	147	P	S4	F	132	10.4	29	15	4525	1755	1375
2.9	2946	190	P	V6	F	143	8.2	26	16	4525	1755	1470
1.9 TD	1905	75	D	S4	F	100	17.6	41	–	4525	1755	1300
2.0 HDi	1997	90	D	S4	F	111	12.7	50	13	4525	1755	1310
2.0 HDI	1997	109	D	S4	F	118	12.5	51	13	4525	1755	1435
XM												
2.0	1998	132	P	S4	F	127	10.8	29	14	4710	1795	1415
2.0 Turbo	1998	147	P	S4	F	133	9.3	27	15	4710	1795	1460
2.9 V6	2946	190	P	V6	F	144	8.4	24	15	4710	1795	1550
2.1 TD	2088	109	D	S4	F	119	12.9	40	14	4710	1795	1465
2.5 TD	2446	129	D	S4	F	125	12.1	37	14	4710	1795	1580
Berlingo Multispace												
1.1	1124	60	P	S4	F	87	21.6	38	–	4110	1720	995
1.4	1361	75	P	S4	F	93	14.6	40	–	4110	1720	1125
1.8	1762	90	P	S4	F	99	12.2	31	5	4110	1720	1170
1.9 Diesel	1769	58	P	S4	F	84	27.4	42	–	4110	1720	1150
1.9 Diesel	1769	68	P	S4	F	88	16.3	43	–	4110	1720	1185
1.9 Diesel	1769	71	P	S4	4x4	82	–	–	–	4110	1720	1175
Picasso												
1.6	1587	88	P	S4	F	105	15.0	32	–	4275	1750	1250
1.8	1762	115	P	S4	F	112	12.5	32	–	4275	1750	1280
2.0 TD	1998	109	P	S4	F	112	12.5	46	–	4275	1750	1300
Synergie												
1.8	1762	99	P	S4	F	102	16.2	27	–	4455	1820	1445
2.0	1998	121	P	S4	F	110	15.1	28	10	4455	1820	1510
2.0 Turbo	1998	147	P	S4	F	121	11.0	25	–	4455	1820	1575
1.9 TD	1905	90	D	S4	F	99	16.8	35	10	4455	1820	1585
2.1 TD	2088	109	D	S4	F	109	14.1	34	–	4455	1820	1615
DACIA												
1310												
1.4	1397	63	P	S4	F	88	–	35	–	4365	1635	940
1.6	1557	72	P	S4	F	93	–	33	–	4365	1635	940
DAEWOO												
Matiz												
0.8	796	52	P	S3	F	89	17.0	44	2	3595	1495	725
Tico												
0.8	796	41	P	S3	F	89	17.5	47	–	3340	1400	620
Lanos												
1.4	1349	75	P	S4	F	105	15.0	36	4	4075	1680	1005
1.5	1498	86	P	S4	F	106	12.5	33	–	4075	1680	1025
1.6	1598	106	P	S4	F	112	11.5	34	6	4075	1680	1090
Nubira												
1.5	1500	106	P	S4	F	115	11.0	32	–	4495	1700	1080
1.6	1598	105	P	S4	F	115	11.0	36	7	4495	1700	1080
1.8	1800	133	P	S4	F	121	9.0	30	–	4495	1700	1230
2.0	1998	133	P	S4	F	121	9.0	33	11	4495	1700	1230
Leganza												
1.8 8v	1796	95	P	S4	F	112	13.5	28	–	4670	1780	1220
2.0 8v	1998	116	P	S4	F	116	12.2	30	–	4670	1780	1220
2.0 16v	1998	136	P	S4	F	128	10.2	31	11	4670	1780	1370
2.2 16v	2198	133	P	S4	F	124	10.0	30	–	4670	1780	1400
Korando												
2.0	1995	128	P	S4	4x4	91	–	22	–	4260	1840	1755
2.3	2295	140	P	S4	4x4	102	12.5	22	14	4260	1840	1755
3.2	3199	209	P	S6	4x4	115	10.9	20	–	4260	1840	1830
2.3 D	2299	77	D	S4	4x4	78	25.0	30	–	4260	1840	1750
2.9 D	2874	98	D	S5	4x4	87	19.0	29	–	4260	1840	1750
2.9 TD	2874	129	D	S5	4x4	93	19.8	29	12	4260	1840	1830
Musso												
2.3	2295	140	P	S4	4x4	110	12.0	23	14	4660	1860	1890
3.2	3199	220	P	S6	4x4	118	10.2	19	–	4660	1860	1935
2.3 D	2299	77	D	S4	4x4	84	25.0	30	–	4660	1860	1795
2.9 D	2874	98	D	S5	4x4	90	19.0	29	–	4660	1860	1850
2.9 TD	2874	120	D	S5	4x4	99	16.0	31	13	4660	1860	1850
DAIHATSU												
Move – 0.8	847	42	P	S3	F	82	17.6	47	2	3310	1395	745
Cuore												
0.7	659	45	P	S3	F	84	–	55	–	3410	1475	690
1.0	989	56	P	S3	F	87	12.8	57	3	3410	1475	720
Sirion												
1.0	989	56	P	S3	F	90	16.0	44	5	3675	1595	810
0.7 Turbo	713	120	P	S4	4x4	112	–	43	–	3675	1595	840
Charade												
1.3	1296	84	P	S4	F	107	11.0	42	6	3780	1620	830
1.5	1499	90	P	S4	F	105	10.8	38	7	3780	1620	840
1.6	1590	105	P	S4	F	115	9.6	38	–	3780	1620	875
Grand Move												
1.5	1499	90	P	S4	F	102	13.3	37	8	4050	1640	1010
1.6	1590	91	P	S4	F	99	14.4	34	–	4050	1640	1040
Hijet – 1.3	1296	64	P	S4	F	80	–	38	7	3370	1395	–
Terios – 1.3	1296	83	P	S4	4x4	90	15.2	32	7	3845	1555	1045
Feroza – 1.6	1590	95	P	S4	4x4	93	13.3	28	–	3770	1590	1255
Fourtrak												
2.2	2237	91	P	S4	4x4	81	–	25	–	3840	1690	1380
2.8 D	2765	73	D	S4	4x4	81	18.1	30	–	3840	1690	1620
2.8 TD	2765	98	D	S4	4x4	86	18.1	30	8	3840	1690	1620
FERRARI												
355 Spider	3495	381	P	V8	R	183	4.6	18	20	4250	1900	1450
360M	3586	405	P	V8	R	183	4.5	16	20	4475	1920	1390
550M	5474	485	P	V12	R	198	4.4	12	20	4550	1935	1690
456M GT	5474	442	P	V12	R	186	5.2	15	20	4730	1920	1790
FIAT												
Seicento												
0.9	899	39	P	S4	F	87	18.0	45	1	3320	1510	705
1.1	1108	54	P	S4	F	93	13.8	49	3	3320	1510	710
Palio												
1.0	994	61	P	S4	F	94	16.3	43	–	3740	1610	890
1.2	1241	73	P	S4	F	103	13.2	41	–	3740	1610	1025
1.4	1372	69	P	S4	F	101	12.9	42	–	3740	1610	925
1.5	1497	76	P	S4	F	102	12.8	42	–	3740	1610	925
1.6	1581	106	P	S4	F	117	9.5	37	–	3740	1610	960
1.7 TD	1698	69	D	S4	F	102	14.9	44	–	3740	1610	1110
Punto												
1.1	1108	54	P	S4	F	93	16.5	44	–	3760	1625	840
1.2	1242	60	P	S4	F	99	14.5	42	3	3760	1625	865
1.2	1242	73	P	S4	F	105	12.0	40	–	3760	1625	880
1.2	1242	86	P	S4	F	110	10.9	41	6	3760	1625	900
1.4 GT	1372	131	P	S4	F	124	7.9	34	14	3760	1625	1000
1.7 TD 60	1698	63	D	S4	F	96	16.8	43	4	3760	1625	1010
1.7 TD 70	1698	69	D	S4	F	101	14.8	46	5	3760	1625	1035
Bravo												
1.2	1242	82	P	S4	F	107	12.5	42	6	4025	1755	985
1.4	1369	80	P	S4	F	105	13.8	42	–	4025	1755	985
1.6	1581	103	P	S4	F	114	11.0	37	8	4025	1755	1025
1.8	1747	113	P	S4	F	120	10.0	34	10	4025	1755	1100
2.0	1998	155	P	S5	F	132	8.0	30	16	4025	1755	1165
1.9 Diesel	1929	65	D	S4	F	96	17.3	42	–	4025	1755	1100
1.9 TD 75	1910	75	D	S4	F	102	15.1	45	6	4025	1755	1120
1.9 TD 100	1910	101	D	S4	F	113	11.8	44	8	4025	1755	1155
1.9 TD 105	1910	105	D	S4	F	116	10.4	52	10	4025	1755	1145
Brava												
1.2	1242	82	P	S4	F	107	13.0	41	6	4190	1755	1015
1.4	1369	80	P	S4	F	105	13.9	42	–	4190	1755	1015
1.6	1581	103	P	S4	F	112	11.5	36	9	4190	1755	1065
1.8	1747	113	P	S4	F	118	10.3	34	11	4190	1755	1130
1.9 Diesel	1929	65	D	S4	F	96	17.8	42	–	4190	1755	1130
1.9 TD	1910	75	D	S4	F	102	15.5	44	6	4190	1755	1145
1.9 TD 100	1910	101	D	S4	F	112	11.0	44	8	4190	1755	1180
1.9 TD 105	1910	105	D	S4	F	115	10.6	51	10	4025	1755	1170
Marea												
1.4	1369	80	P	S4	F	107	13.7	36	–	4390	1740	1085
1.6	1581	103	P	S4	F	116	10.7	34	10	4390	1740	1140
1.8	1747	113	P	S4	F	121	10.0	35	11	4390	1740	1195
2.0	1998	155	P	S5	F	130	8.6	29	14	4390	1740	1255
2.0 Turbo	1998	182	P	S5	F	141	7.4	31	–	4390	1740	1310
1.9 TD 75	1910	75	D	S4	F	104	15.2	43	8	4390	1740	1185
1.9 TD 105	1910	105	D	S4	F	115	10.8	50	10	4390	1740	1215
2.4 TD	2387	130	D	S5	F	122	10.0	42	12	4390	1740	1280
barchetta – 1.8	1747	131	P	S4	F	124	8.9	34	16	3915	1640	1060
Coupe												
1.8	1747	131	P	S4	F	127	9.2	32	–	4250	1770	1180
2.0	1998	155	P	S5	F	133	8.4	29	17	4250	1770	1270
2.0 Turbo	1998	220	P	S5	F	155	6.5	28	19	4250	1770	1310
Multipla												
1.6	1581	103	P	S4	F	105	12.6	33	–	3995	1870	1300
1.9 TD	1910	105	P	S4	F	105	12.4	44	–	3995	1870	1370
Ulysse												
1.8	1762	99	P	S4	F	102	14.3	27	–	4455	1830	1445
2.0	1998	121	P	S4	F	110	13.1	28	10	4455	1830	1510
2.0 Turbo	1998	147	P	S4	F	121	10.1	26	–	4455	1830	1575
1.9 TD	1905	92	D	S4	F	99	15.1	35	10	4455	1830	1565
2.1 TD	2088	109	D	S4	F	109	13.3	34	–	4455	1830	1615
FORD												
Ka												
1.3	1299	60	P	S4	F	96	15.4	42	2	3620	1640	890
1.3	1299	50	P	S4	F	91	17.7	48	–	3620	1640	870

	Engine – CC	Power – bhp	Fuel	Engine config.	Driven wheels	Top speed – mph	0–60 mph – secs	mpg – average	Insurance group	Length – mm	Width – mm	Weight – Kg
Fiesta												
1.3	1299	50	P	S4	F	89	19.5	41	–	3830	1635	930
1.3	1299	60	P	S4	F	96	15.5	42	4	3830	1635	930
1.25 16v	1242	75	P	S4	F	109	12.2	40	5	3830	1635	940
1.4 16v	1388	90	P	S4	F	113	10.8	38	7	3830	1635	945
1.8 Diesel	1753	60	D	S4	F	98	17.6	47	5	3830	1635	1015
Escort												
1.3	1299	60	P	S4	F	95	16.8	46	–	4140	1700	1005
1.4	1391	75	P	S4	F	105	14.4	33	–	4140	1700	1050
1.6	1597	90	P	S4	F	110	12.2	35	7	4140	1700	1080
1.8	1796	116	P	S4	F	122	9.9	35	–	4140	1700	1080
1.8 Diesel	1753	60	D	S4	F	101	15.8	43	–	4140	1700	1125
1.8 TD	1753	90	D	S4	F	107	11.6	44	7	4140	1700	1130
Focus												
1.4	1398	75	P	S4	F	106	14.1	44	4	4150	1700	1070
1.6	1596	101	P	S4	F	115	10.9	42	5	4150	1700	1070
1.8	1796	116	P	S4	F	123	10.2	37	6	4150	1700	1125
2.0	1988	131	P	S4	F	125	9.2	32	8	4150	1700	1145
1.8 TD	1753	91	D	S4	F	114	12.4	58	5	4150	1700	1185
Mondeo												
1.6i	1597	95	P	S4	F	115	12.7	37	7	4560	1750	1240
1.8i	1796	116	P	S4	F	121	10.9	37	9	4560	1750	1240
2.0i	1988	131	P	S4	F	128	9.9	35	11	4560	1750	1245
2.5i	2544	170	P	V6	F	139	8.3	30	15	4560	1750	1335
2.5i ST 200	2544	200	P	V6	F	146	8.3	30	17	4560	1750	1335
1.8 TD	1753	90	D	S4	F	112	13.2	44	7	4560	1750	1285
Puma												
1.4	1388	90	P	S4	F	112	11.9	39	9	3895	1670	1035
1.7	1679	125	P	S4	F	126	9.2	38	12	3895	1670	1040
Cougar												
2.0	1988	131	P	S4	F	130	9.6	35	11	4700	1770	1315
2.5	2544	170	P	V6	F	140	8.1	30	14	4700	1770	1390
Galaxy												
2.0	1998	116	P	S4	F	110	13.1	28	–	4620	1810	1650
2.3	2295	145	P	S4	F	120	10.7	28	12	4620	1810	1650
2.8	2792	174	P	V6	F	123	10.5	25	15	4620	1810	1690
2.8	2792	174	P	V6	4x4	120	11.6	22	15	4620	1810	1810
1.9 TD	1896	90	D	S4	F	99	17.1	42	11	4620	1810	1645
1.9 TD 110	1896	110	D	S4	F	107	10.8	43	12	4620	1810	1645
Explorer												
4.0	3996	162	P	V6	4x4	105	12.7	21	–	4815	1875	1670
4.0	3996	213	P	V6	4x4	106	10.9	21	16	4815	1875	1670
FORD US												
Escort – 2.0	1988	111	P	S4	F	115	–	40	–	4440	1700	1120
Contour												
2.0	1988	126	P	S4	F	121	–	36	–	4690	1760	1275
2.5 V6	2544	173	P	V6	F	136	8.6	30	–	4690	1760	1375
2.5 V6	2544	203	P	V6	F	143	7.9	30	–	4690	1760	1390
Taurus												
3.0 V6	2986	147	P	V6	F	112	–	27	–	5020	1850	1495
3.0-24v V6	2967	203	P	V6	F	130	–	30	–	5020	1850	1515
3.4-32v V8	3392	238	P	V8	F	140	–	26	–	5020	1850	1560
Crown Victoria												
4.6 V8	4601	203	P	V8	R	124	–	25	–	5380	1980	1715
Mustang												
3.8 V6	3813	193	P	V6	R	112	–	30	–	4655	1855	1390
4.6 V8	4601	264	P	V8	R	133	–	27	–	4655	1855	1490
Windstar												
3.0 V6	2979	152	P	V6	F	112	13.5	24	–	5125	1915	1710
3.8 V6	3797	203	P	V6	F	109	–	25	–	5125	1915	1690
Expedition												
4.6 V8	4601	243	P	V8	4x4	105	11.0	21	–	5195	2000	2200
5.4 V8	5403	264	P	V8	4x4	112	10.0	19	–	5195	2000	2200
FORD Australia												
Falcon												
4.0	3987	213	P	S6	R	130	8.0	23	–	4910	1870	1515
4.0 XR6	3987	223	P	S6	R	136	7.5	23	–	4910	1870	1515
4.0 Fairmont	3987	228	P	S6	R	136	7.5	23	–	4910	1870	1515
4.0 VCT	3987	234	P	S6	R	–	–	–	–	4910	1870	1515
4.9	4942	238	P	V8	R	136	–	23	–	4900	1860	1515
4.9	4942	252	P	V8	R	136	–	23	–	4900	1860	1515
FSO												
Caro												
1.5	1481	75	P	S4	R	92	18.8	35	–	4320	1650	1190
1.9 D	1905	69	D	S4	R	87	21.8	42	–	4320	1650	1210
HINDUSTAN												
Ambassador												
1.8	1818	73	P	S4	R	87	–	26	–	4325	1660	1105
1.5 Diesel	1488	37	D	S4	R	68	–	31	–	4325	1660	1200
2.0 Diesel	1995	56	D	S4	R	81	–	30	–	4325	1660	1200
HOLDEN												
Statesman/Caprice												
3.8	3791	197	P	V6	R	–	–	24	–	5237	1847	1678
3.8	3791	229	P	V6	R	–	–	20	–	5237	1847	1718
5.7	4981	295	P	V8	R	–	–	21	–	5237	1847	1735
Commodore/Calais												
3.8	3791	197	P	V6	R	–	9.0	27	–	4884	1842	1512
3.8	3791	229	P	V6	R	–	8.5	21	–	4884	1842	1586
5.7 SS	4981	295	P	V8	R	–	6.5	22	–	4884	1842	1576
HONDA												
Logo – 1.3	1343	65	P	S4	F	99	14.5	45	–	3785	1645	940
Civic												
1.3	1343	91	P	S4	F	117	10.2	42	–	4190	1695	1075
1.4	1396	75	P	S4	F	102	14.6	42	–	4190	1695	1040
1.4	1396	90	P	S4	F	110	10.8	40	7	4190	1695	1040
1.5	1493	114	P	S4	F	117	10.2	42	8	4190	1695	1075
1.6	1590	116	P	S4	F	105	10.7	43	9	4190	1695	1105
1.6	1590	126	P	S4	F	118	11.8	38	–	4190	1695	1105
1.6 VTi	1595	160	P	S4	F	128	8.0	33	15	4190	1695	1165
1.8 VTi	1797	169	P	S4	F	138	8.3	32	15	4190	1695	1190
2.0 TD	1994	86	D	S4	F	105	14.4	50	–	4190	1695	1225
Accord												
1.6	1590	116	P	S4	F	118	12.2	34	–	4595	1750	1330
1.8	1850	136	P	S4	F	127	10.4	33	8	4595	1750	1405
2.0	1997	147	P	S4	F	130	9.9	33	10	4595	1750	1405
2.2 Type R	2157	212	P	S4	F	141	7.2	29	16	4595	1750	1405
3.0 V6	2997	200	P	V6	F	140	8.5	26	17	4595	1750	1470
2.0 TD	1994	105	P	S4	F	105	–	46	–	4595	1750	1405
Legend – 3.5	3474	205	P	V6	F	139	9.1	23	17	4995	1820	1625
Integra												
1.8	1834	142	P	S4	F	124	–	33	–	4525	1710	1190
1.8 Type-R	1797	190	P	S4	F	144	6.7	32	18	4400	1695	1120
Prelude												
2.0	1997	133	P	S4	F	125	9.2	31	15	4545	1750	1240
2.2	2157	185	P	S4	F	141	7.5	28	18	4545	1750	1319
S 2000 – 2.0	1997	240	P	S4	R	150	6.2	29	19	4135	1750	1260
NSX												
3.0	2977	256	P	V6	R	161	6.5	24	20	4430	1810	1430
3.2	3179	280	P	V6	R	167	6.0	24	20	4430	1810	1410
Shuttle – 2.3 auto	2154	150	P	S4	F	115	12.0	26	15	4760	1790	1490
HR-V – 1.6	1590	105	P	S4	4X4	102	12.0	33	8	4010	1695	1125
CR-V												
2.0	1973	128	P	S4	4X4	108	10.5	28	9	4520	1750	1440
2.0	1973	147	P	S4	4X4	–	–	28	–	4520	1750	1440
HYUNDAI												
Atoz – 1.0	999	56	P	S4	F	88	15.1	45	2	3495	1495	810
Accent												
1.3	1341	60	P	S4	F	–	–	38	–	4105	1630	935
1.3	1341	75	P	S4	F	–	–	38	–	4105	1630	935
1.3	1341	84	P	S4	F	108	12.8	38	6	4105	1630	935
1.5 12v	1495	90	P	S4	F	112	11.7	40	7	4105	1630	935
1.5 16v	1495	99	P	S4	F	112	10.5	35	–	4105	1630	970
Lantra												
1.5	1495	88	P	S4	F	–	–	–	–	4420	1700	1130
1.6	1600	114	P	S4	F	120	11.2	34	9	4420	1700	1130
1.8	1796	128	P	S4	F	122	9.4	33	–	4420	1700	1200
2.0	1975	139	P	S4	F	125	–	34	14	4420	1700	1280
Sonata												
2.0	1997	136	P	S4	F	124	9.6	32	10	4710	1820	1320
2.4	2351	150	P	S4	F	118	–	31		4710	1820	1320
2.5 V6	2494	160	P	S4	F	136	9.3	28	14	4710	1820	1320
XG												
2.5	2494	160	P	S6	R	132	9.1	26	–	4865	1825	1640
3.0 V6	2972	182	P	V6	R	135	9.3	23	–	4865	1825	1670
Coupe												
1.6	1600	114	P	S4	F	120	11.2	34	9	4340	1730	1235
1.8	1796	132	P	S4	F	118	–	32	–	4340	1730	1165
2.0	1975	139	P	S4	F	125	8.6	32	12	4340	1730	1250
ISUZU												
Vehi-Cross – 3.2	3165	215	P	V6	4x4	105	–	22	–	4130	1790	1750
Trooper												
3.5	3494	212	P	V6	4x4	112	11.3	21	15	4760	1835	1890
3.0 D	2999	157	D	S4	4x4	99	15.8	26	14	4760	1835	1990
JAGUAR												
S-Type												
3.0	2967	238	P	V6	R	146	7.5	28	15	4860	1820	1630
4.0	3996	276	P	V8	R	150	6.6	25	19	4860	1820	1720
XJ8												
3.2	3253	237	P	V8	R	140	8.5	24	16	5022	1800	1710
4.0	3996	284	P	V8	R	149	7.3	24	17	5022	1800	1710
4.0 S'charged XJR	3996	363	P	V8	R	155	5.6	22	19	5022	1800	1775
XK8												
4.0	3996	284	P	V8	R	155	6.7	23	18	4760	1830	1615
4.0 S'charged XKR	3996	363	P	V8	R	155	5.4	22	20	4760	1830	1640
KIA												
Pride												
1.2	1139	62	P	S4	F	–	–	–	–	3565	1605	770
1.3	1324	64	P	S4	F	93	11.8	42	5	3565	1605	770
Sephia/Mentor												
1.5	1498	80	P	S4	F	105	11.8	36	–	4425	1710	1040
1.5	1498	88	P	S4	F	112	–	36	–	4425	1710	1040
1.8	1793	111	P	S4	F	121	10.3	34	–	4425	1710	1115
Shuma												
1.5	1498	88	P	S4	F	112	11.8	36	–	4475	1711	1040

Model	Engine – CC	Power – bhp	Fuel	Engine config.	Driven wheels	Top speed – mph	0–60 mph – secs	mpg – average	Insurance group	Length – mm	Width – mm	Weight – Kg
1.8	1793	111	P	S4	F	121	10.3	31	–	4475	1711	1115
Clarus												
1.8	1793	116	P	S4	F	115	10.7	30	–	4730	1770	1195
2.0	1998	133	P	S4	F	121	10.9	28	–	4730	1770	1220
Sportage												
2.0	1998	95	P	S4	R	99	–	24	–	4245	1730	1420
2.0 16v	1998	128	P	S4	R	107	14.7	24	9	4245	1730	1420
2.0 TD	1998	83	D	S4	R	90	20.4	30	–	4245	1730	1540
LADA												
Samara												
1.1	1100	53	P	S4	F	87	16.0	35	–	4010	1620	900
1.1	1100	58	P	S4	F	–	–	33	–	4010	1620	900
1.3	1288	67	P	S4	F	93	14.5	37	–	4010	1620	920
1.3	1288	73	P	S4	F	–	–	–	–	4010	1620	920
1.5	1500	71	P	S4	F	97	14.0	36	–	4010	1620	920
1.5	1500	79	P	S4	F	96	13.0	27	–	4010	1620	920
1.5-16v	1500	90	P	S4	F	112	12.0	42	–	4010	1620	920
Niva												
1.7	1690	80	P	S4	4x4	85	22.0	25	–	3720	1680	1210
1.8	1774	91	P	S4	4x4	99	17.0	26	–	3720	1680	1210
1.9 D	1905	64	D	S4	4x4	78	25.0	35	–	3720	1680	1240
1.5 TD	1524	65	D	S4	4x4	78	25.0	38	–	3720	1680	1250
110												
1.5	1500	76	P	S4	F	106	13.4	33	–	4265	1675	1040
1.5 16v	1500	94	P	S4	F	115	11.5	33	–	4265	1675	1080
2.0 GTI	1998	150	P	S4	F	128	9.0	27	–	4265	1675	1100
2.0 Rallye	1998	240	P	S4	F	137	6.5	–	–	4265	1675	980
2.0 Rotor Sport	1998	190	P	Wankel	F	150	5.6	18	–	4250	1780	960
LAMBORGHINI												
Diablo												
5.7 V12	5707	530	P	V12	R	198	3.8	11	20	4470	2040	1530
5.7 V12	5707	585	P	V12	R	213	3.6	11	20	4470	2040	1530
5.7 V12	5707	640	P	V12	R	212	3.6	12	20	4470	2040	–
LANCIA												
Y												
1.1	1108	54	P	S4	F	93	15.0	45	–	3725	1690	850
1.2	1242	60	P	S4	F	99	13.3	42	–	3725	1690	860
1.2	1242	86	P	S4	F	110	10.9	43	–	3725	1690	910
Delta												
1.6	1581	103	P	S4	F	118	11.0	34	–	4010	1705	1130
1.8	1747	131	P	S4	F	124	9.4	32	–	4010	1705	1200
2.0 Turbo	1995	193	P	S4	F	140	7.5	27	–	4010	1705	1330
1.9 TD	1929	90	D	S4	F	112	12.0	43	–	4010	1705	1280
Dedra												
1.6	1581	103	P	S4	F	117	11.0	36	–	4345	1700	1175
1.8	1747	131	P	S4	F	126	10.0	32	–	4345	1700	1255
1.9 TD	1929	90	D	S4	F	112	13.5	42	–	4345	1700	1245
Lybra												
1.6	1581	103	P	S4	F	115	11.3	40	–	4466	1743	1290
1.8	1747	131	P	S4	F	125	10.3	40	–	4466	1743	1340
2.0	1998	154	P	S4	F	130	9.6	34	–	4466	1743	1390
1.9 JTD	1910	105	D	S4	F	115	11.3	57	–	4466	1743	1310
2.4 JTD	2387	134	D	S4	F	124	9.9	49	–	4466	1743	1370
Kappa												
2.0	1998	155	P	S5	F	131	9.2	26	–	4685	1825	1440
2.0 Turbo	1995	220	P	S5	F	151	7.3	26	–	4685	1825	1480
2.4	2446	175	P	S5	F	135	8.7	26	–	4685	1825	1450
3.0	2959	204	P	V6	F	140	8.0	24	–	4685	1825	1520
2.4 TD	2387	136	D	S5	F	125	10.0	37	–	4685	1825	1510
Z												
2.0	1998	132	P	S4	F	115	13.4	27	–	4470	1835	1555
2.0 Turbo	1998	147	P	S4	F	121	10.1	25	–	4470	1835	1575
2.1 TD	2088	109	P	S4	F	109	12.7	33	–	4470	1835	1615
LAND ROVER												
Freelander												
1.8	1795	120	P	S4	4x4	102	11.1	27	10	4380	1805	1380
2.0 TD	1994	98	D	S4	4x4	96	15.2	36	10	4380	1805	1405
Defender												
2.5 TD	2495	122	D	S5	4x4	84	16.8	28	7	3880	1790	1695
3.9	3947	182	P	V8	4x4	87	–	18	–	3880	1790	1630
Discovery												
2.5 TD	2496	138	D	S5	4x4	97	15.3	30	13	4710	1860	2075
3.9	3947	185	D	V8	4x4	105	11.7	17	14	4710	1860	2020
Range Rover												
4.0	3947	185	P	V8	4x4	118	10.5	17	13	4715	1850	2090
4.6	4552	218	P	V8	4x4	124	9.9	16	15	4715	1850	2120
2.5 TD	2497	136	D	S6	4x4	105	14.3	27	13	4715	1850	2070
LEXUS												
IS200	1988	155	P	S6	R	133	9.5	31	–	4400	1720	1300
GS300	2997	228	P	S6	R	138	8.2	25	17	4810	1800	1665
GS400	3969	294	P	V8	R	155	5.7	25	–	4810	1800	1665
SC300	2997	228	P	S6	R	146	7.9	30	–	4850	1790	1610
LS400	3969	294	P	V8	R	155	6.9	23	19	5005	1830	1780
RX300	2995	223	P	V6	4x4	112	8.5	26	–	4575	1815	1675
LIGIER AMBRA	505	5.4	D	S2	F	45	–	85	–	2470	1400	350
LINCOLN												
Continental	4601	279	P	V8	F	133	–	25	–	5260	1870	1760
Town Car	4601	208	P	V8	R	112	–	25	–	5470	1985	1820
Navigator	5403	264	P	V8	4x4	118	–	20	–	5200	2030	2335
5.4 V8	5403	304	P	V8	4x4	–	–	–	–	5200	2030	2335
LS6/8												
3.0 V6	2967	190	P	V6	R	130	–	28	–	4925	1860	1700
4.0 V8	3950	245	P	V8	R	136	–	25	–	4925	1860	1700
LOTUS												
Elise												
1.8	1795	120	P	S4	R	125	5.9	40	17	3730	1700	690
1.8	1795	145	P	S4	R	133	5.3	39	20	3730	1700	690
1.8 Sprint	1795	150	P	S4	R	127	5.5	–	–	3730	1700	690
1.8 Sport	1795	190	P	S4	R	130	4.4	–	–	3730	1700	670
Esprit – 3.5	3506	354	P	V8	R	175	4.6	21	20	4370	1880	1380
MAHINDRA												
2.1	2112	63	D	S4	4x4	65	–	28	–	3810	1800	1285
2.5	2523	55	D	S4	4x4	65	–	30	–	3800	1800	1285
2.5	2498	72	D	S4	4x4	70	–	28	–	4340	1800	1610
MARCOS												
MantaRay												
2.0 turbo	1994	200	P	S4	R	136	–	27	–	4005	1680	1050
4.0	3946	193	P	V8	R	140	5.6	–	–	4005	1680	1050
4.6	4601	254	P	V8	R	149	5.2	–	–	4005	1680	1050
LM500												
LM 4.0	3950	190	P	V8	R	143	5.4	–	–	4260	1830	1075
LM 4.6	4601	254	P	V8	R	149	5.2	–	–	4260	1830	1075
Mantis – 4.6	4601	355	P	V8	R	164	4.2	19	–	4260	1830	1075
MASERATI												
3200 GT – 3.2 V8	3217	368	P	V8	R	174	5.1	17	20	4510	1820	1590
Quattroporte												
2.8 twin-turbo	2790	280	P	V6	R	161	5.9	21	20	4550	1810	1545
3.2 twin-turbo	3217	336	P	V8	R	167	5.8	18	20	4550	1810	1645
MAZDA												
121												
1.3	1299	60	P	S4	F	96	15.9	40	4	3830	1635	930
1.25	1242	75	P	S4	F	105	12.7	41	5	3830	1635	940
1.8 D	1753	60	D	S4	F	96	17.4	45	–	3830	1635	1015
Demio												
1.3	1324	63	P	S4	F	94	14.0	41	–	3810	1670	950
1.3	1324	72	P	S4	F	98	13.2	41	5	3810	1670	950
1.5	1498	99	P	S4	F	105	–	38	–	3810	1670	970
323												
1.3	1324	73	P	S4	F	104	14.2	38	6	4200	1705	980
1.5	1498	88	P	S4	F	110	11.9	38	7	4200	1705	1010
1.8	1840	114	P	S4	F	120	9.8	34	9	4200	1705	1105
2.0 Diesel	1998	71	P	S4	F	104	16.9	38	–	4200	1705	1105
2.0 TD	1998	90	P	S4	F	110	12.2	55	7	4200	1705	1160
Premacy												
1.8	1840	100	P	S4	F	108	11.8	34	6	4295	1705	1150
1.8	1840	115	P	S4	F	112	11.4	34	7	4295	1705	1150
2.0TD	1998	90	P	S4	F	106	–	50	6	4295	1705	1150
626												
1.8	1840	90	P	S4	F	112	12.6	37	8	4575	1710	1185
2.0	1991	116	P	S4	F	123	9.9	36	10	4575	1710	1185
2.0	1991	136	P	S4	F	129	9.6	35	12	4575	1710	1175
2.5	2497	200	P	V6	4x4	136	–	26	–	4575	1710	1500
2.0 TD	1998	101	D	S4	F	115	11.5	54	9	4575	1710	1275
Xedos 6												
1.6	1598	107	P	S4	F	114	11.9	35	–	4560	1700	1135
2.0 V6	1995	140	P	V6	F	133	9.4	31	16	4560	1700	1190
Xedos 9												
2.0 V6	1995	143	P	V6	F	125	10.7	32	–	4825	1770	1415
2.3 V6	2255	211	P	V6	F	143	9.4	29	–	4825	1770	1500
2.5 V6	2497	167	P	V6	F	136	8.6	29	17	4825	1770	1415
MX-5												
1.6	1598	110	P	S4	R	118	9.7	35	11	3975	1680	1015
1.8	1840	140	P	S4	R	127	–	33	12	3975	1680	1025
RX-7 – 2.6	2616	280	P	R2	R	155	5.3	24	–	4285	1760	1240
MCC												
Smart	599	45	P	S3	R	84	18.9	50	–	2500	1515	720
0.6	599	54	P	S3	R	–	17.2	–	–	2500	1515	720
0.8 TD	799	40	P	S3	R	84	17.5	67	–	2500	1515	720
MERCEDES-BENZ												
A-Class												
A140	1397	82	P	S4	F	105	12.9	40	5	3575	1720	1020
A160	1598	102	P	S4	F	113	10.8	39	6	3575	1720	1040
A190	1998	125	P	S4	F	123	8.8	37	8	3575	1720	1040
A160 TD	1689	60	D	S4	F	96	18.0	63	–	3575	1720	1070
A170 TD	1689	90	D	S4	F	109	12.5	58	6	3575	1720	1085
C-Class												
C180	1799	122	P	S4	R	120	12.0	31	11	4515	1725	1350
C200	1998	136	P	S4	R	126	11.0	30	12	4515	1725	1365
C200 K S'charged	1998	192	P	S4	R	140	–	32	–	4515	1725	1420
C230 K S'charged	2250	193	P	S4	R	143	8.4	32	14	4515	1725	1420

	Engine – CC	Power – bhp	Fuel	Engine config.	Driven wheels	Top speed – mph	0–60 mph – secs	mpg – average	Insurance group	Length – mm	Width – mm	Weight – Kg
C240 V6	2398	170	P	V6	R	135	9.3	27	13	4515	1725	1420
C280 V6	2799	197	P	V6	R	144	8.3	28	15	4515	1725	1430
C43 AMG V8	4266	306	P	V8	R	155	6.5	24	19	4515	1725	1570
C220 CDi	2151	102	D	S4	R	113	13.4	46	–	4515	1725	1340
C220 CDi	2151	125	D	S4	R	123	10.5	46	12	4515	1725	1340
C250 TD	2497	150	D	S5	R	126	9.9	36	13	4515	1725	1480
E-Class												
E200	1998	136	P	S4	R	127	11.4	31	13	4800	1800	1365
E240 V6	2398	170	P	V6	R	138	9.6	27	14	4800	1800	1375
E280 V6	2799	204	P	V6	R	145	8.5	28	15	4800	1800	1465
E320 V6	3199	224	P	V6	R	148	7.7	27	16	4800	1800	1505
E430 V8	4266	279	P	V8	R	155	6.6	25	17	4800	1800	1575
E55 AMG V8	5439	354	P	V8	R	155	5.7	22	19	4800	1800	1635
E220 CDi	2151	102	D	S4	R	114	13.9	46	–	4800	1800	1395
E220 CDi	2151	125	D	S4	R	123	11.0	46	13	4800	1800	1395
E290 TD	2874	129	D	S5	R	121	11.5	42	–	4800	1800	1465
E300 TD	2996	177	D	S6	R	136	8.9	33	15	4800	1800	1555
E320 CDi	3226	197	D	S6	R	143	8.3	36	–	4800	1800	1555
S-Class												
S280	2799	204	P	V6	R	143	9.5	26	15	5040	1855	1695
S320	3199	224	P	V6	R	149	8.2	25	16	5040	1855	1695
S430	4266	279	P	V8	R	155	7.3	23	18	5040	1855	1780
S500	4966	306	P	V8	R	155	6.5	21	19	5040	1855	1780
CL-Coupe	Details unavailable at time of going to press											
CLK												
2.0	1998	136	P	S4	R	129	11.0	30	13	4565	1720	1300
2.0 S'charged	1998	192	P	S4	R	145	8.4	30	–	4565	1720	1320
2.3 S'charged	2295	193	P	S4	R	145	8.4	29	15	4565	1720	1350
3.2	3199	218	P	V6	R	149	7.4	28	18	4565	1720	1420
4.3	4266	279	P	V8	R	155	6.3	25	18	4565	1720	1480
5.5 AMG	5500	347	P	V8	R	155	5.4	–	–	4565	1720	1480
SLK												
200	1998	136	P	S4	R	129	9.3	31	–	4000	1720	1195
200 K S'charged	1998	192	P	S4	R	141	7.6	32	–	4000	1720	1250
230 K S'charged	2295	193	P	S4	R	143	7.7	30	17	4000	1720	1250
SL												
SL280	2799	204	P	V6	R	144	9.7	25	20	4500	1810	1740
SL320	3199	224	P	V6	R	148	8.4	25	20	4500	1810	1760
SL500	4966	306	P	V8	R	155	6.5	22	20	4500	1810	1820
SL600	5987	394	P	V12	R	155	6.1	18	20	4500	1810	1980
V-Class												
2.3	2300	143	P	S4	R	109	14.5	24	14	4659	1880	–
2.8	2800	174	P	S4	R	118	12.7	21	16	4659	1880	–
2.2 CDi	2200	122	P	S4	R	103	17.5	38	14	4659	1880	–
M-Class												
ML230	2295	150	P	S4	4x4	112	12.3	22	–	4590	1830	1785
ML320	3199	218	P	V6	4x4	112	9.5	22	16	4590	1830	1915
ML430	4266	272	P	V8	4x4	124	7.9	21	–	4590	1830	2000
MERCURY												
Tracer – 2.0	1988	111	P	S4	F	115	–	40	–	4440	1700	1115
Sable												
3.0 V6	2986	147	P	V6	F	118	–	29	–	5070	1850	1535
3.0 V6	2967	203	P	V6	F	124	–	27	–	5070	1850	1545
Grand Marquis – 4.6	4601	203	P	V8	R	118	–	25	–	5380	1980	1720
Villager – 3.3 V6	3275	173	P	V6	F	109	–	25	–	4950	1900	1735
MITSUBISHI												
Colt												
1.3	1299	75	P	S4	F	105	12.5	41	5	4290	1690	945
1.5	1468	110	P	S4	F	112	10.5	35	–	4290	1690	945
1.6	1597	90	P	S4	F	115	10.5	38	6	4290	1690	975
1.6	1597	175	P	S4	F	130	7.5	28	–	4290	1690	1020
1.8	1829	135	P	V6	F	118	–	30	–	4290	1690	1120
1.8 Turbo	1834	205	P	S4	F	136	7.0	26	–	4290	1690	1240
2.0 Turbo (Lancer)	1997	280	P	S4	4x4	150	4.4	–	–	4350	1770	1360
2.0 TD	1998	88	D	S4	F	99	14.0	40	–	4290	1690	1080
Carisma												
1.6	1597	100	P	S4	F	115	12.1	39	7	4475	1710	1175
1.8 GDi	1834	125	P	S4	F	125	10.4	42	10	4475	1710	1200
1.9 TD	1870	90	D	S4	F	112	13.2	46	8	4475	1710	1215
Galant												
1.8	1834	140	P	S4	F	133	9.0	40	–	4630	1740	1240
2.0	1997	126	P	S4	F	–	–	–	–	4630	1740	1240
2.0	1997	134	P	S4	F	131	9.7	34	–	4630	1740	1240
2.4 GDi	2351	147	P	S4	F	134	9.1	34	–	4630	1740	1320
2.5 V6	2498	161	P	V6	F	140	8.2	31	–	4630	1740	1290
2.5 V6 Turbo	2498	280	P	V6	4x4	140	–	25	–	4630	1740	1460
2.0 TD	1998	90	D	S4	F	112	–	42	–	4630	1740	1300
Eclipse												
2.0	1997	145	P	S4	F	136	9.4	32	–	4375	1735	1320
2.4	2400	143	P	S4	F	–	–	–	–	4375	1735	1320
2.0 Turbo	1997	213	P	S4	F	136	–	25	–	4320	1735	1315
FTO												
1.8	1834	125	P	S4	F	124	–	26	–	4320	1735	1100
2.0 V6	1999	170	P	V6	F	136	–	29	–	4320	1735	1150
2.0 V6	1999	200	P	V6	F	143	–	29	–	4320	1735	1150
3000 GT												
3.0	2972	224	P	V6	4x4	143	–	25	–	4600	1840	1600
3.0	2972	280	P	V6	4x4	155	5.9	24	20	4600	1840	1670
Space Star												
1.3	1299	86	P	S4	F	105	13.4	42	7	4030	1700	1120

	Engine – CC	Power – bhp	Fuel	Engine config.	Driven wheels	Top speed – mph	0–60 mph – secs	mpg – average	Insurance group	Length – mm	Width – mm	Weight – Kg
1.8 GDi	1834	122	P	S4	F	118	10.4	40	10	4030	1700	1195
Space Runner												
1.8 GDi	1834	150	P	S4	F	115	11.0	32	–	4280	1695	1380
2.0	1997	230	P	S4	4x4	136	–	22	–	4480	1740	1570
2.4 GDi	2351	165	P	S4	4x4	121	10.0	28	–	4280	1695	1560
Space Wagon - 2.4 GDi	2351	150	P	S4	F	118	10.7	29	12	4600	1775	1510
Space Gear												
2.0	1997	113	P	S4	R	99	–	24	–	4595	1695	1625
2.4	2351	128	P	S4	R	103	–	24	–	4595	1695	1660
3.0	2972	185	P	V6	R	105	–	23	–	4595	1695	2030
2.5 TD	2477	99	D	S4	R	92	–	26	–	4595	1695	1650
2.8 TD	2835	125	D	S4	R	–	–	–	–	4595	1695	2020
Pinin – 1.8	1834	118	P	S4	4x4	104	10.2	38	–	3735	1695	1250
Shogun												
3.0	2972	177	P	V6	4x4	109	11.1	22	14	4725	1785	1725
3.5	3497	208	P	V6	4x4	115	9.9	21	15	4725	1785	1890
2.5 TD	2477	100	D	S4	4x4	90	16.4	27	13	4725	1785	1720
2.8 TD	2835	125	D	S4	4x4	96	15.0	25	13	4725	1785	1720
Challenger/Montero												
3.0 V6	2972	177	P	V6	4x4	109	11.1	22	16	4550	1775	1830
3.5 V6	3497	245	P	V6	4x4	118	10.0	22	–	4550	1775	1900
2.5 TD	2477	100	D	S4	4x4	90	16.4	27	13	4550	1775	1720
2.8 TD	2835	125	D	S4	4x4	96	15.0	25	–	4550	1775	1810
MITSUOKA GALUE												
2.0	1998	130	P	S6	R	121	–	21	–	4860	1740	1285
MORGAN												
4/4	1796	111	P	S4	R	112	8.0	37	13	3890	1500	870
Plus 4 – 2.0	1994	136	P	S4	R	121	7.5	30	14	3960	1630	920
Plus 8												
4.0	3948	190	P	V8	R	124	5.6	22	16	3960	1630	940
4.6	4552	194	P	V8	R	128	6.0	21	–	3960	1630	975
NISSAN												
Micra												
1.0	998	54	P	S4	F	93	16.4	47	3	3720	1585	775
1.3	1275	75	P	S4	F	105	12.0	46	4	3720	1585	810
1.5 Diesel	1527	57	P	S4	F	91	18.7	57	–	3720	1585	900
Almera												
1.4	1392	87	P	S4	F	107	12.6	40	4	4320	1690	1035
1.6	1597	99	P	S4	F	112	11.0	39	6	4320	1690	1065
2.0	1998	143	P	S4	F	130	8.2	35	14	4320	1690	1155
2.0 TD	1974	90	D	S4	F	97	16.8	43	5	4320	1690	1140
Primera												
1.6	1597	100	P	S4	F	113	12.0	39	8	4522	1715	1235
1.8	1769	114	P	S4	F	123	11.0	39	10	4522	1715	1250
2.0	1998	140	P	S4	F	131	9.6	33	8	4522	1715	1285
2.0 TD	1974	90	D	S4	F	109	14.0	44	8	4522	1715	1335
Skyline												
2.0	1998	155	P	S6	R	124	–	28	–	4705	1720	1360
2.5	2499	200	P	S6	R	130	–	25	–	4705	1720	1400
2.5 Turbo	2499	280	P	S6	R	143	–	25	–	4705	1720	1430
2.6 twin-turbo	2568	280	P	S6	4x4	155	6.0	25	20	4600	1785	1540
QX												
2.0 V6	1995	140	P	V6	F	125	11.3	29	12	4770	1770	1310
2.5 V6	2496	190	P	V6	F	130	–	28	–	4770	1770	1340
3.0 V6	2988	193	P	V6	F	143	8.3	27	14	4770	1770	1360
200 SX												
2.0	1998	165	P	S4	R	130	–	32	–	4440	1695	1200
2.0 Turbo	1998	200	P	S4	R	146	7.5	29	18	4440	1695	1260
Serena												
1.6	1597	97	P	S4	R	93	18.1	26	10	4315	1695	1250
2.0	1998	140	P	S4	R	105	12.2	27	12	4315	1695	1485
2.3 Diesel	2283	75	D	S4	R	84	26.5	27	10	4315	1695	1485
Terrano II												
2.4	2389	116	P	S4	4x4	99	13.7	23	10	4665	1755	1630
2.7 TD	2664	125	D	S4	4x4	96	15.7	29	10	4585	1735	1745
Patrol												
4.5	4479	200	P	S6	4x4	105	–	19	–	4965	1840	2210
2.8 TD	2826	129	D	S6	4x4	93	–	25	13	4965	1840	2070
4.2 TD	4169	145	D	S6	4x4	93	–	20	–	4965	1840	2320
OLDSMOBILE												
Alero												
2.4	2392	152	P	S4	F	124	10.5	31	–	4740	1780	1340
3.4 V6	3350	173	P	V6	F	124	9.2	30	–	4740	1780	1370
Intrigue												
3.5 V6	3473	218	P	V6	F	136	–	29	–	4975	1870	1555
3.8 V6	3791	197	P	V6	F	124	–	29	–	4975	1870	1555
Cutlass												
3.1 V6	3135	152	P	V6	F	112	9.0	30	–	4880	1765	1400
Eighty-Eight												
3.8 V6	3791	208	P	V6	F	124	–	29	–	5090	1880	1570
3.8 V6 Supercharged	3791	243	P	V6	F	124	–	27	–	5090	1880	1590
Aurora – 4.0 V8	3995	253	P	V8	F	135	8.2	26	–	5220	1890	1789
Silhouette – 3.4 V6	3350	188	P	V6	F	118	11.0	26	–	4760	1835	1700
Bravada – 4.3 V6	4300	193	P	V6	4x4	112	10.0	23	–	4660	1720	1835
PERODUA – Nippa	847	42	P	S3	F	84	15.8	52	3	3345	1395	–

	Engine – CC	Power – bhp	Fuel	Engine config.	Driven wheels	Top speed – mph	0–60 mph – secs	mpg – average	Insurance group	Length – mm	Width – mm	Weight – Kg
PEUGEOT												
106												
1.0	954	50	P	S4	F	93	19.4	45	–	3680	1590	815
1.1	1124	60	P	S4	F	102	15.4	44	3	3680	1590	815
1.4	1361	75	P	S4	F	110	13.2	41	–	3680	1590	815
1.6 16v	1587	118	P	S4	F	127	8.7	35	13	3680	1590	950
1.5 D	1527	57	D	S4	F	98	18.5	54	3	3680	1590	875
206												
1.1	1124	60	P	S4	F	98	16.5	46	3	3835	1650	910
1.4	1361	75	P	S4	F	105	14.2	43	4	3835	1650	950
1.6	1587	88	P	S4	F	115	12.5	40	5	3835	1650	1025
2.0 16v	1997	135	P	S4	F	130	8.4	36	–	3835	1650	1050
1.9 D	1868	69	D	S4	F	100	17.2	50	3	3835	1650	1040
306												
1.4	1361	75	P	S4	F	105	14.7	41	4	4265	1690	1010
1.6	1587	88	P	S4	F	111	13.5	39	5	4265	1690	1090
1.8	1762	101	P	S4	F	109	15.1	31	–	4265	1690	1115
1.8 16v	1762	110	P	S4	F	119	11.2	34	6	4265	1690	1095
2.0	1998	133	P	S4	F	125	10.4	31	11	4265	1690	1160
2.0 GTi-6	1998	163	P	S4	F	136	8.8	30	15	4265	1690	1215
1.9 D	1868	69	D	S4	F	100	16.9	46	4	4265	1690	1080
2.0 TD	1997	90	D	S4	F	112	12.6	52	5	4265	1690	1135
406												
1.8	1762	90	P	S4	F	112	14.6	34	–	4600	1765	1245
1.8	1762	110	P	S4	F	119	12.5	34	10	4600	1765	1245
2.0	1997	135	P	S4	F	129	10.8	34	13	4600	1765	1350
3.0 V6	2946	190	P	V6	F	144	8.2	26	16	4600	1765	1455
2.0 HDi	1997	90	D	S4	F	110	14.5	50	12	4600	1765	1330
2.0 HDi	1997	110	D	S4	F	118	12.5	51	12	4600	1765	1410
Coupe												
2.0	1997	137	P	S4	F	129	10.4	37	15	4602	1765	1350
3.0 V6	2946	194	P	V6	F	146	7.9	26	18	4602	1765	1455
605												
2.0	1998	133	P	S4	F	127	10.9	29	–	4765	1800	1440
2.0 Turbo	1998	145	P	S4	F	132	10.0	27	–	4765	1800	1515
3.0 V6	2946	190	P	V6	F	145	8.4	24	–	4765	1800	1540
2.1 TD	2088	109	D	S4	F	119	13.1	40	–	4765	1800	1500
2.4 TD	2446	129	D	S4	F	125	12.1	50	–	4765	1800	1600
806												
1.8	1762	99	P	S4	F	102	16.2	27	–	4455	1835	1445
2.0	1998	121	P	S4	F	110	14.6	27	10	4455	1835	1585
2.0 Turbo	1998	147	P	S4	F	121	11.0	25	–	4455	1835	1650
1.9 TD	1905	92	D	S4	F	99	17.2	34	10	4455	1835	1565
2.1 TD	2088	109	D	S4	F	109	14.1	33	–	4455	1835	1615
PLYMOUTH												
Prowler – 3.5 V6	3518	253	P	V6	R	130	6.5	25	–	4200	1945	1295
PONTIAC												
Grand Am												
2.4	2392	152	P	S4	F	118	9.0	31	–	4730	1790	1385
3.4 V6	3350	173	P	V6	F	118	9.8	29	–	4730	1790	1385
Grand Prix												
3.1 V6	3135	162	P	V6	F	121	–	30	–	4990	1845	1550
3.8 V6	3791	203	P	V6	F	124	–	30	–	4990	1845	1550
3.8 V6 S'charged	3791	243	P	V6	F	140	8.5	28	–	4990	1845	1550
Bonneville												
3.8 V6	3791	208	P	V6	F	124	–	29	–	5120	1890	1565
3.8 V6 Supercharged	3791	243	P	V6	F	136	8.5	25	–	5120	1890	1625
Firebird												
3.8 V6	3791	203	P	V6	R	124	–	29	–	4920	1890	1515
5.7 V8	5665	309	P	V8	R	155	6.0	28	–	4920	1890	1565
Montana – 3.4 V6	3350	185	P	V6	F	118	–	26	–	4750	1845	1680
PORSCHE												
Boxster												
2.7	2700	220	P	F6	R	155	6.6	–	–	4315	1780	–
3.2	3200	252	P	F6	R	162	5.9	27	–	4315	1780	1295
911												
3.4	3387	300	P	F6	R	174	5.4	24	20	4430	1765	1320
GT3	3600	360	P	F6	R	174	4.8	20	–	4430	1780	1320
PROTON												
Compact												
1.3	1299	75	P	S4	F	102	13.6	35	7	3990	1700	960
1.5	1468	87	P	S4	F	107	12.1	34	8	3990	1700	965
1.6	1597	120	P	S4	F	118	10.7	34	10	3990	1700	1000
Persona												
1.5	1468	87	P	S4	F	107	12.1	34	9	4360	1680	965
1.6	1597	120	P	S4	F	118	10.7	34	10	4360	1680	1000
1.8	1834	135	P	S4	F	119	10.4	32	12	4360	1680	1105
1.8	1834	140	P	S4	F	126	8.9	32	14	4220	1690	1105
2.0 Diesel	1998	68	D	S4	F	99	18.5	54	–	4360	1680	1125
2.0 TD	1998	82	D	S4	F	105	14.3	36	10	4360	1680	1125
Reliant Robin 0.8	848	40	P	S4	F	–	–	–	6	3410	1450	794
RENAULT												
Twingo – 1.2	1149	58	P	S4	F	93	13.4	40	–	3435	1630	820
Clio												
1.2	1149	58	P	S4	F	99	15.0	46	2	3775	1640	880
1.4	1390	75	P	S4	F	105	12.1	42	4	3775	1640	940

	Engine – CC	Power – bhp	Fuel	Engine config.	Driven wheels	Top speed – mph	0–60 mph – secs	mpg – average	Insurance group	Length – mm	Width – mm	Weight – Kg
1.6	1598	90	P	S4	F	112	10.6	39	5	3775	1640	965
1.6 16v	1598	107	P	S4	F	121	9.6	39	–	3775	1640	995
1.9 Diesel	1870	64	D	S4	F	100	15.4	47	3	3775	1640	975
Kangoo												
1.1	1149	58	P	S4	F	87	17.2	41	–	3995	1660	1020
1.4	1390	75	P	S4	F	96	14.3	38	–	3995	1660	1065
1.9 D	1870	64	P	S4	F	90	19.5	45	–	3995	1660	1110
Megane												
1.4	1390	75	P	S4	F	105	13.8	43	6	4130	1700	1015
1.4	1390	95	P	S4	F	114	11.8	42	6	4130	1700	1050
1.6	1598	90	P	S4	F	114	11.5	39	–	4130	1700	1055
1.6	1598	107	P	S4	F	121	9.8	40	7	4130	1700	1095
2.0	1998	114	P	S4	F	122	9.7	34	–	4130	1700	1085
2.0 16v	1998	150	P	S4	F	130	8.7	30	13	4130	1700	1150
1.9 Diesel	1870	64	D	S4	F	99	16.6	43	5	4130	1700	1090
1.9 TDi	1870	94	D	S4	F	112	12.3	44	–	4130	1700	1115
1.9 TDi	1870	98	D	S4	F	113	12.3	53	6	4130	1700	1115
Megane Scenic												
1.4	1390	75	P	S4	F	99	16.2	35	–	4130	1720	1215
1.4	1390	95	P	S4	F	107	12.9	40	–	4130	1720	1235
1.6	1598	90	P	S4	F	102	16.0	31	–	4130	1720	1220
1.6	1598	110	P	S4	F	115	11.2	39	–	4130	1720	1250
2.0	1998	114	P	S4	F	115	11.1	33	–	4130	1720	1270
2.0	1998	140	P	S4	F	122	10.2	35	–	4130	1720	1270
1.9 Diesel	1870	64	D	S4	F	94	18.9	40	–	4130	1720	1275
1.9 TD	1870	94	D	S4	F	–	–	–	–	4130	1720	1290
1.9 TDi	1870	100	D	S4	F	108	12.7	49	–	4130	1720	1290
Laguna												
1.6	1598	107	P	S4	F	121	11.5	38	9	4510	1750	1230
1.8	1783	120	P	S4	F	126	10.7	36	13	4510	1750	1265
2.0	1998	114	P	S4	F	118	11.6	31	–	4510	1750	1290
2.0 16v	1948	139	P	S4	F	130	9.8	32	13	4510	1750	1310
3.0	2946	190	P	V6	F	146	7.7	26	15	4510	1750	1395
1.9 TD	1870	98	D	S4	F	115	12.5	51	10	4510	1750	1310
2.2 TD	2188	113	D	S4	F	121	11.8	40	13	4510	1750	1425
Safrane												
2.0	1948	136	P	S4	F	128	10.5	31	14	4770	1820	1450
2.5	2435	165	P	S5	F	136	9.1	28	15	4770	1820	1495
3.0 V6	2946	190	P	V6	F	140	9.5	24	–	4770	1820	1580
2.2 TD	2188	113	D	S4	F	119	13.2	39	–	4770	1820	1575
Espace												
2.0	1998	114	P	S4	F	109	13.7	29	13	4515	1810	1490
2.0 16v	1998	140	P	S4	F	115	11.6	31	–	4515	1810	1490
3.0 V6	2963	194	P	V6	F	128	10.6	24	–	4515	1810	1680
2.2 TD	2188	113	D	S4	F	109	14.5	38	12	4515	1810	1630
ROLLS-ROYCE												
Silver Seraph – 5.4	5379	326	P	V12	R	140	6.9	16	20	5390	1930	2300
ROVER												
Mini – 1.3	1275	63	P	S4	F	92	12.5	43	5	3050	1410	695
200												
211	1113	60	P	S4	F	96	15.0	42	4	3970	1690	985
214	1396	75	P	S4	F	103	13.3	42	5	3970	1690	985
214 16v	1396	103	P	S4	F	115	10.7	40	6	3970	1690	1000
216	1588	111	P	S4	F	118	9.9	39	7	3970	1690	1025
218	1795	120	P	S4	F	121	9.0	39	9	3970	1690	1025
200vi	1795	145	P	S4	F	127	8.0	38	14	3970	1690	1060
220D Turbo	1994	86	D	S4	F	105	13.0	50	7	3970	1690	1105
220D Turbo	1994	105	D	S4	F	115	10.4	53	7	3970	1690	1105
400												
414	1396	103	P	S4	F	115	11.8	42	8	4490	1700	1120
416	1588	111	P	S4	F	118	10.0	40	10	4490	1700	1125
420	1994	136	P	S4	F	123	9.0	33	13	4490	1700	1265
420 D Turbo	1994	86	D	S4	F	105	13.0	50	11	4490	1700	1220
420 Di Turbo	1994	105	D	S4	F	115	10.4	53	11	4490	1700	1220
75												
1.8	1795	120	P	S4	F	121	11.6	36	8	4745	1780	1315
2.0 V6	1991	150	P	V6	F	130	10.2	30	10	4745	1780	1370
2.5 V6	2497	175	P	V6	F	136	8.8	29	14	4745	1780	1370
2.0 TD	1951	116	P	S4	F	120	11.7	50	8	4745	1780	1410
MG												
MGF												
1.8	1795	120	P	S4	R	120	8.5	38	12	3920	1630	1060
1.8 VVC	1795	145	P	S4	R	130	7.0	36	14	3920	1630	1070
SAAB												
9-3												
2.0	1985	131	P	S4	F	124	10.6	31	10	4634	1710	1295
2.0 Turbo	1985	154	P	S4	F	130	8.2	30	–	4634	1710	1320
2.0 Turbo	1985	185	P	S4	F	143	7.5	31	14	4634	1710	1380
2.0 Turbo	1985	205	P	S4	F	146	6.9	30	–	4634	1710	1380
2.0 Turbo	1985	230	P	S4	F	155	6.5	29	–	4634	1710	1380
2.2 TD	2172	116	D	S4	F	124	10.3	46	10	4634	1710	1350
9-5												
2.0 Turbo	1985	150	P	S4	F	135	9.8	30	13	4810	1790	1485
2.0 Turbo	1985	190	P	S4	F	146	8.3	–	–	4810	1790	1485
2.3 Turbo	2290	170	P	S4	F	140	8.7	29	14	4810	1790	1485
3.0 Turbo	2962	200	P	V6	F	146	8.3	25	16	4810	1790	1600
San Storm Streak 1.1	1149	60	P	S4	F	100	10.5	45	–	3543	1504	600

Model	Engine – CC	Power – bhp	Fuel	Engine config.	Driven wheels	Top speed – mph	0–60 mph – secs	mpg – average	Insurance group	Length – mm	Width – mm	Weight – Kg
SATURN EV1 – 1.0	999	50	P	S4	F	94	17.4	50	2	3535	1640	86
Saturn												
1.9	1901	101	P	S4	F	93	10.5	32	–	4495	1695	1055
1.9 16v	1901	126	P	S4	F	99	9.0	32	–	4495	1695	1085
SEAT												
Arosa												
1.0	999	50	P	S4	F	94	17.4	49	2	3535	1640	865
1.4	1390	60	P	S4	F	99	14.1	46	3	3535	1640	895
1.7D	1716	60	D	S4	F	97	16.8	64	3	3535	1640	960
Ibiza												
1.0	999	50	P	S4	F	90	19.4	46	–	3855	1640	910
1.4	1390	60	P	S4	F	97	15.1	43	4	3855	1640	920
1.4 16v	1390	101	P	S4	F	117	10.7	40	–	3855	1640	985
1.6	1598	75	P	S4	F	104	12.7	38	–	3855	1640	975
1.6	1595	101	P	S4	F	117	10.7	36	–	3855	1640	1005
2.0	1984	116	P	S4	F	123	9.8	36	10	3855	1640	1045
2.0 16v	1984	150	P	S4	F	134	8.3	34	14	3855	1640	995
1.9 D	1896	64	D	S4	F	97	16.5	49	–	3855	1640	1030
1.9 TD	1896	90	D	S4	F	112	12.0	59	7	3855	1640	1050
1.9 TD	1896	110	D	S4	F	120	10.2	59	–	3855	1640	1060
Cordoba												
1.4	1390	60	P	S4	F	97	15.7	43	–	4145	1640	975
1.4 16v	1390	101	P	S4	F	117	10.9	39	–	4145	1640	1025
1.6	1598	75	P	S4	F	102	13.2	38	5	4145	1640	1015
1.6	1595	101	P	S4	F	117	10.9	36	–	4145	1640	1050
2.0	1984	116	P	S4	F	123	10.2	36	–	4145	1640	1080
2.0 16v	1984	150	P	S4	F	134	8.5	34	15	4145	1640	1120
1.9 D	1896	64	D	S4	F	97	17.1	49	–	4145	1640	1050
1.9 TD	1896	90	D	S4	F	112	12.5	58	8	4145	1640	1095
1.9 TD	1896	110	D	S4	F	120	10.6	58	–	4145	1640	1105
Toledo												
1.6	1595	101	P	S4	F	117	11.5	37	7	4440	1740	1155
1.8	1781	125	P	S4	F	124	10.5	34	9	4440	1740	1225
2.3	2324	150	P	S5	F	134	9.2	30	13	4440	1740	1305
1.9 TD	1896	90	P	S4	F	112	13.0	55	–	4440	1740	1245
1.9 TD 110	1896	110	P	S4	F	120	11.2	57	9	4440	1740	1270
Alhambra												
1.8T	1781	150	P	S4	F	120	12.0	28	11	4515	1810	1755
2.0	1984	116	P	S4	F	110	15.4	29	11	4615	1810	1730
1.9 TD	1896	90	D	S4	F	99	19.3	43	11	4615	1810	1755
1.9 TD 110	1896	110	D	S4	F	107	16.0	44	11	4615	1810	1755
SHELBY												
Series 1	3995	253	P	V8	R	170	5.0	20	–	–	–	1045
Spectre – R45	4601	355	P	V8	R	175	5.0	24	–	4325	1905	1250
SKODA												
Felicia												
1.3	1289	54	P	S4	F	94	15.5	44	4	3885	1635	935
1.3	1289	68	P	S4	F	100	13.5	43	4	3855	1635	935
1.6	1598	75	P	S4	F	105	12.0	41	6	3855	1635	965
1.9 D	1896	64	D	S4	F	97	16.5	50	5	3855	1635	1020
Octavia												
1.6	1598	75	P	S4	F	105	14.4	37	7	4510	1730	1165
1.6	1595	101	P	S4	F	116	11.7	37	8	4510	1730	1195
1.8	1781	125	P	S4	F	125	10.6	34	11	4510	1730	1285
1.8 Turbo	1781	150	P	S4	F	135	8.9	36	–	4510	1730	1295
1.9 D	1896	68	D	S4	F	96	–	46	8	4510	1730	1270
1.9 TD 90	1896	90	D	S4	F	110	13.7	55	9	4510	1730	1265
1.9 TD 110	1896	110	D	S4	F	119	11.5	57	11	4510	1730	1265
SUBARU												
Vivio												
0.7	658	48	P	S4	4x4	81	21.2	46	–	3300	1400	710
0.7	658	64	P	S4	4x4	87	–	43	–	3300	1400	750
Justy – 1.3	1298	68	P	S4	4x4	96	13.6	41	6	3745	1590	845
Impreza												
1.5	1493	97	P	F4	4x4	–	–	–	–	4350	1690	1115
1.6	1597	85	P	F4	4x4	109	12.3	34	–	4350	1690	1005
2.0	1994	125	P	F4	4x4	118	9.7	31	13	4350	1690	1170
2.0 Turbo	1994	218	P	F4	4x4	143	6.3	28	17	4350	1690	1255
2.0 Turbo WRX	1994	280	P	F4	4x4	136	–	23	–	4350	1690	1250
2.5	2457	167	P	F4	4x4	130	–	31	–	4350	1690	1280
Legacy												
2.0	1994	125	P	F4	4x4	120	10.3	31	–	4600	1700	1370
2.0	1994	155	P	F4	4x4	124	–	29	–	4600	1700	1170
2.0 Turbo	1994	280	P	F4	4x4	155	6.8	22	–	4600	1700	1380
2.5	2457	150	P	F4	4x4	127	9.7	27	15	4600	1700	1315
Forester												
2.0	1994	125	P	F4	4x4	110	11.4	31	11	4450	1735	1380
2.0 Turbo	1994	250	P	F4	4x4	124	–	29	–	4450	1735	1405
2.5	2457	150	P	F4	4x4	118	–	29	–	4450	1735	1780
SUZUKI												
Alto												
0.7	657	55	P	S3	F	78	–	51	–	3395	1475	590
0.7 Turbo	658	64	P	S3	F	93	–	43	–	3395	1475	660
1.0	993	54	P	S4	F	93	15.5	48	3	3495	1495	730
Wagon R												
1.0	997	65	P	S4	F	87	–	48	2	3410	1575	845
1.0 Turbo	997	101	P	S4	F	109	–	42	–	3410	1575	810
1.2	1171	69	P	S4	F	87	–	48	4	3410	1575	875
Swift												
1.0	993	53	P	S3	F	90	–	51	4	3745	1590	730
1.3	1299	68	P	S4	F	102	–	49	5	3745	1590	755
Baleno												
1.3	1299	86	P	S4	F	99	–	43	–	3900	1690	915
1.6	1590	96	P	S4	F	114	–	42	7	3900	1690	950
1.8	1840	121	P	S4	F	112	–	40	–	3900	1690	935
1.9 TD	1905	75	P	S4	F	99	–	41	–	3900	1690	1030
Jimny – 1.3	1298	80	P	S4	4x4	87	–	34	7	3625	1600	1025
Vitara												
1.6	1590	97	P	S4	4x4	93	–	27	8	3620	1630	1115
2.0	1995	132	P	S4	4x4	99	–	29	–	3745	1695	1170
2.0 V6	1998	136	P	V6	4x4	99	12.5	28	–	4125	1695	1300
1.9 D	1905	68	D	S4	4x4	84	–	40	–	3620	1630	1305
2.0 TD	1998	87	D	S4	4x4	93	–	36	–	4125	1695	1360
Grand Vitara												
1.6	1590	94	P	S4	4x4	93	–	34	–	3860	1700	1200
2.0	1995	128	P	S4	4x4	99	–	30	–	3860	1700	1260
2.5	2494	144	P	V6	4x4	102	–	27	13	3860	1700	1405
2.0 TD	1998	92	D	S4	4x4	93	–	38	12	3860	1700	1200
TATA												
Indica												
1.4	1405	65	P	S4	F	93	14.0	32	–	3660	1645	930
1.4 D	1405	54	D	S4	F	85	16.0	38	–	3660	1645	930
Safari												
1.9	1948	137	P	S4	4x4	95	–	20	–	4650	1810	2040
1.9 TD	1948	90	D	S4	4x4	81	–	24	–	4650	1810	2040
TOYOTA												
Yaris												
1.0	998	68	P	S4	F	97	12.0	46	2	3610	1660	820
1.3	1299	90	P	S4	F	105	–	46	–	3610	1660	820
Starlet												
1.3	1332	75	P	S4	F	105	11.2	42	4	3740	1625	945
1.3 Turbo	1332	135	P	S4	F	118	–	34	–	3790	1625	920
1.5 D	1454	54	D	S4	F	96	14.5	63	–	3740	1625	980
Corolla												
1.3	1332	86	P	S4	F	109	12.5	41	6	4100	1690	1040
1.6	1587	110	P	S4	F	121	10.2	36	9	4100	1690	1075
1.8	1762	110	P	S4	4x4	112	11.8	30	–	4100	1690	1255
2.0 D	1975	72	D	S4	F	102	14.4	44	7	4270	1690	1145
Prius – 1.5	1497	58	P	S4	F	–	–	–	–	4275	1695	1240
Avensis												
1.6	1587	101	P	S4	F	118	12.1	39	7	4490	1710	1195
1.6	1587	110	P	S4	F	121	11.7	37	–	4490	1710	1195
1.8	1762	110	P	S4	F	121	11.0	40	8	4490	1710	1195
2.0	1998	128	P	S4	F	127	9.3	34	9	4490	1710	1250
2.0 TD	1975	90	D	S4	F	112	12.0	44	8	4490	1710	1280
2.0 TD	1975	112	D	S4	F	–	–	–	–	4490	1710	1280
Camry												
2.2	2164	131	P	S4	F	124	10.4	32	12	4765	1785	1385
3.0 V6	2995	190	P	V6	F	136	9.0	25	14	4765	1785	1445
MR2												
2.0	1998	175	P	S4	R	140	7.5	31	16	4180	1695	1210
2.0 Turbo	1998	245	P	S4	R	149	–	23	–	4180	1695	1260
2.2	2164	137	P	S4	R	124	9.5	32	–	4180	1695	1145
Celica												
1.8	1762	116	P	S4	F	124	10.2	36	12	4420	1750	1110
2.0	1998	170	P	S4	F	136	–	31	15	4420	1750	1210
2.0 Turbo	1998	242	P	S4	4x4	149	6.1	28	–	4420	1750	1380
New Celica												
1.8	1794	140	P	S4	F	127	8.7	37	–	4335	1735	1160
Picnic												
2.0	1998	128	P	S4	F	112	10.8	31	10	4530	1695	1335
2.2 TD	2184	90	D	S4	F	102	13.9	37	10	4530	1695	1420
Previa												
2.4	2438	132	P	S4	R	109	11.5	26	13	4765	1800	1670
2.2 TD	2184	101	D	S4	R	99	–	36	–	4765	1800	1670
RAV4												
2.0	1998	128	P	S4	4x4	104	10.9	29	9	4115	1695	1150
2.0	1998	165	P	S4	4x4	112	–	30	–	4115	1760	1220
Landcruiser Colorado												
2.7	2694	152	P	S4	4x4	103	–	22	–	4750	1820	1680
3.4 V6	3378	176	P	V6	4x4	109	11.5	20	15	4750	1820	1810
3.0 TD	2982	123	D	S4	4x4	99	14.0	26	14	4750	1820	1720
Landcruiser Amazon												
4.7 V8	4664	235	P	V8	4x4	109	11.7	17	15	4890	1940	2260
4.2 TD	4164	204	D	S6	4x4	105	13.6	25	14	4890	1940	2090
4.2 TD	4164	250	D	S6	4x4	–	–	–	–	4890	1940	2090
TVR												
Chimaera												
4.0 V8	3950	238	P	V8	R	152	4.8	23	20	4020	1860	1060
4.6 V8	4552	288	P	V8	R	159	4.7	22	20	4020	1860	1060
5.0 V8	4997	326	P	V8	R	167	4.1	20	20	4020	1860	1060
Griffith 500												
5.0 V8	4997	326	P	V8	R	167	4.1	20	20	3890	1940	1060
Tuscan Speed Six 4.0	3996	364	P	S6	R	161	4.5	21	–	4160	1900	1080
Cerbera												
4.0 V8	3966	355	P	V8	R	167	4.4	–	20	4280	1860	1100

	Engine – CC	Power – bhp	Fuel	Engine config.	Driven wheels	Top speed – mph	0–60 mph – secs	mpg – average	Insurance group	Length – mm	Width – mm	Weight – Kg
4.2 V8	4280	365	P	V8	R	159	4.2	19	20	4280	1860	1100
4.5 V8	4475	426	P	V8	R	159	3.9	19	20	4280	1860	1100
VAUXHALL/OPEL												
Corsa												
1.0	973	54	P	S3	F	93	18.0	50	2	3740	1610	865
1.2	1199	65	P	S4	F	101	14.0	50	3	3740	1610	870
1.4	1389	90	P	S4	F	112	11.0	38	6	3740	1610	965
1.6	1589	106	P	S4	F	119	10.5	36	10	3740	1610	980
1.5 TD	1488	67	D	S4	F	102	14.0	52	5	3740	1610	950
1.7 D	1686	60	D	S4	F	93	16.5	54	4	3740	1610	940
Astra												
1.2	1199	65	P	S4	F	102	16.0	46	–	4250	1710	1035
1.4	1389	90	P	S4	F	112	12.5	40	4	4250	1709	1090
1.6	1598	75	P	S4	F	100	14.5	40	4	4250	1709	1005
1.6	1598	101	P	S4	F	117	11.5	38	6	4250	1709	1005
1.8	1796	116	P	S4	F	124	10.0	36	7	4250	1709	1145
2.0	1998	136	P	S4	F	129	9.0	33	11	4250	1709	1170
1.7 TD	1700	68	D	S4	F	101	17.0	48	4	4250	1709	1145
2.0 TD	1995	82	D	S4	F	109	14.5	50	5	4250	1709	1225
Vectra												
1.6 8v	1598	75	P	S4	F	109	16.1	38	6	4495	1710	1205
1.6 16v	1598	101	P	S4	F	120	12.5	38	7	4495	1710	1215
1.8	1796	116	P	S4	F	126	11.0	38	9	4495	1710	1265
2.0	1998	112	P	S4	F	–	–	–	–	4495	1710	1340
2.0	1998	136	P	S4	F	133	10.0	33	11	4495	1710	1340
2.5 V6	2498	170	P	V6	F	143	8.5	27	15	4495	1710	1355
2.5 V6	2498	195	P	V6	F	148	7.6	28	16	4495	1710	1415
2.0 TD	1995	82	D	S4	F	110	15.5	50	7	4495	1710	1335
2.0 TD	1995	101	D	S4	F	121	13.0	48	8	4495	1710	1330
Omega												
2.0i 8v	1998	116	P	S4	R	121	13.0	30	–	4785	1785	1400
2.0i 16v	1998	136	P	S4	R	130	11.0	30	13	4785	1785	1460
2.2i 16v	2200	144	P	S4	R	131	10.1	–	–	4785	1785	1460
2.5 V6	2498	170	P	V6	R	141	9.5	26	14	4785	1785	1550
3.0 V6	2962	211	P	V6	R	151	8.5	26	16	4785	1785	1590
2.0 TD	1995	101	D	S4	R	115	15.0	42	12	4785	1785	1540
2.5 TD	2498	131	D	S6	R	124	12.0	36	13	4785	1785	1550
Tigra												
1.4	1389	90	P	S4	F	118	11.5	39	10	3920	1600	980
1.6	1598	106	P	S4	F	126	10.5	34	12	3920	1600	1000
Zafira												
1.6	1598	101	P	S4	F	109	13.5	34	–	4320	1740	1300
1.8	1796	116	P	S4	F	114	12.0	33	–	4320	1740	1320
2.0 TD	1995	82	P	S4	F	99	17.0	43	–	4320	1740	1430
Sintra												
2.2	2198	141	P	S4	F	117	12.7	29	12	4670	1830	1655
3.0 V6	2962	201	P	V6	F	125	10.8	25	13	4670	1830	1725
2.2 TD	2172	116	P	S4	F	109	14.5	36	–	4670	1830	1735
Frontera												
2.2	2198	136	P	S4	4x4	102	13.4	25	9	4270	1785	1460
3.2 V6	3165	205	P	V6	4x4	119	9.7	24	12	4270	1785	1780
2.2 TD	2172	116	P	S4	4x4	96	13.9	31	9	4270	1785	1720
Monterey												
3.2 V6	3494	215	P	V6	4x4	112	11.3	21	–	4365	1835	1865
3.0 TD	2999	159	D	S4	4x4	99	15.8	26	–	4365	1835	1965
VENTURI												
Atlantique												
3.0	2975	281	P	V6	R	174	–	–	20	4240	1840	1250
3.0 Twin-turbo	2946	310	P	V6	R	171	4.9	–	–	4240	1840	1250
3.0 (Automatic)	2946	207	P	V6	R	149	7.5	–	20	4240	1840	1250
3.0 Twin-turbo	2975	408	P	V6	R	180	–	–	–	4240	1840	1150
Volga												
2.3	2287	150	P	S4	R	118	11.5	23	–	4940	1800	1500
3.4	3380	170	P	V8	R	125	10.5	17	–	4940	1800	1500
2.1 TD	2134	114	D	S4	R	112	12.5	29	–	4940	1800	1500
VOLKSWAGEN												
Lupo												
1.0	999	50	P	S4	F	94	17.9	49	2	3525	1640	895
1.4	1390	75	P	S4	F	107	12.0	46	3	3525	1640	905
1.4	1390	100	P	S4	F	116	10.0	43	6	3525	1640	950
1.6	1598	120	P	S4	F	124	8.5	40	–	3525	1640	960
1.2 TD	1196	61	P	S3	F	102	16.5	91	–	3525	1640	780
1.7 D	1716	60	P	S4	F	97	16.8	64	3	3525	1640	980
Polo												
1.0	999	50	P	S4	F	94	18.5	49	3	3715	1655	880
1.4 8v	1390	60	P	S4	F	99	14.9	45	4	3715	1655	910
1.4 16v	1390	101	P	S4	F	117	10.5	41	9	3715	1655	950
1.6	1598	75	P	S4	F	107	12.4	41	6	3715	1655	915
1.6 100	1598	100	P	S4	F	117	10.9	38	9	3715	1655	960
1.6 120	1598	125	P	S4	F	124	9.1	40	–	3715	1655	960
1.7 D	1716	60	D	S4	F	97	17.4	64	–	3715	1655	960
1.9 D	1896	64	D	S4	F	99	15.8	50	6	3715	1655	960
1.9 TD	1896	90	D	S4	F	109	12.5	58	6	3715	1655	960
Golf Mk1												
1.3	1349	71	P	S4	F	94	12.8	31	–	3815	1610	–
1.6	1595	82	P	S4	F	–	–	–	–	3815	1610	–
Golf												
1.4	1390	75	P	S4	F	106	13.9	44	4	4150	1735	1090
1.6	1595	101	P	S4	F	117	10.8	37	5	4150	1735	1075
1.8	1781	125	P	S4	F	125	9.9	34	–	4150	1735	1195
1.8 T	1781	150	P	S4	F	134	8.5	36	14	4150	1735	1195
2.0	1984	116	P	S4	F	115	10.9	32	10	4150	1735	1195
2.3 VR5	2324	150	P	V5	F	134	8.8	30	–	4150	1735	1240
1.9 D	1896	68	D	S4	F	99	17.2	54	4	4150	1735	1170
1.9 TD	1896	90	D	S4	F	112	12.6	57	6	4150	1735	1200
1.9 TD 110	1896	110	D	S4	F	120	10.6	58	10	4150	1735	1210
Bora												
1.6	1595	101	P	S4	F	117	11.7	37	5	4375	1735	1185
2.0	1984	116	P	S4	F	121	11.0	36	8	4375	1735	1235
2.3 VR5	2324	150	P	V5	F	134	9.1	30	15	4375	1735	1300
1.9 TD	1896	90	P	S4	F	112	12.9	55	6	4375	1735	1275
1.9 TD	1896	110	P	S4	F	120	10.9	57	7	4375	1735	1285
Beetle												
2.0	1984	116	P	S4	F	115	10.9	32	12	4080	1725	1230
1.9 TD	1896	90	D	S4	F	106	13.1	54	–	4080	1725	1250
Passat												
1.6	1595	101	P	S4	F	119	12.5	35	–	4675	1740	1230
1.8	1781	125	P	S4	F	128	10.9	33	10	4675	1740	1290
1.8 Turbo	1781	150	P	S4	F	138	8.9	36	15	4675	1740	1310
2.3 VR5	2324	150	P	V5	F	138	8.9	29	15	4675	1740	1335
2.8	2771	193	P	V6	4x4	148	7.6	27	17	4675	1740	1450
1.9 TD	1896	90	D	S4	F	114	13.5	53	10	4675	1740	1305
1.9 TD 110	1896	110	D	S4	F	122	11.3	53	10	4675	1740	1310
1.9 TD 116	1896	116	D	S4	F	124	10.7	52	–	4675	1740	1320
2.5 TD 150	2496	150	D	V6	F	137	9.6	42	–	4675	1740	1457
Sharan												
1.8 Turbo	1781	150	P	S4	F	120	12.0	28	11	4620	1810	1640
2.0	1984	116	P	S4	F	110	15.4	29	11	4620	1810	1560
2.8	2792	174	P	V6	F	123	11.8	24	15	4620	1810	1700
1.9 TD	1896	90	D	S4	F	99	19.3	44	11	4620	1810	1660
1.9 TDi 110	1896	110	D	S4	F	109	16.4	44	11	4620	1810	1660
VOLKSWAGEN Brazil/Mexico												
Gol												
1.0	998	54	P	S4	F	91	18.4	40	–	3810	1650	905
1.0 16v	998	69	P	S4	F	100	14.3	40	–	3810	1650	905
1.6	1595	92	P	S4	F	110	11.5	41	–	3810	1650	930
1.8	1781	99	P	S4	F	112	10.9	39	–	3810	1650	990
2.0 8v	1984	111	P	S4	F	118	10.0	36	–	3810	1650	1050
2.0 16v	1984	145	P	S4	F	128	8.7	36	–	3810	1650	1115
Beetle – 1.6	1585	44	P	F4	R	77	27.2	37	–	4060	1550	820
VOLVO												
S40/V40												
1.6	1587	109	P	S4	F	118	12.0	35	8	4480	1720	1230
1.8	1731	116	P	S4	F	121	11.0	29	9	4480	1720	1170
1.8 GDi	1834	125	P	S4	F	124	10.5	37	10	4480	1720	1192
1.9 Turbo	1855	200	P	S4	F	146	7.3	30	16	4480	1720	1225
2.0	1948	140	P	S4	F	127	9.7	35	–	4480	1720	1172
2.0 Turbo	1948	160	P	S4	F	133	8.5	25	–	4480	1720	1210
1.9 TD	1870	90	D	S4	F	112	12.5	40	9	4480	1720	1203
S70/V70												
2.0 10v	1984	126	P	S5	F	121	11.7	28	–	4720	1760	1430
2.0 Turbo	1984	179	P	S5	F	133	9.3	25	–	4720	1760	1430
2.0 Turbo	1984	226	P	S5	F	149	7.7	25	–	4720	1760	1460
2.3 T5	2319	240	P	S5	F	152	7.0	29	16	4720	1760	1460
2.4 Bi-Fuel	2435	122	P	S5	F	112	14.1	25	13	4720	1760	1430
2.4 20v	2435	140	P	S5	F	127	10.1	33	13	4720	1760	1430
2.4 20v	2435	170	P	S5	F	130	8.9	32	13	4720	1760	1430
2.4 20v Turbo	2435	193	P	S5	F	140	7.9	29	13	4720	1760	1430
2.4 R	2435	265	P	S5	F	152	7.4	24	17	4720	1760	1460
2.5 TDi	2461	140	D	S5	F	124	9.9	43	12	4720	1760	1510
C70												
2.0 Turbo	1984	170	P	S5	F	133	8.5	32	14	4720	1820	1450
2.0 Turbo	1984	226	P	S5	F	151	7.5	22	–	4720	1820	1450
2.3 Turbo	2319	240	P	S5	F	155	6.9	29	16	4720	1820	1450
2.4 Turbo	2435	193	P	S5	F	143	7.8	29	15	4720	1820	1450
S80												
2.0 Turbo 163	1984	163	P	S5	F	136	9.2	–	–	4820	1830	1490
2.0 Turbo 226	1984	226	P	S5	F	152	7.2	–	–	4820	1830	1490
2.4 140	2435	140	P	S5	F	127	11.0	33	14	4820	1830	1490
2.4 170	2435	170	P	S5	F	136	9.0	32	14	4820	1830	1490
2.8 Turbo	2783	272	P	S6	F	155	7.2	25	16	4820	1830	1590
2.9	2922	200	P	S6	F	146	8.2	29	15	4820	1830	1550
2.5 TD	2461	140	D	S5	F	127	11.0	44	13	4820	1830	1550
WESTFIELD												
1.6	1597	105	P	S4	R	108	6.3	–	–	3710	1625	–
1.8	1796	115	P	S4	R	110	6.5	–	–	3710	1625	–
1.8 Sport	1796	140	P	S4	R	118	5.8	–	–	3710	1625	–
1.8 Speed Sport	1796	155	P	S4	R	130	5.3	–	–	3710	1625	–
1.8 FW400	1796	145	P	S4	R	135	4.0	–	–	3710	1625	–
1.8 FW400	1796	190	P	S4	R	140	3.5	–	–	3710	1625	–
4.0 V8	3951	200	P	V8	R	138	4.3	–	–	3710	1625	–
ZIL												
41041 7.7	7695	315	P	V8	R	125	11.5	12	–	5750	2085	3030
41047 7.7	7695	400	P	V8	R	125	12.5	10	–	6330	2085	3600

NEW CAR PRICES

The tables give the UK list prices of new cars as the Guide went to press in September 1999. Inevitably prices will change over the coming months. For the most up-to-date listing look in the weekly magazine Auto Express.

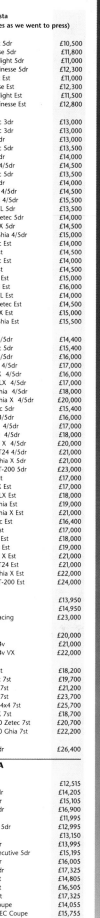

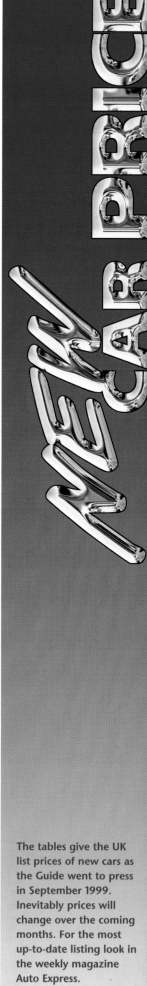

AC

Cobra	
5.0 V8 CRS	£38,950
5.0 V8 Superblower	£69,795
Ace	
5.0 V8	£69,795
4.6 V8	£74,950
5.0 V8 Supercharged	£79,750
Aceca	
4.6 V8	£69,795

ALFA ROMEO

145	
1.6 Twin Spark 3dr	£14,500
1.8 Twin Spark 3dr	£15,299
2.0 Cloverleaf 3dr	£16,772
146	
1.6 Twin Spark 5dr	£14,836
1.8 Twin Spark 5dr	£15,699
2.0 ti 5dr	£17,123
156	
1.8 Twin Spark 4dr	£17,996
1.8 TS Lusso 4dr	£19,198
2.0 Twin Spark 4dr	£20,198
2.0 TS Selespeed 4dr	£21,993
2.5 V6 24v 4dr	£22,801
2.4 JTD 4dr	£20,335
166	
2.0 Twin Spark 4dr	£23,371
2.5 V6 4dr	£26,437
3.0 V6 Super 4dr	£29,171
Spider/GTV	
Spider 2.0 Twin Spark	£23,583
Spider 2.0 TS Lusso	£26,188
GTV 2.0 Twin Spark	£22,183
GTV 2.0 TS Lusso	£24,878
GTV 3.0 V6 Lusso	£28,093
GTV 3.0 V6 6-Speed	£30,000

ASTON MARTIN

DB7	
3.2 Coupe	£84,950
3.2 Volante	£92,500
6.0 V12 Vantage	£92,500
6.0 V12 V'ge Volante	£99,950
Virage	
5.3 Volante	£169,500
Coupe	
5.3 V8	£149,500
Vantage	
5.3 Vantage	£189,950

AUDI

A3	
1.6 3dr	£15,230
1.6 Sport 3dr	£16,905
1.6 SE 3dr	£17,540
1.8 3dr	£16,912
1.8 Sport 3dr	£18,586
1.8 SE 3dr	£19,222
1.8 T Sport 3dr	£19,525
1.8 T Sport quattro	£22,150
1.8 S3 quattro 3dr	£27,150
1.9 TDi 3dr	£16,150
1.9 TDi 110 3dr	£17,050
1.9 TDi SE 3dr	£18,460
1.9 TDi 110 Sport 3dr	£18,725
1.9 TDi 110 SE 3dr	£19,360
1.6 5dr	£15,880
1.6 Sport 5dr	£17,555
1.6 SE 5dr	£18,190
1.8 5dr	£17,562
1.8 Sport 5dr	£19,236
1.8 SE 5dr	£19,872
1.8 T Sport 5dr	£20,175
1.8 T Sport quattro	£22,800
1.9 TDi 5dr	£16,800
1.9 TDi 110 5dr	£17,700
1.9 TDi SE 5dr	£19,110
1.9 TDi 110 Sport 5dr	£19,375
1.9 TDi 110 SE 5dr	£20,010
A4	
1.6 4dr	£17,470
1.6 SE 4dr	£19,267
1.8 4dr	£19,506
1.8 SE 4dr	£21,105
1.8 T Sport 4dr	£23,577
2.4 V6 4dr	£22,193
2.4 V6 SE 4dr	£23,792
2.8 V6 4dr	£25,450
2.8 V6 SE 4dr	£27,049
1.8 T quattro Sport 4dr	£27,150
2.8 V6 quattro 4dr	£28,905
S4 quattro 4dr	£36,645
1.9 TDi 4dr	£19,565
1.9 TDi SE 4dr	£21,154
1.9 TDi 110 4dr	£20,780
1.9 TDi 110 SE 4dr	£22,379
2.5 TDi 4dr	£23,917
2.5 TDi SE 4dr	£25,516
2.5 TDi quattro 4dr	£27,458
Avant 1.6	£18,381
Avant 1.6 SE	£20,367
Avant 1.8	£20,418
Avant 1.8 SE	£22,179
Avant 1.8 T Sport	£24,668
Avant 2.4 V6	£23,105
Avant 2.4 V6 SE	£24,866
Avant 2.8 V6	£26,362
Avant 2.8 V6 SE	£28,123
Avant 1.8T q'ttro Sport	£28,225
Avant 2.8 V6 quattro	£29,980
Avant S4 quattro	£37,720
Avant 1.9 TDi	£20,476
Avant 1.9 TDi SE	£22,238
Avant 1.9 TDi 110	£21,691
Avant 1.9 TDi 110 SE	£23,453
Avant 2.5 TDi	£24,829
Avant 2.5 TDi SE	£26,590
Avant 2.5 TDi quattro	£28,533
Cabriolet	
1.8	£22,298
2.6	£26,059
2.8	£30,946
A6	
1.8T 4dr	£23,708
1.8T SE 4dr	£25,722
1.9 TDi 4dr	£23,150
1.9 TDi SE 4dr	£25,164
2.4 4dr	£26,054
2.4 SE 4dr	£28,068
2.5 TDi SE 4dr	£28,068
2.5 TDi quattro 4dr	£30,025
2.8 quattro 4dr	£31,391
2.7T quattro 4dr	£33,149
4.2 quattro 4dr	£43,403
4.2 S6 quattro 4dr	£52,250
Avant 1.8T	£25,208
Avant 1.8T SE	£26,972
Avant 1.9 TDi	£24,650
Avant 1.9 TDi SE	£26,414
Avant 2.4	£27,555
Avant 2.4 SE	£29,318
Avant 2.5 TDi SE	£29,318
Avant 2.5 TDi quattro	£31,194
Avant 2.8 quattro	£32,560
Avant 2.7T quattro	£34,318
Avant 4.2 quattro	£44,572
Avant 4.2 S6 quattro	£53,420
A8	
2.8 4dr	£37,550
2.8 Sport 4dr	£40,550
3.7 quattro 4dr	£46,550
3.7 quattro Sport 4dr	£49,099
4.2 quattro 4dr	£53,850
4.2 quattro Sport 4dr	£56,400
4.2 S8 quattro 4dr	£65,198
TT	
1.8 quattro 180 Coupe	£26,650
1.8 quattro 225 Coupe	£29,650
1.8 quattro 180 Conv'	£29,150
1.8 quattro 225 Conv'	£32,150

BENTLEY

Arnage 4dr	£145,000
Continental R	£199,750
Continental SC	£245,000
Continental T	£233,350
Azure	£230,890

BMW

New 3-Series	
316i 4dr	£18,495
316i SE 4dr	£19,795
318i 4dr	£19,895
318i SE 4dr	£21,195
323i SE 4dr	£24,895
328i SE 4dr	£28,150
320d 4dr	£21,345
320d SE 4dr	£22,645
318Ci Coupe	£22,150
323Ci Coupe	£25,950
328Ci Coupe	£28,995
Old 3-Series	
316i Compact 3dr	£14,895
318ti 3dr	£16,995
318ti Sport 3dr	£18,995
318tds 3dr	£16,495
318i Convertible	£24,800
323i	£27,650
328i	£31,870
M3 Evolution	£44,220
5-Series	
520i 4dr	£24,595
520i SE 4dr	£26,195
523i 4dr	£26,550
523i SE 4dr	£28,095
528i SE 4dr	£31,095
528i Sport 4dr	£33,995
535i 4dr	£36,995
535i Sport 4dr	£39,595
540i 4dr	£43,695
M5 4dr	£59,995
530d SE 4dr	£29,395
520i Touring	£26,545
520i SE Touring	£28,265
523i Touring	£28,495
523i SE Touring	£29,995
528i SE Touring	£33,145
540i Touring	£45,695
530d SE Touring	£31,395
7-Series	
728i 4dr	£37,550
735i 4dr	£44,940
740i 4dr	£51,500
740iL 4dr	£58,650
750i 4dr	£71,450
750iL 4dr	£76,580
8-Series	
840Ci	£57,500
840Ci Sport	£57,500
Z3/M Coupe	
Z3 1.9	£19,995
Z3 2.0	£22,995
Z3 2.8	£28,350
Z3 3.2M	£40,600
M Coupe 3.2	£40,600

BRISTOL Blenheim

5.9 V8 Coupe	£124,500

CADILLAC Seville

4.6 V8 STS 4dr	£39,900

CATERHAM

Seven	
1.6 Classic	£13,400
1.6 K-Series	£17,655
1.8 K-Series	£18,655
1.6 Superlight	£20,655
1.8 VVC	£20,900
1.8 Superlight R	£26,155
C21	
1.6	£24,105
1.8	£25,105
1.8 VVC	£27,605
1.8 VHPD	£29,105

CHEVROLET

Camaro	
3.8 V6 Coupe	£17,950
3.8 V6 Convertible	£21,475
5.7 Z28 Coupe	£22,875
Blazer	
4.3 V6 LS 5dr	£22,925
4.3 V6 LT 5dr	£24,925
Corvette	
5.7 V8 Coupe	£37,625
5.7 V8 Convertible	£42,225

CHRYSLER

Neon	
2.0 SE 4dr	£10,995
2.0 LX 4dr	£13,495
Jeep Wrangler	
2.5 Sport 3dr	£14,220
4.0 Sport 3dr	£15,720
4.0 Sahara 3dr	£17,875
Jeep Cherokee	
2.5 Sport 5dr	£18,220
2.5TD Sport 5dr	£19,520
2.5TD Limited 5dr	£23,220
2.5TD Orvis 5dr	£25,495
4.0 Sport 5dr	£20,420
4.0 Ltd 5dr	£23,220
4.0 Orvis 5dr	£25,495
Jeep Grand Cherokee	
4.0 Limited 5dr	£29,995
4.7 V8 Limited 5dr	£34,995
Voyager	
2.0 SE	£18,420
2.0 LE	£21,220
2.5TD SE	£19,620
2.5TD LE	£22,420
3.3 LE	£23,720
2.5TD Grand V'ger SE	£21,920
2.5TD Grand V'ger LE	£24,320
3.3 Grand Voyager LE	£26,020
3.3 Grand Voyager LX	£28,995
Viper 8.0 GTS Coupe	£68,825

CITROEN

Saxo	
1.1 X 3dr	£7,985
1.6 VTR 3dr	£10,880
1.6 VTS 3dr	£12,200
1.1 X 5dr	£8,435
1.1 SX 5dr	£9,420
1.4 SX 5dr	£10,535
1.5 D SX 5dr	£10,020
Xsara	
1.4 X 5dr	£11,900
1.4 LX 5dr	£12,610
1.6 X 5dr	£12,400
1.6 LX 5dr	£13,110
1.6 SX 5dr	£13,470
1.8 SX 5dr	£14,315
1.8 Exclusive 5dr	£15,425
1.9 D X 5dr	£12,635
1.9 D LX 5dr	£13,345
1.9 D SX 5dr	£13,705
2.0 HDi X 5dr	£13,580
2.0 HDi LX 5dr	£14,290
2.0 HDi SX 5dr	£14,650
2.0 HDi Exclusive 5dr	£15,760
1.4 X Est	£12,650
1.4 LX Est	£13,360
1.6 LX Est	£13,860
1.8 Exclusive Est	£16,175
1.9 D X Est	£13,385
1.9 D LX Est	£14,095
2.0 HDi X Est	£14,330
2.0 HDi LX Est	£15,040
2.0 HDi SX Est	£15,400
2.0 HDi Exclusive Est	£16,510
1.6 VTR Coupe	£13,570
1.8 VTR Coupe	£15,695
2.0-16v VTS Coupe	£17,420
Xantia	
1.8i 16v X 5dr	£14,000
1.8i 16v LX 5dr	£14,715
1.8i 16v SX 5dr	£15,720
2.0i 16v SX 5dr	£16,900
2.0i 16v Exclusive 5dr	£18,775
2.0i Turbo Activa 5dr	£18,880
3.0i V6 5dr	£22,440
2.0 HDi X 5dr	£15,955
2.0 HDi LX 5dr	£16,670
2.0 HDi SX 5dr	£17,675
2.0 HDi LX 110 5dr	£17,460
2.0 HDi SX 110 5dr	£18,465
2.0 HDi Exclusive 110	£20,340
1.8 16v LX Est	£15,685
2.0 16v SX Est	£17,870
2.0 Turbo Exclusive Est	£20,315
2.0 HDi LX Est	£17,640
2.0 HDi SX Est	£18,645
2.0 HDi LX Est 110	£18,430
2.0 HDi SX Est 110	£19,435
2.0 HDi Exclusive 110	£21,310
XM	
2.0i Turbo VSX 5dr	£23,960
2.1 TD VSX 5dr	£23,960
3.0 V6 Excl 5dr	£29,650
2.0i Turbo VSX Est	£24,505
2.1 TD VSX Est	£24,505
2.5 TD VSX Est	£26,525
Berlingo Multispace	
1.4i Est	£10,830
1.8i Est	£11,180
1.9 D Est	£11,390
Synergie	
2.0i X	£16,865
2.0i SX	£19,205
1.9 TD X	£17,575
1.9 TD SX	£19,915
1.9 TD Exclusive	£23,305

DAEWOO

Matiz	
800 SE 5dr	£6,440
800 SE Plus 5dr	£7,440
Lanos	
1.4S 3dr	£7,995
1.4 SE 3dr	£8,995
1.6 SX 3dr	£10,495
1.4 S 5dr	£8,495
1.4 SE 5dr	£9,495
1.6 SX 5dr	£10,995
1.6 SX 4dr	£10,995
Nubira	
1.6 SE 4dr	£12,225
2.0 CDX 4dr	£13,225
1.6 SE Est	£13,225
2.0 CDX Est	£14,225
Leganza	
2.0 SX 4dr	£14,125
2.0 CDX 4dr	£15,325
2.0 CDX-E 4dr	£17,825
Korando	
2.3 3dr	£15,995
2.9TDi 3dr	£16,995
Musso	
2.3 5dr	£17,995
2.9TDi 5dr	£18,995

DAIHATSU

New Cuore	
1.0 3dr	£6,540
1.0 Plus 5dr	£7,240
Sirion	
1.0 5dr	£8,140
1.0 Plus 5dr	£9,540
Charade	
1.3 LXi 5dr	£9,095
1.3 GLXi 5dr	£10,395
1.5 GLXi 4dr	£10,795
Move	
850 est	£7,240
850 Plus Est	£8,240
Grand Move	
1.6 Est	£11,595
1.6 Plus Est	£13,595
Hijet 1.3	£7,995
Terios	
1.3 5dr	£9,995
1.3 Plus 5dr	£11,995
1.3 SE 5dr	£12,495
Fourtrak Independent	
2.8 TDL Est	£16,095
2.8 TDL-SE Est	£17,795
2.8 TDX Est	£19,095
2.8 TDX-SE Est	£20,795

FERRARI

360M	£101,243
550M	£149,701
456	£167,714

FIAT

Seicento	
900 S 3dr	£6,470
900 SX 3dr	£6,769
900 Citymatic 3dr	£7,069
1.1 Sporting 3dr	£7,525
New Punto	
(no prices as we went to press)	
Bravo	
1.2 SX 3dr	£10,953
1.6 SX 3dr	£11,974
1.6 HLX 3dr	£13,320
1.8 HLX 3dr	£14,272
2.0 HGT 3dr	£15,847
1.9 TD 75 SX 3dr	£11,640
1.9 JTD 105 SX 3dr	£12,407
Brava	
1.2 SX 5dr	£10,953
1.6 SX 5dr	£11,974
1.6 HSX 5dr	£12,496
1.6 ELX 5dr	£13,320
1.8 ELX 5dr	£14,272
1.9 TD 75 SX 5dr	£11,640
1.9 JTD 105 SX 5dr	£12,407
1.9 JTD 105 ELX 5dr	£13,913
Marea	
1.6 SX 4dr	£12,754
1.6 ELX 4dr	£14,537
1.8 ELX 4dr	£13,674
2.0 ELX 4dr	£14,901
2.0 HLX 4dr	£16,505
1.9 TD75 SX 4dr	£13,424
1.9 JTD105 SX 4dr	£14,097
1.9 JTD105 ELX 4dr	£14,705
2.4 JTD130 HLX 4dr	£17,174
1.6 SX Weekend	£13,994
1.6 ELX Weekend	£15,716
1.8 ELX Weekend	£14,704
2.0 ELX Weekend	£15,780
2.0 HLX Weekend	£17,775
1.9 TD75 SX Weekend	£14,401
1.9 JTD105 SX Weekend	£15,107
1.9 JTD105 ELX W'end	£16,054
2.4 JTD130 HLX W'end	£18,522
Barchetta 1.8 Convertible	£15,879
Coupé	
2.0 20v	£20,205
2.0 20v Turbo	£22,855
2.0 20v Turbo Plus	£24,754
Ulysse	
2.0 S	£17,183
2.0 EL	£20,054
1.9 TD S	£18,147
1.9 TD EL	£20,900

FORD

Ka	
1.3 Ka 3dr	£7,495
1.3 Ka 2 3dr	£8,495
1.3 Ka 3 3dr	£9,495
New Fiesta	
(no prices as we went to press)	
Escort	
1.6 Flight 5dr	£10,500
1.6 Finesse 5dr	£11,800
1.8 TDi Flight 5dr	£11,000
1.8 TDi Finesse 5dr	£12,300
1.6 Flight Est	£11,000
1.6 Finesse Est	£12,300
1.8 TDi Flight Est	£11,500
1.8 TDi Finesse Est	£12,800
Focus	
1.6i Zetec 3dr	£13,000
1.8i Zetec 3dr	£13,000
1.4i CL 5dr	£13,000
1.6i Zetec 5dr	£13,500
1.6i LX 5dr	£14,000
1.6iGhia 4/5dr	£14,500
1.8i Zetec 5dr	£13,500
1.8i LX 5dr	£14,000
1.8i Ghia 4/5dr	£14,500
2.0i Ghia 4/5dr	£15,500
1.8 TDi CL 5dr	£13,500
1.8 TDi Zetec 5dr	£14,000
1.8 TDi LX 5dr	£14,500
1.8 TDi Ghia 4/5dr	£15,000
1.6i Zetec Est	£14,000
1.6i LX Est	£14,500
1.8i Zetec Est	£14,000
1.8i LX Est	£14,500
1.8i Ghia Est	£15,000
2.0i Ghia Est	£16,000
1.8 TDi CL Est	£14,000
1.8 TDi Zetec Est	£14,500
1.8 TDi LX Est	£15,000
1.8 TDi Ghia Est	£15,500
Mondeo	
1.6i LX 4/5dr	£14,400
1.8i Zetec 5dr	£15,400
1.8i LX 4/5dr	£16,000
1.8i GLX 4/5dr	£17,000
1.8 TD LX 4/5dr	£16,000
1.8 TD GLX 4/5dr	£17,000
1.8 TD Ghia 4/5dr	£18,000
1.8 TD Ghia X 4/5dr	£20,000
2.0i Zetec 5dr	£15,400
2.0i LX 4/5dr	£16,000
2.0i GLX 4/5dr	£17,000
2.0i Ghia 4/5dr	£18,000
2.0i Ghia X 4/5dr	£20,000
2.5 V6 ST24 4/5dr	£21,000
2.5 V6 Ghia X 5dr	£21,000
2.5 V6 ST-200 5dr	£23,000
1.8i LX Est	£17,000
1.8 TD LX Est	£17,000
1.8 TD GLX Est	£18,000
1.8 TD Ghia Est	£19,000
1.8 TD Ghia X Est	£21,000
2.0i Zetec Est	£16,400
2.0i LX Est	£17,000
2.0i GLX Est	£18,000
2.0i Ghia Est	£19,000
2.0i Ghia X Est	£21,000
2.5 V6 ST24 Est	£21,000
2.5 V6 Ghia X Est	£22,000
2.5 V6 ST-200 Est	£24,000
Puma	
1.4 16v	£13,950
1.7 16v	£14,950
1.7 16v Racing	£23,000
Cougar	
2.0 16v	£20,000
2.5 V6 24v	£21,000
2.5 V6 24v VX	£22,000
Galaxy	
2.3 LX 7st	£18,200
2.3 Zetec 7st	£19,700
2.3 Ghia 7st	£21,200
2.8 Ghia 7st	£23,700
2.8 Ghia 4x4 7st	£25,700
1.9 TD LX 7st	£18,700
1.9 TD 110 Zetec 7st	£20,700
1.9 TD 110 Ghia 7st	£22,200
Explorer	
4.0 V6 5dr	£26,400

HONDA

Civic	
1.4i 3dr	£12,515
1.5 LSi 3dr	£14,205
1.6 ES 3dr	£15,105
1.6 VTi 3dr	£16,900
1.4 S 5dr	£11,995
1.4 Sport 5dr	£12,995
1.5 S 5dr	£13,150
1.6 SE 5dr	£13,995
1.6 SE Executive 5dr	£15,195
1.6 ES 5dr	£16,005
1.8 VTi 5dr	£17,325
1.6 LSi Est	£14,805
1.6i ES Est	£16,505
1.8 VTi Est	£17,325
1.6i LS Coupe	£14,055
1.6 SR VTEC Coupe	£15,755
Accord	
1.8i VTEC S 4dr	£15,550
1.8i VTEC SE 4dr	£16,750
1.8i VTEC SE Exec' 4dr	£19,600
2.0i VTEC SE 4dr	£17,300
2.0i VTEC SE Exec' 4dr	£20,100
2.2i Type-R 4dr	£23,000
2.0i ES Coupe	£21,250
3.0i V6 auto Coupe	£24,350
HR-V 1.6i 3dr	£14,000
CR-V	
2.0i LS 5dr	£16,905
2.0i ES 5dr	£18,155
2.0i ES Executive 5dr	£19,850
Shuttle	
2.3i LS	£18,305
2.3i ES	£20,425
2.3i LS Executive	£20,500

2.3i ES Executive	£22,620
Integra R 1.8	£20,500
Prelude	
2.0	£19,075
2.0 Motegi	£21,570
2.2 VTi	£22,700
2.2 VTi Motegi	£24,195
S 2000 2.0 Convertible	£27,995
Legend 3.5 Saloon 4dr	£31,995
NSX	
3.2	£69,590
3.2-T	£73,090

HYUNDAI
Atoz	
1.0 5dr	£6,949
1.0 Plus 5dr	£7,949
Accent	
1.3 Coupe Siena 3dr	£6,999
1.3 Coupe i 3dr	£7,499
1.3 Coupe Si 3dr	£8,499
1.5 MVi 3dr	£10,699
1.3 Si 5dr	£8,699
1.3 GSi 5dr	£9,499
Lantra	
1.6 Si 4dr	£10,604
1.6 GSi 4dr	£12,004
2.0 CDX 4dr	£13,004
1.6 Si Est	£11,104
1.6 GSi Est	£12,504
2.0 CDX Est	£13,504
Coupe	
1.6	£14,029
1.6 SE	£15,404
2.0 SE	£17,029
2.0 F2 Evolution	£19,299
Sonata	
2.0 GSi 4dr	£14,004
2.0 CDX 4dr	£15,504
2.5 V6 auto 4dr	£19,004

ISUZU
Trooper	
3.5 V6 SWB Duty 3dr	£21,000
3.5 V6 SWB Citation	£23,650
3.0 TD SWB 3dr	£19,100
3.0 TD SWB Duty 3dr	£21,000
3.5 V6 SWB Cit' 3dr	£23,650
3.5 V6 LWB Duty 5dr	£23,500
3.0 TD LWB 5dr	£21,650
3.0 TD LWB Duty 5dr	£23,500
3.0 TD LWB Cit' 5dr	£26,650

JAGUAR
S-Type	
3.0 V6 4dr	£28,300
3.0 V6 SE 4dr	£33,150
4.0 V8 4dr	£37,600
XJ8	
3.2 4dr	£37,405
4.0 4dr	£42,305
4.0 Sovereign 4dr	£45,805
4.0 Sovereign lwb 4dr	£47,605
4.0 XJR 4dr	£54,405
Daimler V8 4dr	£55,005
Daimler Super V8 4dr	£64,305
XK8	
XK8 4.0 Coupe	£50,955
XKR 4.0 Coupe	£60,105
XK8 4.0 Convertible	£57,955
XKR 4.0 Convertible	£67,105

KIA
Pride	
1.3i S 3dr	£5,495
1.3i SX 3dr	£5,995
1.3i SX 5dr	£6,495
Mentor II	
1.5 S 4dr	£8,495
1.5 SX 4dr	£9,995
Shuma	
1.5 S 5dr	£8,495
1.5 SX 5dr	£9,995
1.8 GSX 5dr	£11,595
Clarus	
1.8 SX 4dr	£10,995
2.0 GSX 4dr	£12,495
2.0 Executive 4dr	£13,495
Sportage	
2.0 S 5dr	£12,995
2.0 SX 5dr	£13,995
2.0 GSX 5dr	£14,995

LAMBORGHINI
Diablo	
5.7 SV Coupe	£135,536
5.7 VT Coupe	£160,211
5.7 GT Coupe	£207,211
5.7 VT Roadster	£186,061

LAND ROVER
Defender	
2.5 TD5 3dr	£19,925
2.5 County TD5 3dr	£20,775
2.5 TD5 5dr	£22,654
2.5 County TD5 5dr	£23,565
Freelander	
1.8 Soft Back 3dr	£16,995
1.8 Soft Back Xi 3dr	£18,795
1.8 Soft Back XEi 3dr	£20,695
1.8 Hard Back 3dr	£16,995
1.8 Hard Back Xi 3dr	£18,795
1.8 Hard Back XEi 3dr	£20,695
2.0di Soft Back 3dr	£17,995
2.0di Soft Back Xi 3dr	£19,795
2.0di Soft Back XEi 3dr	£21,695
2.0di Hard Back 3dr	£17,995
2.0di Hard Back Xi 3dr	£19,795
2.0di H'Back XEi 3dr	£21,695
1.8 S/Wagon 5dr	£18,450
1.8 S/Wagon Xi 5dr	£19,995
1.8 S/Wagon XEi 5dr	£21,995
2.0di S/Wagon 5dr	£19,450
2.0di S/Wagon Xi 5dr	£20,995
2.0di S/Wagon XEi 5dr	£22,995
Discovery	
2.5 Td5 S 5dr	£25,505
2.5 Td5 GS 5dr	£27,855
2.5 Td5 XS 5dr	£29,785
2.5 Td5 ES 5dr	£34,605
4.0 V8 GS 5dr	£28,325
4.0 V8 XS 5dr	£30,255
4.0 V8 ES 5dr	£35,075
Range Rover	
2.5 DT 5dr	£39,645
2.5 DT SE 5dr	£42,705
2.5 DT HSE 5dr	£48,710
4.0 V8 5dr	£41,000
4.0 V8 SE 5dr	£44,060
4.6 HSE 5dr	£51,170

LEXUS
IS 200	
2.0 S 4dr	£20,500
2.0 SE 4dr	£22,000
2.0 Sport 4dr	£23,000
GS300	
3.0 S 4dr	£31,230
3.0 SE 4dr	£34,314
LS400 4.0 V8 4dr	£49,999

LOTUS
Elise	
1.8	£22,675
1.8 111S	£26,590
Esprit	
GT3	£39,950
GT V8	£49,950
V8 SE	£59,950
V8 Sport	£64,750

MARCOS
MantaRay	
4.0 V8	£35,248
4.6 V8	£37,749
LM	
4.0 V8 Coupe	£38,249
4.0V8 Spyder	£38,249
4.6 V8 Coupe	£40,750
4.6 V8 Spyder	£40,750
Mantis	
4.6 V8 Coupe	£44,749
4.6 V8 Spider	£44,749
4.6 S'charged Coupe	£50,031
4.6 S'charged Conv'	£50,031

MASERATI
Quattroporte	
2.8 Turbo V6 4dr	£49,146
3.2 Turbo V8 4dr	£56,545
3200 GT	
3.2 Turbo V8 Coupe	£60,575

MAZDA
121	
1.3 GXi 3dr	£8,165
1.25-16v GSi 5dr	£9,335
Demio 1.3 5dr	£10,565
323	
1.3 LXi 5dr	£11,735
1.5 LXi 5dr	£13,485
1.5 GXi 5dr	£14,435
1.8 GSi 5dr	£15,235
1.8 SE 5dr	£16,085
2.0 Di Turbo 5dr	£14,235
Premacy	
1.8 GXi Est	£14.375
1.8 GSi Est	£16,525
2.0 TD GXi Est	£15,375
626	
1.8ie 5dr	£14.035
2.0 LXi 5dr	£14,815
2.0 GXi 5dr	£15,665
2.0 GXi 5dr	£17,035
2.0 GXi Est	£16,035
2.0D GXi 5dr	£16,390
2.0 GXi Est	£16,035
2.0 GXi Est	£16,665
2.0 GSi Est	£18,235
2.0D GXi Est	£17,390
Xedos 6 2.0i V6 SE 4dr	£21,965
Xedos 9	
2.5 V6 S'charged 4dr	£28,665
MX-5	
1.6i	£15,685
1.8i	£16,815
1.8i S	£18,790

MERCEDES-BENZ
A-Class	
A140 Classic 5dr	£14,490
A140 Eleg'/A'garde	£15,990
A160 Classic 5dr	£15,490
A160 Eleg'/A'garde 5dr	£16,990
A170 CDi Classic 5dr	£17,990
A170 CDi Eleg'/A'garde	£17,890
C-Class	
C180 Classic/Esprit 4dr	£20,440
C200 Classic/Esprit	£22,240
C230K Classic/Esprit	£25,190
C240 Classic/Esprit	£25,740
C280 Classic/Esprit	£29,690
C220CDI Cl'c/Esprit	£22,240
C250 Classic/Esprit TD	£24,240
C180 Classic/Esprit Est	£21,870
C200 Classic/Esprit Est	£23,670
C230K Classic/Esprit Est	£26,620
C240 Classic/Esprit Est	£27,170
C280 Classic/Esprit Est	£31,120
C220CDI Classic/Esprit	£23,670
C250 Classic/Esprit TD	£25,670
Elegance, Sport	+£2,050-£3,000
C43 4dr	£47,640
C43 Est	£49,070
E-Class	
E200 Classic 4dr	£26,395
E240 Classic 4dr	£29,310
E280 Classic 4dr	£33,280
E320 Classic 4dr	£37,600
E430 Elegance 4dr	£48,330
E55 AMG 4dr	£60,540
E220CDI Classic 4dr	£26,170
E300DT Classic 4dr	£30,780
E200 Classic Est	£28,695
E240 Classic Est	£31,610
E320 Classic Est	£39,900
E430 Elegance Est	£50,630
E55 AMG Est	£62,840
E300DT Classic Est	£33,080
Elegance	+£1,860-£2,600;
Avant Garde	+£2,120-£2,870
S-Class	
S280 4dr	£43,640
S320 4dr	£49,140
S430 4dr	£57,140
S500 4dr	£69,040
S320L 4dr	£54,140
S430L 4dr	£62,140
S500L 4dr	£74,040
CLK	
200 Sport/Elegance	£27,390
230K Sport/Elegance	£31,590
320 Sport/Elegance	£36,640
430 Sport/Elegance	£45,640
55 AMG Coupe	£59,640
230K Sport/Eleg Conv'	£36,090
320 Sport/Elegance	£41,140
430 Sport/Elegance	£50,140
CL Coupe	
CL420	£72,040
CL500	£83,040
CL600	£107,040
SLK	
230K	£31,640
SL	
SL280	£54,640
SL320	£58,690
SL500	£73,950
SL600	£96,370
V-Class	
V230 Trend/Fashion	£22,390
V230 Ambiente	£26,290
V280 Ambiente	£28,290
V220CDI Trend/F'on	£22,390
V220 CDI Ambiente	£26,290
M-Class	
ML320 5dr	£31,780
ML430 5dr	£42,640

MITSUBISHI
Colt	
1.3 GLX 3dr	£10,825
1.6 GLX 3dr	£12,375
1.6 Mirage 3dr	£13,625
Carisma	
1.6 i 5dr	£12,995
1.6 Classic 4/5dr	£13,995
1.6 Equippe 4/5dr	£15,225
1.8 GDi Equippe 4/5dr	£15,955
1.8 GDi Sport 5dr	£16,495
1.8 GDi Elegance 5dr	£17,995
1.9 TD Classic 5dr	£14,695
1.9 TD Equippe 5dr	£15,955
Galant	
2.0 GLX 4dr	£16,400
2.0 GLS 4dr	£18,000
2.4 GDi 4dr	£19,600
2.5 V6 4dr	£23,200
2.0 GLX est	£17,300
2.0 GLS Est	£18,900
2.4 GDi est	£20,500
2.5 V6 est	£24,100
Colt Space Star	
1.3i	£11,200
1.3i GL	£12,400
1.3i GLX	£13,000
1.8 GDI GLX	£14,000
1.8 GDI GLS	£15,340
Space Wagon	
2.4 GDi GL	£17,800
2.4 GDi GLX	£18,960
2.4 GDi GLS	£22,500
Challenger	
2.5 TD GLX 5dr	£20,370
2.8 TD GLS 5dr	£23,680
3.0 V6 GLS 5dr	£24,500
Shogun	
2.5 TD GLX 3dr	£20,425
2.8 TD GLS 3dr	£23,380
2.8 TD GLS DOP 3dr	£25,680
3.0-24v V6 GLS 3dr	£23,900
3.0-24v V6 GLS DOP	£26,200
2.8 TD GLS 5dr	£24,925
2.8 TD GLS 5dr	£28,230
2.8 TD GLS DOP 5dr	£32,055
3.0-24v V6 5dr	£28,750
3.0-24v V6 DOP 5dr	£32,525
3.5-24v V6 SE 5dr	£40,000
3000 GT 3.0 Turbo Coupe	£45,805

MORGAN
4/4	
1.8 2-seater	£20,592
Plus 4	
2.0 2-seater	£25,357
Plus 8	
4.0 2-seater	£31,020
4.6 2-seater	£33,629

NISSAN
Micra	
1.0 Profile 3dr	£7,940
1.0 GX 3dr	£9,040
1.3 Profile 3dr	£8,395
1.3 GX 3dr	£9,495
1.3 Si 3dr	£9,995
1.0 Profile 5dr	£8,420
1.0 GX 5dr	£9,520
1.3 Profile 5dr	£8,875
1.3 GX 5dr	£9,975
1.3 SE 5dr	£10,900
Almera	
1.4 Equation 3dr	£11,500
1.4 GTi 3dr	£16,600
1.4 Equation 5dr	£12,000
1.4 GX 5dr	£13,100
1.6 GX 5dr	£13,700
1.6 SLX 5dr	£14,600
1.6 GX 4dr	£13,100
1.6 GX 4dr	£13,700
New Primera	
1.6 E 5dr	£14,000
1.8 S 4/5dr	£15,300
2.0 S 4/5dr	£15,900
1.8 Sport 4/5dr	£16,200
1.8 SE 4/5dr	£16,400
2.0 SE 4/5dr	£16,800
2.0 Sport + 4/5dr	£18,000
2.0 SE + 4/5dr	£19,000
2.0 TD S 4/5dr	£15,900
2.0 TD SE 4/5dr	£17,000
1.6 E Est	£14,850
1.8 S Est	£16,150
2.0 S Est	£16,750
1.8 Sport Est	£17,100
1.8 SE Est	£17,300
2.0 Sport Est	£17,700
2.0 SE Est	£17,900
2.0 Sport + Est	£18,900
2.0 SE + Est	£19,900
2.0 TD S Est	£16,750
QX	
2.0 V6 SE 4dr	£22,400
2.0 V6 SEL auto 4dr	£24,800
3.0 V6 SEL auto 4dr	£30,200
200 SX	
2.0 Turbo	£22,000
2.0 Turbo Touring	£24,700
Skyline 2.6 Twin Turbo	£50,000
Serena	
1.6 GX	£15,595
2.0 Excursion	£17,625
2.3 D Occasion	£16,000
Terrano II	
2.7 TDi S 3dr	£18,000
2.7 TDi SE 3dr	£19,995
2.7 TDi SE 5dr	£22,625
2.7 TDi SE Touring 5dr	£25,180
Patrol	
2.8TD S 5dr	£21,500
2.8TD SE 3dr	£24,500
2.8TD 5dr	£24,955
2.8TD SE 5dr	£28,500
2.8TD SE Touring 5dr	£31,200

PERODUA
Nippa	
850 EX 5dr	£5,094
850 GX 5dr	£5,694

PEUGEOT
106	
1.1 Zest 3dr	£7,125
1.1 Zest 2 3dr	£7,825
1.1 Zest 3 3dr	£9,025
1.5D Zest 2 3dr	£8,425
1.5D Zest 3 3dr	£9,625
1.6 GTi 3dr	£12,495
1.1 Zest 2 5dr	£8,275
1.5D Zest 2 5dr	£8,875
206	
1.1 L 3dr	£8,500
1.1 LX 3dr	£9,100
1.4 LX 3dr	£10,000
1.4 GLX 3dr	£10,800
1.6 XS 3dr	£11,450
2.0 GTi 3dr	£13,995
2.0 GT 3dr	£15,695
1.9D L 3dr	£9,300
1.9D LX 3dr	£10,400
1.1 L 5dr	£8,950
1.1 LX 5dr	£9,550
1.4 LX 5dr	£10,450
1.4 GLX 5dr	£11,250
1.6 GLX 5dr	£11,450
1.9D L 5dr	£9,750
1.9D LX 5dr	£10,850
306	
1.8 XS 3dr	£13,245
2.0 XSi 3dr	£14,845
2.0 GTI-6 3dr	£18,195
2.0 HDi D Turbo 3dr	£14,295
1.4 L 5dr	£11,995
1.4 LX 5dr	£12,845
1.6 L 5dr	£12,295
1.6 LX 5dr	£13,145
1.6 GLX 5dr	£13,945
1.8 GLX 5dr	£13,945
2.0 XSi 5dr	£15,245
1.9 D L 5dr	£12,745
1.9 D LX 5dr	£13,445
2.0 HDi L 5dr	£13,795
2.0 HDi LX 5dr	£14,495
2.0 HDi GLX 5dr	£14,995
2.0 HDi D Turbo 5dr	£14,695
1.4 L Est	£12,745
1.4 LX Est	£13,045
1.6 LX Est	£13,895
1.8 GLX Est	£14,695
1.9 D L Est	£13,495
2.0 D LX Est	£14,195
2.0 HDi L Est	£14,545
2.0 HDi LX Est	£15,245
2.0 HDi GLX Est	£15,745
1.8 Cabrio	£17,295
2.0 Cabrio	£19,695
2.0 Roadster	£21,065
406	
1.8 L 4dr	£14,295
1.8 LX 4dr	£15,300
2.0 LX 4dr	£15,950
1.8 GLX 4dr	£16,700
2.0 GLX 4dr	£17,000
2.0 GTX 4dr	£18,020
2.0 Executive 4dr	£20,000
3.0 V6 GTX 4dr	£20,020
3.0 V6 4dr	£22,000
2.0 HDi L 90 4dr	£15,200
2.0 HDi LX 90 4dr	£16,200
2.0 HDi LX 110 4dr	£17,350
2.0 HDi GLX 90 4dr	£17,600
2.0 HDi GLX 110 4dr	£18,400
2.0 HDi GTX 90 4dr	£18,620
2.0 HDi GTX 110 4dr	£19,420
2.0 HDi Executive 110	£21,400
1.8 L Est	£15,295
1.8 LX Est	£16,300
1.8 GLX Est	£17,700
2.0 GLX Est	£18,000
2.0 GTX Est	£19,020
3.0 V6 GTX Est	£21,020
3.0 V6 Est	£23,000
2.0 HDi L 90 Est	£16,200
2.0 HDi LX 90 Est	£17,200
2.0 HDi LX 110 Est	£18,350
2.0 HDi GLX 90 Est	£18,600
2.0 HDi GLX 110 Est	£19,400
2.0 HDi GTX 90 Est	£19,620
2.0 HDi GTX 110 Est	£20,420
2.0 HDi Executive 110	£22,400
2.0 Coupe	£20,875
2.0 Coupe SE Coupe	£22,695
3.0 V6 SE Coupe	£25,995
806	
2.0 LX	£18,100
2.0 GLX	£18,805
2.0 TD LX	£18,810
1.9 TD GLX	£19,515

PORSCHE
Boxster	
2.7	£34,232
3.2 S	£42,161
911	
Carrera	£60,271
Carrera Cabriolet	£67,266
Carrera 4	£64,585
Carrera 4 Cabriolet	£71,580
GT3	£76,500

PROTON
Compact	
1.3 GLi 3dr	£7,499
1.3 LSi 3dr	£7,999
1.3 Duo 3dr	£8,899
1.5 GLSi 3dr	£8,999
1.6 SRi 3dr	£9,999
1.6 SEi 3dr	£9,999
Persona	
1.3 LSi 5dr	£8,799
1.5 GLSi 5dr	£9,999
1.6 XLi 5dr	£10,799
1.8 EXi 5dr	£11,799
1.6 SEi 5dr	£12,299
2.0 GLS TDi 5dr	£10,999
2.0 EX TDi 5dr	£11,399
1.3 LSi 4dr	£8,499
1.3 Si 4dr	£9,499
1.5 GLSi 4dr	£9,699
1.6 XLi 4dr	£10,499
1.8 EXi 4dr	£11,499
1.6 SEi 4dr	£11,999
2.0 GLS TDi 4dr	£10,699
2.0 EX TDi 4dr	£11,099
Coupe 1.8 Evolution	£13,999

RELIANT Robin
850 LX 3dr	£8,137
850 SLX 3dr	£8,459
850 B.R.G./Royale 3dr	£9,654

RENAULT
Clio	
1.2 3dr	£8,350
1.2 RN 3dr	£9,055
1.2 RT 3dr	£9,655
1.4 RT 3dr	£10,155
1.4 Alize 3dr	£10,350
1.6 Si 3dr	£11,000
1.6 RXE 3dr	£11,360
1.6 16v 3dr	£12,800
1.9D 3dr	£9,055
1.2 5dr	£8,805
1.2 RN 5dr	£9,505
1.4 RT 5dr	£10,105
1.4 RT 5dr	£10,605
1.4 Alize 5dr	£10,800
1.6 RXE 5dr	£11,810
1.9D 5dr	£9,505
1.9D RT 5dr	£10,905
Kangoo	
1.4 RN Est	£9,750
1.6 RXE Est	£10,500
1.9 D RN Est	£9,750
Megane	
1.4e 5dr	£11,900
1.4e RT 5dr	£12,600
1.6e RT 4/5dr	£12,900
1.6e Sport 5dr	£13,100
1.4e Alize 5dr	£13,100
1.6e Sport 5dr	£13,400
1.6e Alize 4/5dr	£13,400
1.4e Sport Alize 5dr	£13,600
1.6e Sport Alize 5dr	£13,900
1.6e RXE 4/5dr	£14,400
1.9 D 5dr	£12,300
1.9 TDi RT 4/5dr	£13,900
1.9 TDi Sport 5dr	£14,400
1.9 TDi Alize 4/5dr	£14,400
1.9 TDi Sport Alize 5dr	£14,900
1.9 TDi RXE 4/5dr	£15,400
1.4e Classic 5dr	£12,200
1.4 16v Coupe	£12,850
1.4 16v Sport Coupe	£13,600
1.6 16v Sport Coupe	£13,900
1.4 16v Sport Alize	£14,100
1.6 16v Sport Alize	£14,400
1.6 16v Monaco Coupe	£15,400
2.0 16v Sport Alize	£16,400
2.0 16v Monaco Coupe	£17,400
1.6 16v Convertible	£15,900
1.6 16v Sport Conv'	£17,400
2.0 16v Sport Conv'	£17,900
1.6 16v Monaco Conv'	£18,900
2.0 16v Sport Alize	£19,900
2.0 16v Monaco	£20,900
Scenic	
1.4 16v Est	£13,100
1.4 16v RT Est	£13,900
1.6 16v RT Est	£14,200
1.4 16v Alize Est	£14,400
1.4 16v Sport Est	£14,400
1.6 16v Alize Est	£14,700
1.6 16v Sport Est	£14,700
1.6 Sport Alize Est	£15,200
1.6 16v RXE Est	£15,700
1.6 16v Monaco Est	£16,300
2.0 16v Sport Alize Est	£16,400
2.0 16v RXE Est	£16,900
2.0 16v Monac Est	£17,500
1.9 TDi RT Est	£15,200
1.9 TDi Alize Est	£15,700
1.9 TDi Sport Est	£15,700
1.9 TDi Sport Alize Est	£16,200
1.9 TDi RXE Est	£16,700
1.9 TDi Monaco Est	£17,300
Laguna	
1.6 RT 5dr	£14,075
1.6 Alize 5dr	£14,925
1.6 Sport 5dr	£15,375
1.8 Alize 5dr	£15,375
1.8 Sport 5dr	£15,825
1.8 RXE 5dr	£16,825
2.0 RXE 5dr	£17,625
1.6 RTi 5dr	£16,575
2.0 RXE 5dr	£17,575
2.0 Monaco 5dr	£20,575
3.0 V6 RTi 5dr	£18,575
3.0 V6 Monaco 5dr	£22,575
1.9dTi RT 5dr	£15,075
1.9dTi Alize 5dr	£15,925
1.9dTi Sport 5dr	£16,375
1.9dTi RXE 5dr	£18,375
2.2 dT RXE 5dr	£18,375
2.2 dT Monaco 5dr	£21,375
1.6 RT Est	£15,075
1.8 Alize Est	£16,375
1.8 Sport Est	£16,825
2.0 Alize Est	£17,125
2.0 Sport Est	£17,575
2.0 RXE Est	£18,575
2.0 Monaco Est	£21,575
1.9dTi RT est	£16,075
1.9dTi Alize Est	£16,925
1.9dTi Sport Est	£17,375
2.2 dT RXE Est	£19,375
2.2 dT Monaco Est	£22,375
Safrane	
2.0i 16v Executive 5dr	£21,910
2.5i 20v Executive 5dr	£24,410
Espace	
2.0 Alize	£19,200
2.0 RT-X	£21,200
2.2 Alize dT	£20,800
2.2 RT-X dT	£22,800
2.2 RXE dT	£25,595
3.0 V6 RXE	£27,695
Grand 2.0 RT-X	£22,300
Grand 2.2 RT-X dT	£23,900
Grand 2.2 RXE dT	£26,695
Grand 3.0 V6 RXE	£28,795

ROLLS-ROYCE
Silver Seraph 4dr	£155,000

ROVER
Mini	
1.3i 2dr	£9,325
1.3i Cooper 2dr	£9,625
200	
(no 25 prices as we went to press)	
211i SE 3dr	£7,995
211i iE 3dr	£9,995
214i-8v SE 3dr	£9,495
214i-8v iE 3dr	£10,495
214i-16v iE 3dr	£11,495
214i-16v iL 3dr	£12,495
214i-16v iS 3dr	£12,495
216i iE 3dr	£12,495
216i iL 3dr	£13,495
216i iS 3dr	£13,495
200 vi 3dr	£15,995
220 TD SE 3dr	£9,995
220 TD iE 3dr	£10,995
220 TD iE 3dr	£11,995
220 TD iL 3dr	£12,995
220 TD iS 3dr	£12,995
211i SE 5dr	£8,495
211i iE 5dr	£10,495
214i-8v SE 5dr	£9,995
214i-8v iE 5dr	£10,995
214i-16v iE 5dr	£11,995
214i-16v iL 5dr	£12,995
214i-16v iS 5dr	£12,995
216i iE 5dr	£12,995
216i iL 5dr	£13,995
216i iS 5dr	£13,995